A Sense of Higher Design

The Kohlers of Kohler

A Sense of Higher Design

The Kohlers of Kohler

Richard Blodgett

GREENWICH PUBLISHING GROUP, INC.
LYME, CONNECTICUT

Produced and published by Greenwich Publishing Group, Inc.
Lyme, Connecticut
www.greenwichpublishing.com

Design by Clare Cunningham Graphic Design

Separation and film assembly by Scan Communications Group, Inc.

Library of Congress Catalog Card Number: 97-77059

ISBN: 0-944641-26-1

First Printing: October 2003

10 9 8 7 6 5 4 3 2 1

*P*ages 2-3, sôk overflowing bath; pages 4-5, Fountain Courtyard of The American Club,
including The Greenhouse garden café at right edge of photo; page 7, The American Club;
pages 8-9, Fountain Courtyard in summer.

Table of Contents

*K*ohler Co., with annual revenues of $3 billion, has been described by *Business Week* as "one of the largest and most innovative family-run companies" in the United States. Pictured is the company's general office in Kohler, Wisconsin.

The Kohlers of Kohler, Wisconsin, one of the great business families in America, have prospered for a century and a quarter despite — or perhaps because of — the differing personalities and management styles of their company's leaders over the years. If there is one thing you can say about the Kohlers, it is that each generation has marched to the beat of a different drummer. To be a Wisconsin Kohler is to be a rugged individualist. Self-reliance and independent thinking, occasionally even to the point of eccentricity, have always been encouraged within the family. Maybe that is one reason why Kohler Co., founded in 1873, has succeeded so consistently for so long. Given the imaginativeness of its leaders, Kohler Co. has never wanted for original ideas.

Kohler Co. is a diversified enterprise participating in four business fields: kitchen and bath, including plumbing fixtures, faucets and cabinetry; power systems, including electrical generators, small engines and generator rental services; interiors, including furniture, accessories and tile; and hospitality and real estate.

To many consumers, it is best known for one of those businesses, plumbing products, and for having single-handedly changed the look of the bathroom. Indeed, Kohler Co.'s success in continuously reinventing the bathroom is a prime example of the company's creativity from generation to generation of family leadership.

Until the turn of the twentieth century, Kohler Co. was a small regional supplier of quality plumbing products, a mere speck on the competitive scene in comparison to Standard Sanitary Manufacturing Company (a predecessor of today's American Standard Companies Inc.) and Crane Co., which dominated the industry. Then matters began to change. At that time, bathtubs and other plumbing products were considered to be boring utilitarian necessities. The majority of American homes still had outhouses, and indoor plumbing fixtures were rudimentary. However, Walter J. Kohler, a son of company founder John Michael Kohler, championed a new idea — that plumbing products could be beautiful as well as practical. With that notion, he launched a plumbing products revolution.

Under Walter's leadership, Kohler Co. introduced stylish new products, beginning with its elegant Windsor line in 1908. In the 1920s, it developed pastel and jet black toilets and other fixtures, defying the industry convention that plumbing products came only in white. Kohler's jet black products were so unusual, even spectacular, for their time that they were featured in a 1929 show on

John Michael Kohler, above, founded Kohler Co. in 1873. He was a civic leader and supporter of the arts, in addition to being a successful businessman, and led the company until his death in 1900. He was succeeded as president by his son, Robert J. Kohler, right, who led the company until 1905.

*A*nother of John Michael's sons, Walter J. Kohler, ran the company from 1905 to 1940. The inclusion of Kohler plumbing products in a 1929 Metropolitan Museum of Art exhibition, below left, was an important endorsement of the company's design leadership. Above, Kohler entered the electrical generator business in 1920 with the development of the Kohler Automatic Power & Light.

industrial design at New York's Metropolitan Museum of Art.

Kohler Co. innovated in other fields as well, such as its development in 1920 of the world's first engine-powered electrical generator, the Kohler Automatic Power & Light. Unique for its era, the unit started automatically when an electrical appliance or light was turned on. "This 1,500-watt unit brought electricity to rural America for the first time without the use of 32-volt batteries," *Construction Equipment*

*W*alter was succeeded as Kohler Co. president by another of John Michael's sons, Herbert V. Kohler Sr., who was CEO from 1940 to 1968. During his watch, the company began producing small engines, manufactured precision controls, built its first plant outside the state of Wisconsin and launched The Bold Look of Kohler theme.

remarks. Beginning with that pioneering generator, Kohler has become a major force in the power systems industry.

Kohler Co. withstood the Great Depression of the 1930s, converted to military production during World War II and resumed its innovation and growth after the war. In 1948, it opened a factory to manufacture small engines. Today the company supplies engines to customers such as Sears Roebuck, John Deere and Toro to power their garden tractors and other equipment. Kohler entered both the generator and engine businesses through internal development, drawing on the engineering, manufacturing and marketing skills of its

people, a far tougher road than diversifying through acquisition.

In plumbing products, the next great creative burst occurred in the 1960s, when the company — now headed by Walter's brother, Herbert V. Kohler Sr. — unveiled the industry's first products in "accent" colors. These colors were richer and more vibrant than the pastels of the 1920s, and they offered an array of new design possibilities.

The concept of accent colors originated with three Kohler executives in the advertising and public relations department — Charles Pagnucco, Alfred Ellrodt and Armond "Bud" Grube. They took their idea to Herbert Sr., who quickly

gave his blessing. Not being color experts themselves, the three executives approached an editor of *House & Garden* magazine who helped them select five stylish colors to which distinctive names were assigned: Antique Red, Blueberry, Citron, Expresso and Jade.

The new products were introduced at the National Home Builders Show and at regional meetings of home builders and Kohler distributors. With appropriate hoopla, a large satin bed sheet was pulled aside to reveal five lavatories (the industry term for bathroom sinks), each a different color, unadorned on the stage. Audiences went wild. In San Francisco, the entire crowd of Kohler distributors rose to its feet and cheered. Speaking of the response, Bud Grube said, "They were salespeople and they were excited. They had waited a long time for something new in the plumbing industry."

More important still, the new products were an immediate hit with consumers, capturing an emergent public taste for upscale household design. The company kept the color pot boiling, offering fresh colors virtually every year beginning in 1965.

However, it was not just the accent colors that were new. It was also the style and functionality of the products. Starting with the renewed growth of the plumbing market after World War II and continuing to this day, hundreds of new products — bathtubs, whirlpools, toilets, urinals, bidets, lavatories, kitchen sinks, faucets — flowed from Kohler Co.'s factories, featuring beautiful designs as well as the latest technological advances, such as toilets that used less water and innovative whirlpool baths.

Some people, though, had trouble talking about toilets and other bathroom accouterments, or they poked fun at those who did. When Kohler advertised its products on *The Tonight Show*, Johnny Carson, the show's host, referred to them coyly as "Kohler conveniences." And when Kohler advertised its luxurious new bathtubs for two, picturing a man and woman bathing together in a relaxed and thoroughly wholesome manner, some consumers saw sexual innuendo and

The industry's first "accent" color plumbing products were introduced during Herbert Sr.'s tenure under The Bold Look of Kohler tag line. Pictured is the Lady Vanity lavatory, designed for use as a shampoo center/baby bath.

wrote letters of protest to the company — and still do. Unfazed, Kohler Co. stuck to its advertising approach.

In 1967, Kohler's advertising team dreamed up the tag line, The Bold Look of Kohler, for its accent-color plumbing products. Today, The Bold Look of Kohler is one of the memorable advertising slogans in America and remains the company's signature, underscoring the originality, quality and elegance of Kohler products.

Propelled by its leadership in new products for the bathroom and kitchen — and led now by yet another Kohler, Herbert Sr.'s son, Herbert V. Kohler Jr. — Kohler Co. soon caught up with and, in the 1970s, breezed right by its two larger

competitors, establishing a lead in the plumbing products industry it has never relinquished.

Kohler is today "the undisputed king of the American bathroom," in the words of *Forbes* magazine, and the industry's design and innovation leader. Its relentless rise to the top of the industry is one of the great business success stories of our time.

The bathroom has come a long way from those first Kohler Windsor products in 1908. No longer viewed as a mere humdrum necessity, the bathroom has evolved into a center of design and luxury in the home. Today's state-of-the-art bathrooms have amenities such as whirlpools, body sprays, dual lavatories, decorative tile and cabinetry. Homeowners talk about their bathrooms and show them off to friends and neighbors. Each year, Kohler Co. introduces a profusion of new products that are innovative, functional and beautiful. A recent catalog of Kohler products for the bath and powder room ran 140 pages and contained nearly 500 full-color photographs of bathtubs, lavatories, toilets and other products, and an entirely separate catalog of Kohler faucets ran 90 pages.

The bathroom has changed forever. And it all began early in the twentieth century with Kohler.

Taking Independent Thinking to New Heights

Kohler Co.'s innovation in plumbing products, generators, engines and other fields has been made possible by the long-term stability of its management and the willingness of its leaders to explore new opportunities and take risks. As the company celebrates its 130th anniversary, direct descendants of the founder still own and manage the business and still live in Kohler, Wisconsin.

The company is headed today by Herbert Jr., a grandson of founder John Michael Kohler. Demanding and incredibly energetic, Herb

*D*istinctive consumer advertising has been a key to Kohler Co.'s success since the 1920s. The ad at left, titled "Out of the Blue," is from the company's "As I See It" series which features images by contemporary artists and photographers. Pictured is a Kohler Vessels over-the-counter lavatory (bathroom sink).

Kohler is a bigger-than-life character who has been described as "the most controversial and charismatic personality" in the plumbing products industry. He has embraced the Kohler family legacy while pursuing a singular vision of what the company can become.

True to the family tradition of innovation, Herb has led Kohler Co. in entirely new directions, such as developing and operating golf courses and manufacturing furniture. In explaining the company's product and service diversity, he says, "Fundamentally, we are in the business of creating and marketing living environments."

Herb was just 33 years old when he took the reins as CEO in 1972, following the death of his father, Herbert Sr., four years earlier. One of his first major decisions was to build the world's largest and most efficient cast-iron molding line, replacing the company's antiquated coke-fired foundry with modern electric-induction melting technology. To help finance this and other investments, Kohler Co. sold $8 million of debentures, the first and only public offering of securities in its history. (Having an outstanding issue of public securities forced Kohler Co. to disclose its financial results, which Herb did not like in the least. The debentures were repaid in 1978, and since that time Kohler Co. has returned to keeping its financial results private.)

Not long after Kohler Co. began

*H*erbert V. "Herb" Kohler Jr., pictured in 1989, a grandson of founder John Michael Kohler, assumed leadership of the company in 1972 at age 33. He has expanded the company's plumbing products business in the U.S. and overseas, and has broadened operations to include furniture manufacturing and the creation of a world-class resort in Kohler Village. He continues as CEO today. Upper right, Kohler Co. invested in modern cast-iron manufacturing capacity in the 1970s when many other manufacturers were phasing out of the material.

building its new foundry, a senior executive of American Standard gave a speech proclaiming that the use of cast iron for plumbing products was obsolete. He predicted that cast iron would be replaced by acrylics and other new materials. "And here I was staking a good part of our company's future on cast iron," Herb recalls. "It put me on the edge of my seat."

As it turned out, Herb Kohler was right and American Standard was wrong. With its high quality and exceptional durability, cast iron remains a staple of the plumbing products market. The key is to process the material as efficiently as possible. Kohler Co. is able to manufacture cast-iron bathtubs, kitchen sinks and lavatories less expensively than any of its competitors thanks to in-line casting technology and the electric-melt facility installed in the 1970s, as well as to more recent investments in robotics. It also makes products from acrylics, fiberglass-reinforced plastic, sheet-molded compound fiberglass and other materials. "There are great synthetics, and ceramics are a wonderful material, and we make many products in these materials," Herb points out. "However, cast iron continues to be a core material for this company."

That investment in modern cast-iron production technology helped define Herb Kohler's management style — think boldly and invest for the long term. Herb says one reason he is able to do this is Kohler Co.'s generational approach to investing. "As a family-owned business," he asserts, "we can invest to create lasting value rather than to please the financial analyst who wants a quick payoff."

No decision was bolder (or more outlandish to some at the time) than the renovation of The American Club, in the heart of Kohler Village 50 miles north of Milwaukee, into a luxury resort hotel. The structure was built by Kohler Co. in 1918 to provide clean rooms, hearty meals and recreational facilities for single male employees, including immigrant employees, until they could afford homes of their own. By the late 1970s, it had long since outlived its original purpose and was being used as a village inn, badly in need of repair. Many Kohler Co. executives thought the time had come to tear the building down. But Herb is never one to destroy anything associated with the Kohler legacy. He says he feels "essentially an obligation" to preserve and build upon the accomplishments of his predecessors. He therefore decided to restore the historic facility and turn it into an upscale inn the village could be proud of. The fact that The American Club stands directly across the street from an 8,000-employee

Kohler Co. factory did not concern him in the least, especially since he had visited Michigan's Dearborn Inn, near a Ford Motor Company manufacturing complex, and saw how well that worked. Setting out to create a charming inn, he exceeded even his own expectations. Opened in 1981, the 125-room hostelry was successful from the start. Soon, Kohler Co. began expanding the facility, adding more rooms and developing it into a superb resort hotel.

Five years after its opening, through persistence and attention to detail, the remodeled facility achieved Five Diamond status, the highest rating of the American Automobile Association. Today, a decade and a half later, The American Club remains the only resort hotel in the Midwest to carry that top AAA ranking.

Jeffrey P. Cheney, Kohler Co.'s senior vice president-finance, puts the matter in perspective as follows: "When bankers visit me in Kohler, they love to stay at The American Club. And when they rave about it, as they often do, I respond by asking whether they would have loaned Herb Kohler the money for its renovation. Without hesitation they say, 'No.' And I say, 'That's the point. None of us would have given it to him.'" Cheney adds that opening a luxury hotel in a small community, across the street from a cast-iron foundry, "is almost the definition of folly in some people's minds, yet it works beyond anyone's wildest dreams."

With The American Club as an anchor, Kohler Co. proceeded to develop an entire hospitality business, opening other upscale facilities in the village. These include Sports Core (a health and racquet club) and River Wildlife (an 800-acre outdoor recreational area and wildlife preserve). The biggest draw of all, however, is golf. Since the late 1980s, Kohler Co. has built four 18-hole championship courses, all designed by Pete Dye, the renowned golf course architect. The River Course and Meadow Valleys Course at Blackwolf Run are situated in Kohler Village, while the Straits Course and Irish Course at Whistling Straits are perched along two miles of prime Lake Michigan shoreline northeast of the village.

Golf has been both a commercial and critical success for Kohler Co., punctuated by a rising chorus of media accolades. In 1999, *GOLF Magazine* rated the River Course at Blackwolf Run one of the nation's top three public/resort courses, joining an elite triad that also includes Pebble Beach and Pinehurst No. 2. Subsequently, a *GOLF Magazine* senior editor called the Straits Course at Whistling Straits "the best new golf course I have seen in the last 10 years." In 2000, the low-handicap readers of *Golf Digest* voted Sheboygan County in Wisconsin the seventh best golf destination in the world, lauding the county's "two five-star courses at Blackwolf Run and the magnificent two-year-old Whistling Straits." In

2001, *Forbes* and *The Robb Report* named Blackwolf Run and Whistling Straits, together with The American Club, the nation's best golf resort. The chorus grew even louder in 2002 when *Golf Odyssey* labeled Blackwolf Run and Whistling Straits "the best 72 holes in the world."

Not a single hole of golf existed in Kohler Village prior to 1988. Yet, in direct competition with the other

*K*ohler Co.'s 25,000 employees around the world are dedicated to a higher level of gracious living in kitchen and bath products, furniture, engines, power systems and hospitality. Above, molten iron is transferred between crucibles.

16,000 public, private and resort golf courses in North America, Kohler Co. has ascended rapidly to the highest echelons of this demanding field of enterprise.

An absolute dedication to a single level of quality and leading-edge design has been a winning formula in golf, just as it has been in plumbing products, furniture and other Kohler Co. businesses.

*K*ohler Co. entered the plumbing products business in 1883. Today its Kitchen & Bath Group is a world leader in innovation, quality, technology and design. The PRO CookCenter, above, includes the CookSink in which to boil, steam and poach food and then drain the water with the turn of a dial, eliminating the need to tote hot water from stove to sink.

Kohler Co. Today: Four Core Businesses

Kohler Co.'s four business groups encompass an array of premier brands:

Kitchen & Bath — Kohler, Sterling, Kallista, Jacob Delafon, Neomediam, Mira, Hytec, Englefield and Karat in plumbing products, and Canac, Robern and Sanijura in cabinetry.

Global Power — The Kohler brand in electrical generators, transfer switches and switchgear, generator rental services and small engines.

Interiors — Baker, Milling Road, McGuire and Dapha in fine furniture and accessories, and Ann Sacks in tile, stone and plumbing complements.

Hospitality & Real Estate — The American Club resort hotel and The Inn on Woodlake, the Blackwolf Run and Whistling Straits golf venues, Kohler Waters Spa, Riverbend and other resort facilities in the village.

While some people have a hard time seeing a connection among these diverse products and services, there is a method to Herb's madness. By bringing together leading-edge plumbing fixtures, cabinetry, tile and furniture under one corporate roof, the Kohlers have emerged as "probably the most influential family in the world of interiors," in the view of *House & Garden* magazine.

The company's design presence extends also to power systems. Kohler residential standby generators and the Kohler engines that power lawn and garden tractors are not only attractive in appearance, but also perform quietly and efficiently, contributing to consumers' quality of life.

The company's design leadership is a vital asset, opening distribution channels and selling products. In fact, design originality is one of four characteristics that help define the company and unite its businesses.

Quality is another of these defining characteristics. "In most categories," Herb Kohler says, "we go from a price point for the lower middle income market all the way up to the very high end of the mass market and even somewhat into the custom market. But across these price points, all our products are made to a single high level of quality. We differentiate price through materials, functions and levels of detail, not through quality."

Technological innovation is another defining characteristic,

The Global Power Group traces its roots to 1920, when Kohler Co. introduced the Kohler Automatic generator. Today, Kohler is a major producer of electrical generators, left, as well as small engines, right. Its engines are sold to other manufacturers for use in lawn mowers, garden tractors and other equipment.

exemplified by products such as state-of-the-art small engines and the WaterHaven Shower System, which can be customized to the preferences of each user.

Completing the list is service — from providing a high level of attention and care at The American Club to ensuring that product instructions are easy to understand and that all customer inquiries and complaints are handled promptly and courteously.

There are synergies across markets. For instance, many of the kitchen and bath products made by Kohler Co.

and its operating units are specified by the same interior designers who select furniture from its Baker and McGuire subsidiaries. And the garden tractors powered by Kohler engines and the Kohler standby generators that operate around the home are purchased by the same consumers who buy Kohler plumbing products.

Most importantly, however, these four defining characteristics — design, quality, technology and service — are the threads that bind Kohler Co.'s businesses into a unified whole. Herb contends that, in combi-

*K*ohler Co. entered the fine furniture business in 1986 with the purchase of Baker Furniture. Today, the Interiors Group encompasses Baker, Milling Road and McGuire in furniture, Dapha in custom upholstery, and Ann Sacks in tile, stone and plumbing accessories. Baker products pictured from front to back are the Hide Everything Coffee Table, a Sunday Sectional sofa and an Entertainment Center cabinet from the Haven from Barbara Barry Collection.

nation, these characteristics lead to the creation of functional art. "The concept is true of our plumbing products, it's true of our furniture, it's true of our generators for the home," he says. "And it's the reason we can put a Five Diamond resort hotel across the street from a factory. If the factory looked and smelled like most factories, it wouldn't work."

Golf is perhaps the most surprising of Kohler Co.'s activities, since it seems so unrelated to the others. Yet, as Alice Edland, group vice president-hospitality and real estate, puts it, "The people who come here to play golf are among the same people who buy Kohler plumbing fixtures and other products. So golf is not only a good business in its own right. It also helps sell products by reinforcing the Kohler image of leadership, quality and the highest sense of design."

It doesn't hurt either that the guest rooms at The American Club display Kohler plumbing fixtures, cabinetry, tile and furniture in a striking setting. Each bathroom at The American Club is unique, and some guests even request a different room each night to try different fixtures. Just down the street from The American Club is the 36,000-square-foot Kohler Design Center, which displays a panoply of the latest Kohler plumbing fixtures and furniture, as well as engines and generators for the consumer market. The Design Center is open to the public at no charge and attracts more than 140,000

consumers, designers, architects and builders each year. Kohler is also one of the few industrial companies in the United States that allows the public into its factory to see how its products are made. Two-and-one-half-hour walking tours are conducted each morning, Monday through Friday, by Kohler Co. retirees. The *Wall Street Journal* quoted one visitor who took the tour as proclaiming it "just blew me away." Even more unusual is the Arts/Industry residency program, conceived by Herb's sister, Ruth Kohler, who is director of the John Michael Kohler Arts Center in nearby Sheboygan. Artists selected for the program work in studios in the heart of the Kohler Co. factory. They can utilize the pottery, foundry and enamel shop to create whatever art they want and can call on employees for technical help, all without cost to

*B*aker not only manufactures fine furniture, such as the mahogany serpentine chest, below, but is also a leading furniture distributor. Above is the Baker Tribeca retail store in New York City.

the artist. More than a dozen artists take part each year. Artists love the program because it allows them to create works they couldn't make in their own studios. Employees benefit, Herb believes, through the inspiration that their collaboration with the artists brings to their lives. And the program is one of the ways in which the company expresses its support of art. Such support contributes to the company's success, he says, by keeping it abreast of emerging artistic ideas that can ultimately influence product designs.

What many visitors to Kohler, Wisconsin, find especially surprising is that all these facilities and activities — including tennis, fishing, swimming,

*S*ince the late 1970s, the Hospitality & Real Estate Group has developed Kohler Village into a premier resort with many activities and amenities, including golf. At left is The American Club hotel, flagship of the resort. Above is the par three 17th hole, Pinched Nerve, of the Straits Course. *Forbes* magazine and *The Robb Report* have described The American Club as the best golf resort in the U.S., while *Golf Odyssey* has lauded Kohler's four courses as "the best 72 holes in the world."

hiking, fine dining and the Kohler Waters Spa, in addition to golf, The American Club, the Design Center and factory tours — are located in a charming residential community, population 1,900, with winding tree-lined streets. The village has been described as "one of the prettiest towns in the United States" and "a garden at a factory gate." And that, too, is part of the Kohler heritage of functional art.

What Comes Next?

Kohler Co.'s earnings increased at a compound annual rate of 10.9% from 1970 through 2000, an excellent long-term growth record. However, building a larger, more profitable company is just one of Herb's obsessions. Ensuring that the company remains privately controlled is another. He believes the independence that comes with private ownership gives Kohler Co. a competitive advantage. "Because of private ownership," he states, "we can pursue strategic initiatives that public shareholders would not tolerate since the payoffs are not necessarily immediate. For example, if we were publicly owned, we could not have started our hospitality business. That was a 20-year investment, and the returns today are significant. But we went through a lengthy period of developing that business without an immediate profit."

During the 1960s and 1970s, a small percentage of Kohler Co.'s shares got into the hands of public investors due to sales and loan pledges by two of Herb's cousins. As these shares became more widely distributed, the number of Kohler Co. stockholders approached 500, the threshold at which the company would be publicly owned under federal securities laws. This concerned Herb. To deal with the situation, in 1978 the company executed a 1-for-20 reverse stock split, buying back the holdings of many outside investors who owned less than one full share after the split. In this way, the company pared its stockholder list to fewer than 200.

More recently, in 1998, Kohler Co. implemented a recapitalization plan that established separate voting and non-voting classes of stock. This action not only solidified the company's closely held status, but also provides an effective means to transfer control to future generations. Some stockholders who were required to sell or exchange their Kohler Co. shares challenged the price in court, but in April 2000 Kohler Co. and the dissenting stockholders reached a settlement. With the recap completed, Kohler's future as a private company is assured.

Speaking of the dilemma of many family-controlled enterprises, Jeff Cheney asserts, "There is often the generation that builds it, the generation that builds it bigger and the generation that spends it. This has not happened to Kohler. We don't seem to be getting close to the generation that wants to spend it. They believe in the vision."

Herb's three children, Laura, Rachel and David, have all come into the business and hold senior management positions after having started their careers elsewhere. Even given the normal stresses and strains of working for their father, who expects a great deal of them, Laura, Rachel and David have all bought into the Kohler family heritage. They are bright, hard-working and unpretentious, which may say something about the merits of being raised in a small town like Kohler Village.

Herb, who was born in 1939, is still in the prime of his career. He loves his job as much as ever and continues to work long hours with no sense whatever of a nine-to-five day. Like his father, he drives colleagues batty with meetings that start whenever they happen to start and sometimes keep going into the early morning hours. "There's a saying that very few Kohlers have watches or calendars, if you get the drift," according to Walter Cleveland, Kohler Co.'s president from 1968 to 1974.

With annual revenues of approximately $3 billion, Kohler Co. is one of the largest, oldest and most successful privately owned enterprises in America. Let's take a closer look at this unique company — how it started, how it got to be what it is today and, most importantly, where Herb Kohler, who is always springing surprises, plans to take it next.

*H*erb Kohler, center, poses with members of his family. Left to right are daughter Laura, senior vice president-human resources; son David, group president-kitchen & bath; wife Natalie Black, general counsel, senior vice president of communications and corporate secretary; sister Ruth, director of the John Michael Kohler Arts Center; and daughter Rachel, group president-interiors.

*T*his is the earliest known photograph of Kohler employees and the company's original factory at 9th Street and St. Clair Avenue in Sheboygan, Wisconsin. John Michael Kohler, the company's founder, is just left of center, holding the child. For its first 10 years, the company manufactured plows and other cast-iron farm implements. The plow on the roof is a trade sign, while the barrels are believed to have been filled with water as a safeguard against fire.

ur story begins with an unlikely chain of events: a cheesemaker from a tiny village in the Austrian Alps, where his ancestors have lived for centuries, suddenly pulls up stakes and moves his family to the American frontier. The cheesemaker's son, who is 10 years old at the time, adapts quickly to life in America. He attends college in Chicago, becomes a traveling salesman, moves to Sheboygan, Wisconsin, to be closer to his sweetheart and ends up as a theater impresario and successful entrepreneur, founding what would become one of America's leading private companies, with a premier brand name.

The cheesemaker was Johann Kohler. His enterprising son was John Michael Kohler. And the company founded by John Michael was (and is) Kohler Co.

We know a few basic facts about Johann Kohler. He came from a long line of dairy farmers and cheesemakers. He was very independent-minded. And he was prolific, fathering 17 children by two marriages.

Johann was a native of Schnepfau in the picturesque Alpine valley of Bregenzerwald. In 1838, he married Maria Anna Moosbrugger from the neighboring village of Schoppernau, where her family had operated an inn, the Rössle (Little Horse), since the 1600s. Johann and Maria Anna had eight children, five of whom survived beyond infancy. However, her death in 1853 at age 36 set in motion dramatic change within the family. Not long thereafter, Johann, 48 years old, married his young housekeeper, Maria Theresia Natter. That union produced another nine children. It was with Maria Theresia, pregnant with their first child, and his five surviving children by Maria Anna — Jodok, 15; Kasper, 13; Theresia, 11; John Michael, 10; and Maria, 3 — that Johann left for America in May 1854.

What prompted Johann to pull up stakes and take his family to a distant land is today a matter of conjecture. Perhaps he was driven by the political turmoil of the times. The failure of the revolutions of 1848 had stopped democracy in its tracks all across Europe and led to widespread political repression, prompting an exodus to America's welcoming shores. Or maybe he was influenced by his brother-in-law, Gaspard Moosbrugger, who had departed a decade earlier to become one of the first European

John Michael Kohler, Kohler Co.'s founder, was a businessman, impresario and community leader who lived life to its fullest. At right is a cast-iron wheel made in the original Kohler factory.

*J*ohn Michael's parents were Johann Kohler and Maria Anna Moosbrugger Kohler. Both were natives of the Bregenzerwald Valley in Austria, where their ancestors had lived for centuries. Maria died when John Michael was only nine. Johann thereupon remarried and took his family to the United States, where he became a dairy farmer.

settlers in Minnesota, clearing an 80-acre farm in wilderness five miles north of what is now downtown St. Paul.

Whatever the reason, Johann was an independent thinker, even to the point of obstinacy, as illustrated by an incident on the voyage to America. When the ship, the *Regulator*, ran into a storm, the captain ordered all adult male passengers on deck to help the crew. Johann flatly refused, saying his ticket did not require him to work. According to family legend, the captain responded by threatening to throw him overboard, whereupon Johann concluded that assisting the crew wasn't such a bad idea after all.

Although Johann had prospered in Austria, he was not rich. Indeed, the Kohlers traveled steerage, the least expensive class, and cooked their own meals on the 54-day voyage from LeHavre. Arriving in New York, they continued on to Galesburg, Illinois, where they lived briefly. They then moved to Minnesota, where Johann purchased 160 acres adjacent to the property of his brother-in-law and cleared the land for a dairy farm. Johann's land became something of a local legend. It continued to be farmed by Kohlers for the next 135 years, outlasting all the other original farms in the county as urbanization took hold. The family branch that owned and worked the farm finally sold it to a real estate developer in 1989. Although the farm is now gone,

many Kohlers still live in the St. Paul area. For years, there was even a Kohler brand ice cream. These Minnesota Kohlers are cousins of the Kohlers of Kohler, Wisconsin.

Like many other nineteenth century immigrants, Johann was very proud to be an American. On reaching Minnesota, he anglicized his name to John and applied almost immediately for citizenship, which he was granted in 1860.

Native Americans still outnumbered newcomers in the region around St. Paul when the Kohlers arrived in 1854. One day Indians dropped by the Kohler farmhouse unannounced and were fascinated by the pendulum of a clock. Frightened

and attempting to avoid trouble, Maria Theresia offered the Indians some cheese, which any friendly Austrian would do. As the story was recounted years later by Julia Kohler, of the family branch that continued to own the farm, "It must have been the first cheese they ever had, because they spit it right out." The Indians left soon thereafter — and, as far as we know, never visited the Kohler farm again.

John Michael Kohler and the Founding of Kohler Co.
How difficult these times must have been for young John Michael. In quick order, his mother died, his father remarried and the family

The company's early products included this primitive "engine," which consisted of a series of iron gears turned by teams of horses. The mechanical energy provided by the horses was transmitted by means of a universal joint and drive shaft to the farmer's hay baler, feed chopper or pump.

moved 5,000 miles to a remote wilderness. On the other hand, as an adult John Michael would have wide-ranging personal interests, including the arts, community service, business and family, and would make friends easily. So there was something in his upbringing that fostered an open mind and a love of life.

In 1862, at age 18, John Michael left the family farm and headed for Chicago to attend Dyhrenfurth College at night while working days. He stayed in Chicago nine years, eventually becoming a traveling salesman for a furniture company, a job that took him regularly to Sheboygan, Wisconsin, on the Lake Michigan shoreline north of Milwaukee. On

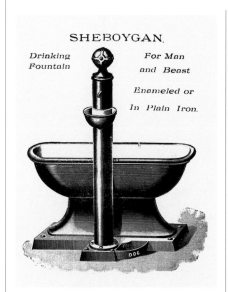

SHEBOYGAN.

Drinking Fountain

For Man and Beast

Enameled or In Plain Iron.

*R*ight, newspaper ads announced in 1873 that John Michael Kohler and Charles Silberzahn had purchased a Sheboygan foundry from Kohler's father-in-law, Jacob Vollrath. Kohler Co. traces its origins to this transaction. Opposite, a handbill shows some of the company's early cast-iron products. Above is a detail from that handbill — a water fountain that conveniently serves people (the spigot on the post), horses (the trough) and dogs (the little dish on the bottom).

one of these visits he met Lillie Vollrath, daughter of a Sheboygan businessman, Jacob Vollrath.

Like the Kohlers, the Vollraths were German-speaking immigrants, having come to the United States from the Rhineland in 1845. John Michael and Lillie fell in love and were married in 1871. Jacob Vollrath immediately took John Michael under his wing, giving him a job in the family-owned foundry and two years later selling the business to him for $5,000. Kohler Co. traces its birth to that transaction, which took place December 3, 1873, when John Michael was 29 years

old. After selling the foundry to John Michael, Jacob launched another business for himself, and that business grew into today's Vollrath Company, a successful Sheboygan manufacturer of products for the food service, health care and consumer markets.

As it happened, John Michael bought the foundry at a most inopportune time: just three months earlier, the nation had plunged into the most severe financial depression of the nineteenth century. The Panic of 1873 would last five years,

> Messrs. Kohler & Silberzahn have bought the interest of J. J. Vollrath in the Sheboygan Union Iron and Steel Foundry, and will hereafter carry on the business in all its branches, at the old stand, corner of Ninth and St. Clair streets. See advertisement of dissolution and new firm in another column.

forcing thousands of companies into bankruptcy. To make matters worse for John Michael, his company manufactured plowshares and other agricultural equipment, and farmers were especially hard-hit by the panic. Yet, somehow the company survived. Especially in those early years, when farmers lacked cash, John Michael often sold products for "payment in kind" — that is, for potatoes, geese, blankets, firewood, bacon or any other commodity the farmer might have on hand. Although we don't know for sure, it's likely that John

The Sheboygan Times.

H. N. ROSS, Publisher.

SATURDAY, DEC. 6, 1873.

CITY AND COUNTY.

☞ S. M. PETTENGILL & CO., 10 State Street Boston, 37 Park Row, New York, and 701 Chestnut Street, Philadelphia, are our Agents for procuring advertisements for THE SHEBOYGAN TIMES in the above cities, and authorized to contract for advertising at our lowest rates.

The mercury fell to zero yesterday (Friday) morning.

Matter for publication has crowded upon us this week, and much has had to be left over for next week.

Dissolution--New Firm.

Notice is hereby given that the firm of J. J. VOLLRATH & CO., proprietors of the Union Iron and Steel Foundry, at Sheboygan, Wis., was dissolved by mutual consent on the 26th day of Nov. 1873. All accounts of the said firm will be settled by Messrs KOHLER & SILBERZAHN, who have succeeded to its business.

J. J. VOLLRATH,
J. M. KOHLER.

The undersigned, having purchased the interest of Mr. J. J. Vollrath in the Sheboygan Union Iron and Steel Foundry, have formed a co-partnership under the firm name of KOHLER & SILBERZAHN, and will continue the business of Iron, Steel and Brass Castings, in their various branches, and would respectfully solicit the continued patronage of the public, guaranteeing that their work shall be the best of its kind. Cast Cast-Steel and other Plows kept constantly on hand, and work of any kind in our line made to order.

JOHN M. KOHLER.
CHAS. SILBERZAHN.

Sheboygan, Dec, 3, 1873. 40w2

KOHLER, HAYSSEN & STEHN MFG. CO.

Office and Works 702-722 Jefferson Ave.

ESTABLISHED 1873. INCORPORATED 1887.

SHEBOYGAN, WISCONSIN, U. S. A.

We manufacture the Champion Agricultural Implements and other goods hereon illustrated. Engines and Boilers for Dairymen and Creameries, Pulleys of all sizes, Shafting and Hangers of latest improved construction. Outside Iron Stairs, Brackets, Balusters, Railings, Columns and Crestings a speciality. Estimates given on application. Bridge Bolts and Caps, Reach and Bolster Plates also Cast Iron Enameled Bath Tubs, Sinks and other Sanitary Goods. Cast Iron Lawn and Cemetery Fences, Vases, Settees and Cast Iron Enameled Crosses and Monuments for Cemeteries.

WRITE FOR ILLUSTRATED AND DESCRIPTIVE CATALOGUES AND PRICE LISTS. DISCOUNTS ON APPLICATION.

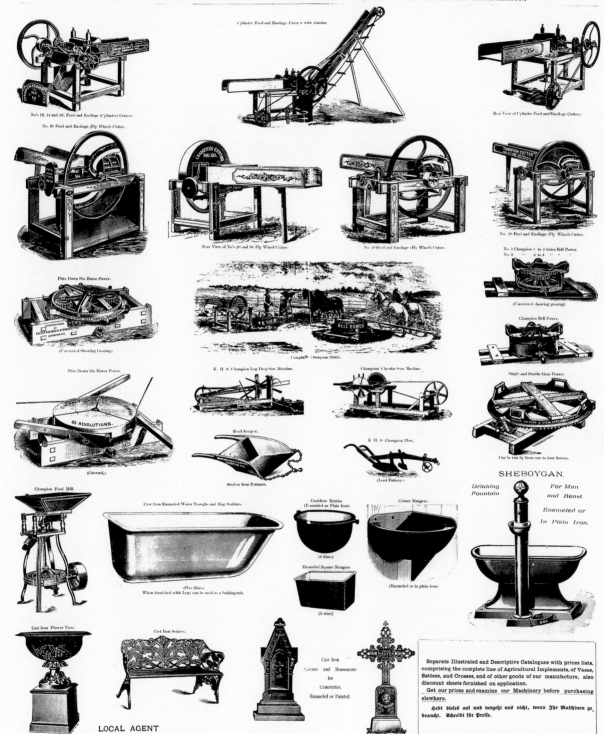

LOCAL AGENT

Separate Illustrated and Descriptive Catalogues with prices lists, comprising the complete line of Agricultural Implements, of Vases, Settees, and Crosses, and of other goods of our manufacture, also discount sheets furnished on application.

Get our prices and examine our Machinery before purchasing elsewhere.

Hebt dieses auf und vergeßt uns nicht, wenn Ihr Maschinen gebraucht. Schreibt für Preise.

The Kohler, Hayssen & Stehn Mfg. Company.

Michael, in turn, distributed these goods to his employees in lieu of paying cash wages.

In addition to producing farm implements, the foundry made cast-iron ornaments for residential yards, including statues of deer and angels, and an assortment of other products such as cemetery gates and hitching posts. Nearly a century later in 1972, Lyman Conger, at that time Kohler Co.'s chairman of the board, recalled

*A*bove, by the late nineteenth century, as it shifted out of farm products and into plumbing products, Kohler was operating from a sizable manufacturing plant in Sheboygan. At right is a receipt for pin catchers and lasts.

Kettles.

Cast Iron Enameled Steam Jacket Kettle.

Mortors.

Bell Shape.   Cast Iron Ground.

Chafing and Vegetable Dishes,
FOR HOTELS AND RESTAURANTS.

Cast Iron Enameled Oval Chafing Dish.

Cast Iron Flower Vase.

*T*he company made virtually any type of cast-iron product for which there was a market, including the assortment at left. At right is an early product catalog.

having once received a request from the Kohler archives, which was running out of storage space, to throw away the old wooden pattern for the angel. "I made a little note, rather humorously, saying I didn't know how you could dispose of an angel," Conger, a devout Roman Catholic, remarked. He gave permission to throw it out. Some today would cringe at the idea of discarding such a rare relic of American industrial history. However, antique industrial tools were often viewed as little more than junk 30 or 40 years ago.

Kohler Co.'s Early Years

In buying the foundry, John Michael Kohler had a minority partner, Charles Silberzahn, an employee in the plant. In fact, Kohler Co.'s original name was Kohler & Silberzahn. The company employed 21 men, mostly German-speaking immigrants, and was located in a small frame building at 9th Street and St. Clair Avenue in Sheboygan. Mounted on the roof were a plow (Kohler Co.'s first advertisement) and several wooden barrels filled with water, to be tipped over in the event of fire. The barrels notwithstanding, when the building caught fire in 1880, it was consumed in minutes. The company thereupon moved to larger quarters at 7th Street and Jefferson Avenue.

Meanwhile, in 1878, Silberzahn sold his interest to Herman Hayssen and John Stehn, German immigrants who worked at the company as machinists, and the company was renamed Kohler, Hayssen & Stehn Manufacturing Company. Shortly after the turn of the century, Hayssen and John Stehn's widow sold their holdings to the Kohler family, and the company was reorganized as J. M. Kohler Sons Co. Subsequently, in 1910, Hayssen invented the automatic bread-wrapping machine and founded

Cast Iron Enameled Water Troughs and Hog Scalders.

(Five Sizes)
When furnished with Legs can be used as a bathing tub.

Kohler got into the plumbing products business in 1883 when John Michael Kohler took a cast-iron water trough, left, and added feet, turning it into a bathtub, below. Within four years, plumbing products and enamelware accounted for 70 percent of the company's sales.

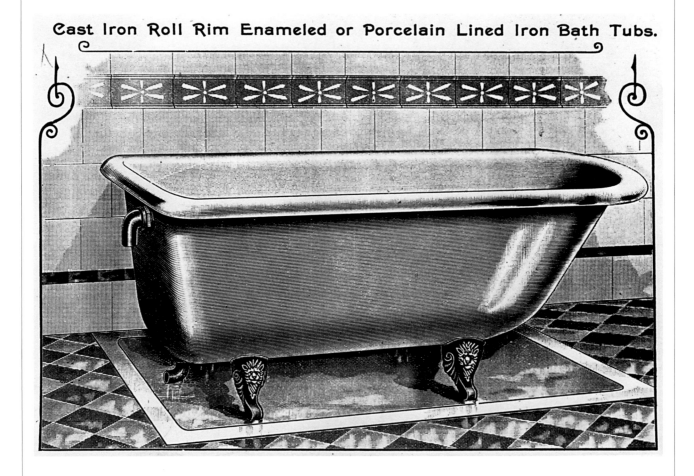

Cast Iron Roll Rim Enameled or Porcelain Lined Iron Bath Tubs.

Hayssen Manufacturing Co. to produce and market the device. Today, as a division of Barry-Wehmiller Companies, Inc., Hayssen Manufacturing is one of the world's leading producers of flexible-packaging equipment for cheese, meats and other items.

The early history of Kohler Co. is one of growth and change. By the late 1870s, the company had broadened its product line by becoming an agent for J. I. Case Threshing Machine Co. and Knowlton Mfg. Co. (which produced reapers, mowers and hayrakes). In 1880, when the company moved to larger quarters following the fire, John Michael added an enamel shop to produce tea kettles and other enamelware.

But the biggest change of all came in 1883. Scouring about for new products, John

Michael took a cast-iron basin, which he sold to farmers for use as a combination hog scalder and watering trough; he then enameled it and added four ornamental feet, turning it into a bathtub. According to company lore, that first bathtub was sold to a local farmer for one cow and 14 chickens.

Plumbing products quickly became the engine for the company's growth — and have been ever since. Prior to 1883, farm implements accounted for about 80 percent of sales. By 1887, plumbing fixtures and other enamelware accounted for 70 percent.

Civic Leader... Family Man... Impresario

What was John Michael Kohler really like? Pictures from the era show a pleasant, kindly face, with a neatly trimmed mustache and goatee

and a robust build like that of a well-fed Austrian bürgermeister. Oscar A. Kroos, who joined Kohler Co. as a young man late in the nineteenth century, described John Michael as being "gentle and kind." John Michael "sympathized with suffering, and his sympathy was expressed in practical ways," Kroos said.

With his outgoing personality and natural leadership abilities, John Michael became a pillar of the community. He was the first signer of a petition for the Humane Society in Sheboygan and he established Friendship House, a youth services institution which still exists a century later. He was a member of the County Board of Supervisors and the City Council and was elected mayor of Sheboygan in 1892, serving one term.

John Michael and Lillie had six children: Evangeline, born in 1872; Robert, in 1873; Walter, in 1875; Marie, in 1876; Lillie II, in 1878; and

A Kohler employee examines a cast-iron bathtub, about 1905. Kohler quickly gained a reputation for consistent product quality.

*J*ohn Michael Kohler, above, was outgoing and energetic. His four sons, left to right, were Carl, Herbert (foreground), Walter and Robert. All went into the family business.

Carl, in 1880. After Lillie died in 1883 at age 35, John Michael married her younger sister, Wilhelmina Vollrath, affectionately known as Minnie, and they had a son, Herbert, in 1891. The Kohlers lived in a large Victorian house near the center of town. By all accounts, the Kohler home was filled with warmth and happy activity. Gossip and spiteful talk were frowned on. John Michael's daughter Evangeline inscribed on the mantel, "Around this hearth let no evil word be spoken." That inscription has never been removed, surviving to this day. (The building now houses the John Michael Kohler Arts Center, a nonprofit institution open to the public.) John Michael loved Wagnerian music and, for lighter entertainment, Gilbert and Sullivan. With their parents' encouragement, all the children learned to play musical instruments. For exercise, John Michael rode horses, a passion that continues among many of his descendants.

There was still another side to John Michael — that of the impresario. For years, he owned and managed the Sheboygan Opera House, where plays and other performances were staged in German and English. He brought to the community many of the best-known touring actors of that time, including Sol Smith Russell, Frederick War, William Courtney and Grace Strickland. Like the Renaissance man who could do anything and everything, John Michael even acted in some of the

Kohler employees pose in a typical group photograph of the day. Many were German-speaking immigrants who had come to the United States in search of a better life.

theater's productions.

John Michael grew up a Roman Catholic, but had a falling out with the church. According to family lore, when one of his sisters, a nun, lay ill in a convent, he tried to visit her but was denied entrance. He never did see her before she died. Angered by that experience, he left the Catholic Church and became an Episcopalian, and his descendants generally remain so today. But rancor of that sort was unusual for John Michael.

The Move to Riverside and John Michael's Death

In 1899, John Michael took an extraordinary business risk that would establish the future course of the company: he purchased 21 acres of farmland in the tiny settlement of Riverside, four miles west of Sheboygan, for $1,400. He then announced plans to build a foundry on the site and move his business there to concentrate solely on the manufacture of cast-iron enamelware

J.M. KOHLER SONS CO.

*R*iverside, Wisconsin, was a tiny settlement when John Michael Kohler moved the company there in 1900. Pictured is the Riverside plant, rebuilt in 1902 after a fire, and two-story office building. The citizens of Riverside renamed their community the Village of Kohler in 1912.

and other plumbing products. His successors, notably his son Walter, would eventually buy dozens of farms in the region, expanding the company's holdings to several thousand acres.

Many residents of Sheboygan found it difficult to understand why John Michael would relocate to the countryside, away from their city's skilled workforce, away from utilities and away from city services. A Sheboygan newspaper even ran an editorial titled "Kohler's Folly," mocking his plan. Although that newspaper ceased publication 50 years ago, Kohler Co. is still going strong in the same location, now called the Village of Kohler, selected by John Michael.

John Michael's idea was to move to a wonderful natural environment with clean air and unlimited room for expansion. The new foundry was completed in October 1900 and began operation that same month with a workforce of 250.

John Michael loved the foundry business and was excited about the prospect of operating his new plant. As fate would have it, though, he did not live to enjoy his dream. John Michael Kohler died on November 5, 1900, just days after the foundry was completed. He was 56 years old and had led the company for its first 27 years.

Reeling from the loss of their father, John Michael's three adult sons — Robert, Walter and Carl, all

in their 20s and novices at managing a business — were suddenly in charge. Robert, the oldest, became president; Walter, the middle, treasurer; and Carl, the youngest of the three, secretary. John Michael's fourth son, Herbert, was a nine-year-old schoolchild.

However, like the onset of a plague, the bad times were just beginning. In February 1901, less than four months after it had been completed, the new foundry was gutted by fire. The loss was estimated at $66,000, of which insurance paid $62,000. Scrambling to keep the company going, the brothers rented foundry space in Sheboygan until they could decide whether to rebuild in Riverside.

Then, one month after the foundry burned, the company's two non-family partners — Herman Hayssen and Magdalena Stehn — withdrew from the business and sold their stock to the company, perhaps because they did not want to undertake the expense of rebuilding the Riverside factory. Already pressed for cash, the company paid $27,000 to purchase their stock. With their departure, the company became wholly owned by members of the Kohler family and was renamed J. M. Kohler Sons Co. (The name was shortened to Kohler Co. in 1912.)

The three Kohler brothers were now faced with one of the most momentous decisions in Kohler Co.

Above is the early 1900s Kohler Co. office building in a photograph taken later than the photo on page 44. Note the streetcar tracks, over which trolleys brought employees from Sheboygan four miles away. The building still exists today, right, and is used as an administrative office.

history: whether to rebuild in Riverside and, if so, how to finance construction. The decision was far from cut-and-dried. On March 15, 1901, four weeks after the fire, the *Sheboygan Telegram* reported, "It has not yet been decided definitely that Kohler, Hayssen & Stehn Manufacturing Co. will rebuild its enameling plant at Riverside. The company has received some flattering offers from other cities, who are desirous of securing the institution, which it is considering."

Ultimately, the brothers chose to stay and rebuild, borrowing $50,000 — a large sum at the time — to help finance construction. The refur-

bished facility was completed in 1902, and Kohler Co. was back in business in Riverside.

But the turmoil was not yet over. Tragedy struck again in 1904 when Carl, the youngest of the three brothers and the company's secretary, died at age 24 after drinking carbolic acid. The death certificate listed "melancholia" as the primary cause of death. Rumors of the time suggested that Carl took his own life in hopes of saving the company from financial ruin through the payment of his life insurance. Walter had the horrible experience of walking into the room as his brother expired. A year later, Robert, the oldest of the brothers

and the company's president, died at age 31 from a stroke.

The Kohlers were a close-knit family, and we can only imagine the pain that Walter endured as a result of the loss of his father and two of his brothers, combined with the business difficulties brought on by the fire at the plant — all within a period of five years. But Walter was an unusually strong individual. He was an optimist by nature and had the fortitude to push ahead even in the face of the direst problems. Following Robert's death, Walter, age 30, became Kohler Co.'s president. He would lead the company for the next 35 years.

*K*ohler Co. experimented with various methods of distributing its products, including the formation in 1903 of a captive organization, Kohler-Smith Company, right, to distribute products to the plumbing trade in Illinois. Kohler-Smith was dissolved in 1905, when Kohler Co. adopted its current practice of distributing products through independent wholesalers.

Sheboygan, Wis., April 25, 1903.

The undersigned each for himself subscribes and agrees to take the number of shares of stock at One Hundred Dollars each in the Kohler-Smith Co. as stated opposite their names respectively and to pay therefore full par value as stated in cash, as it is called for by the Board of Directors of said corporation:

Ezra Smith	11 Shares @ $100.00 each	= $1,100.00
Roy L. Kohler	11 " " "	= 1,100.00
Walter J. Kohler	11 " " "	= 1,100.00
Carl J. Kohler	11 " " "	= 1100.00
O. A. Kroos	6 " " "	= 600.00

*W*alter Kohler was a legendary businessman in the history of Wisconsin. He conducted himself at all times with humor, intelligence and style. He loved white carnations and almost always wore one in his lapel.

ℛecovering from the terrible events of 1900-1905, and taking charge of a company that was in precarious financial condition because of the costs of building and rebuilding the foundry, Walter Kohler would emerge as one of the great leaders in Kohler Co.'s history. The business desperately needed a strong, steady hand at the helm, and Walter was that able captain.

Growing Up in the Family Business

Walter Jodok Kohler was a bright young man in a hurry. Born in 1875, he quit school at age 15, having completed eighth grade, to join his father's company. "He felt work was too important to wait," according to his grandson, John M. "Mike" Kohler Jr. Walter was a voracious reader all his life and, in effect, educated himself.

He began in the foundry, became a foreman at 18 and factory superintendent at 24, taking on the additional title of company treasurer at 25 following the death of his father. Five years later, after his two brothers had died, he was thrust into the presidency.

Intelligent, articulate and poised, Walter had a natural instinct for managing and a willingness to take calculated risks. In addition to heading Kohler Co. from 1905 to 1940, he served as governor of Wisconsin from 1929 to 1931 while continuing to run the company and was even briefly considered for the Republican nomination for U.S. president in 1936.

𝒫roduct quality has been a Kohler Co. hallmark from the earliest years. Because their family name is on their company's products, the Kohlers are sticklers about producing the best.

Walter espoused a philosophy of hard work and integrity. "Talent, even genius," he maintained, "can never take the place of sincere effort." In his view, anything could be accomplished with determination.

He recognized also that art and creativity are indispensable to life. One of Walter's favorite quotations was by the British art critic John Ruskin:

Life without labor is guilt;
Labor without art is brutality.

This belief in artistry is one of the great generational ideas that has guided Kohler Co. for the past century. It is evinced in many ways, including the company's design leadership in kitchen and bath products, furniture and golf; the Arts/Industry program that provides studio space for artists in the factory; the beauty of the grounds surrounding The American Club; and the beauty of the village itself. While this generational idea is stronger today than ever, helping drive the company's success, it was John Michael who laid the groundwork for the idea and Walter who first infused it with life.

In managing the company, Walter believed in the merits not only of art, but also wit and grace. Under his leadership, the employee magazine, *Kohler of Kohler News*, was filled with anecdotes and amusing stories that helped humanize Kohler Co. A 1917 article, titled "How Wise Is an Owl?," read: "All kinds of queer things happen in the foundry. Not long ago an owl

was seen perched on one of the sprinkler pipes. A number of the men were debating about the best way to capture the bird. John Hertziger, being an expert hunter, advised one of the men to attract the attention of the owl by walking around it and looking intently into its eyes so that the bird would follow his gaze. His argument was that after a few trips

had been made the owl would twist its head off. If you have any hunting or trapping problems, refer them to John."

Anyone who ever met Walter never forgot him. A handsome, dapper man with a magnetic personality, he turned heads when he walked into a room. At the same time, he had an ability to put people at ease and

command their respect by treating them with honesty and fairness.

Kohler Co.'s Emergence on The National Scene

The early years of the twentieth century were a period of enormous opportunity and growth in the plumbing products business. Not unlike the progressive incorporation of head-

Shortly after the turn of the twentieth century, Kohler Co. began reinventing the bathroom by introducing beautiful new products. Many of the designs from that period transcend time. For instance, the bathtub, from the 1908 model bathroom at right, was recently reintroduced in an elegant modern version called Vintage. Below is an early product catalog.

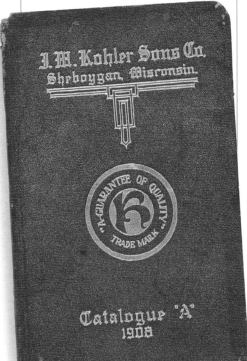

lights, windshield, self-starter and bumpers in the automobile, new fixtures and fittings were being added to the bathroom and kitchen at a rapid rate. Walter recognized this opportunity and capitalized on it by developing new products, investing in state-of-the-art manufacturing equipment and expanding Kohler Co.'s distribution network. Taking what was then a small regional manufacturer of cast-iron bathtubs, he systematically built Kohler Co. into one of the "big three" plumbing products companies in the United States.

Walter was an energetic, hands-on manager. Eager to know every detail of the business, he donned a blue clerk's jacket and old felt hat late each afternoon to visit the factory floor and personally put in his two cents' worth on any manufacturing problems or new product ideas. As a result, he almost always arrived home late for dinner. His wife, Charlotte, a former art teacher in the local public schools, was very understanding. They got along famously and were a popular

The postcard at right depicts Kohler Co.'s factory and general office in 1914. The company had, by now, grown dramatically from the days of its original factory. Above, this 1918 photograph, titled "Our Snow Plow," shows a team of 10 horses (too many for the camera) pulling a massive blade fabricated in the Kohler foundry.

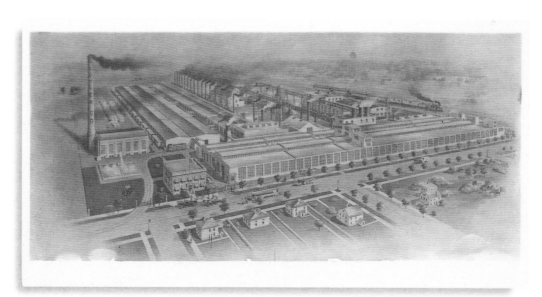

THE KOHLER STABLES

The Kohler name has been associated with horses for many years. Having grown up in the Austrian Alps and on a Minnesota farm, John Michael Kohler, the company's founder, was an avid horseman. He taught all his children to ride, but it was not until 1924 that Walter Kohler, then chairman and president, established the now-famous Kohler Stables. In the early years, many Kohler Co. executives bought horses and kept them at the stables. Although they had to pay for the care of their horses, access to the stables was one of the perks of being a Kohler executive and helped recruit and retain many talented people.

It was a wonderful way of life. "On weekends, 10 or 15 men would have their horses saddled up and ride out to Oostburg or Black River," Allen "Red" Smith, manager of the stables from 1945 to 1972, said in a 1984 interview. At their destination, a huge barbecue prepared by a chef from The American Club would be awaiting their arrival. Wives of the executives also kept horses at the stables and rode together, separately from the men, on Sunday mornings.

In its early years, the stables housed more than 20 horses. By the 1960s, however, just two remained — one belonging to Herbert V. Kohler Sr. and the other to Arthur Kroos, a Kohler Co. vice president. All the others had died

Walter Kohler was a fine athlete and an excellent horseman.

and were buried in an equine graveyard across the road from the stables.

It was Herbert V. Kohler Jr. who revived the stables and brought them to their current preeminence in the field of Morgan horses. All Morgans are descended from Justin Morgan, a champion stallion that lived from 1792 to 1821. Known for their stamina, vivacity and handsome, well-muscled appearance, Morgans are popular in the military, for police work, on cattle ranches, with families and for show. Herb acquired his first Morgan in 1969. On a trip to buy horses for his children, he saw the champion Morgan stallion Vigilmarch, who had been abused and was seriously undernourished. Herb first rode alone at age two, and he has an eye for a good horse. He paid a mere $5,700 for Vigilmarch at a bankruptcy sale. With proper care, Vigilmarch regained his health and, under a breeding program at the Kohler Stables, became one of the great Morgan sires of all time.

Eighteen years after buying Vigilmarch, Herb bought his second Morgan stallion — a young steed named Noble Flaire. Again, Herb's eye for horses won the day. Noble Flaire became the 1989 and 1991 World Grand Champion Stallion and the World Champion in Park Harness in 1988, 1989 and 1991, and he was named Morgan Horse of the

PEOPLE'S CHOICE MORGAN AWARDS

Kohler Stables has made a consistently strong showing in the annual People's Choice Morgan Awards of *Horse World* magazine. In 1997, it pulled off the rare feat of winning Breeder of the Year (Herbert V. Kohler Jr.), Trainer of the Year (Thomas L. Caisse), Horse of the Year (HVK Bell Flaire) and Sire of the Year (Noble Flaire).

Below is a partial list for 2000 and 1999. All the horses are owned or were bred by Kohler Stables.

2000

Breeder of the Year — Herbert V. Kohler Jr.

Horse of the Year — HVK Courageous Flaire

Sire of the Year — Noble Flaire

Reserve Overall Park Saddle — HVK Bell Flaire

Reserve Park Saddle Stallion — HVK Bell Flaire

Park Saddle Gelding — HVK Acclamation

Reserve Park Saddle Gelding — HVK Trafalgar

Reserve Overall Four-Year-Old Park Saddle — HVK Madonna

Four-Year-Old Park Saddle Mare/Gelding — HVK Madonna

Overall Three-Year-Old Park Saddle — HVK Classic Design

Three-Year-Old Park Saddle Mare/Gelding — HVK Classic Design

Overall Amateur Park Saddle — HVK Courageous Flaire

Reserve Overall Amateur Park Saddle — HVK Trafalgar

Amateur Park Saddle Stallion — HVK Courageous Flaire

Amateur Park Saddle Gelding — HVK Trafalgar

Reserve Overall Junior Exhibitor Park Saddle — HVK Noble Flame

Reserve Overall Park Harness — HVK Pavarotti

Reserve Park Harness Stallion — HVK Pavarotti

Park Harness Mare — HVK Tiz Flaire

Four-Year-Old Park Harness Mare/Gelding — HVK Carmen

Reserve Amateur Pleasure Driving Stallion — HVK Grand Entrance

1999

Breeder of the Year — Herbert V. Kohler Jr.

Reserve Horse of the Year — HVK Bell Flaire

Sire of the Year — Noble Flaire

Overall In Hand Mare — HVK Crystal Bay

Five & Over In Hand Mare — HVK Stueben

Four-Year-Old In Hand Mare — HVK Crystal Bay

Reserve Four-Year-Old In Hand Mare — HVK Noble Countess

Reserve Overall Park Saddle — HVK Courageous Flaire

Reserve Park Saddle Stallion — HVK Courageous Flaire

Reserve Three-Year-Old Park Saddle Mare/Gelding — HVK Madonna

Overall Amateur Park Saddle — HVK Courageous Flaire

Amateur Park Saddle Stallion — HVK Courageous Flaire

Reserve Amateur Park Saddle Mare — HVK Dreamscape

Reserve Overall Park Harness — HVK Bell Flaire

Reserve Park Harness Stallion — HVK Bell Flaire

Overall Four-Year-Old Park Harness — HVK Constantinoble

Four-Year-Old Park Harness Mare/Gelding — HVK Constantinoble

Reserve Three-Year-Old Park Harness Mare/Gelding — HVK Obsidian

English Pleasure Stallion — HVK Man About Town

Reserve English Pleasure Mare — HVK Victoria's Secret

Reserve Pleasure Driving Amateur Ladies — HVK Grand Entrance

Special Awards (1999)

Morgan Breeder of the Decade — Herbert V. Kohler Jr.

Reserve Morgan Horse of the Decade — Noble Flaire

Morgan Sire of the Decade — Noble Flaire

Park Harness Horse of the Decade — HVK Bell Flaire

Reserve Roadster Horse of the Decade — HVK Derigueur

Park Harness Horse of the Century — Noble Flaire

Reserve Pleasure Driving Horse of the Century — HVK Frango

Decade for the 1980s by *Horse World* magazine.

In his entire life, Herb has purchased just two stallions — Vigilmarch and Noble Flaire. The Morgan breeding program of Kohler Stables has been built on these two sires.

Kohler Stables is today quite an operation. It breeds Morgans for show, and also trains, shows and sells them. Horses from the stables are in great demand among breeders, trainers and other buyers. "The very serious person coming into the breed often seeks our bloodlines for a foundation," says Tom Caisse, Kohler Stables' manager/trainer. Horses bred by Kohler Stables are identified by the HVK prefix (for Herbert V. Kohler), a kind of trademark of quality. At any Morgan show anywhere in the world, HVK horses are invariably among the winners.

In addition to selling its HVK horses, the stables keeps some and shows them itself. Among that group is its recent great champion, HVK Pavarotti, sired by Noble Flaire. "HVK Pavarotti has been on the cover of virtually every horse magazine, and you can't believe the amount of e-mail he receives," Caisse reports.

Branching out, in 1989 the stables won the United States pair driving championship with its Warmbloods and led the U.S. Equestrian Team to a world championship in Austria.

But Morgans remain the primary focus. "Morgans are very important to Herbert and his family," Caisse says. "He has given me the permission, the tools and the guidance to go forward, and we are by far the leading breeding farm in the world for Morgan horses."

*T*he Morgan breeding program of Kohler Stables has been built entirely on two sires — Noble Flaire, below, and Vigilmarch, above. Horses from their bloodlines are highly sought after by breeders, trainers and other buyers of Morgans.

*H*erb Kohler's favorite horse was Comic Strip, above, bought in the 1960s. Half pinto and half thoroughbred, Comic Strip became a world-champion jumper and was also a family horse. Herb and his children often rode him on the trails in and around Kohler Village.

*D*uring World War I, Kohler Co. produced materials, such as this projectile, for the American troops in Europe. Far right is the projectile mold in a closed position.

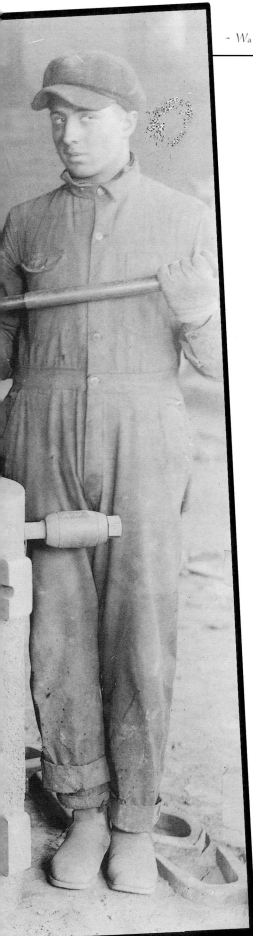

This flag-draped truck is carrying test projectiles made at the Kohler factory.

couple at parties and other social events in Sheboygan County.

The first new technical breakthrough came in 1911, when Kohler Co. introduced the one-piece built-in bathtub, a product we take for granted today. Prior to that time, built-in bathtubs were cast in two separate parts: the tub itself and the exposed side or apron. The two parts were fitted together by the plumber doing the installation. Overcoming technical challenges, Kohler Co. employees learned to cast the entire unit in a single piece. The one-piece bathtub eliminated crevices, joints and seams and is still the industry standard.

Kohler Co. followed up quickly on that success by introducing the industry's first one-piece bathroom lavatory and the first one-piece kitchen sink.

As the company launched new products, it rapidly expanded its marketing network. As of 1914, the company had five branch offices (sales offices) — in San Francisco, Chicago, New York, Boston and London. Within two years, the number had increased to 15 as a result of new offices being opened in Los Angeles, Houston, Philadelphia and seven other U.S. cities. Moreover, Kohler Co.'s workforce had now reached 950. When the United States entered World War I, the company shifted production to mine anchors, projectiles and shells, then resumed its growth in plumbing products following the 1918 armistice.

A Flurry of Activity After World War I

Walter really hit his stride in the decade following the war. In short order, he:

- developed Kohler Village into one of the most beautiful residential-industrial communities in America (see Chapter Four);

- took Kohler Co. into the manufacture of electrical generators;

- added china fixtures and brass fittings to Kohler Co.'s product line, building new facilities to manufacture both;

- broke off a long standing business relationship with a major competitor, Crane Co.; and

- became a corporate aviation pioneer.

When Kohler Co. began manufacturing electrical generators in 1920, one Kohler salesman devised this unusual truck to promote the sale of generators to farmers. The truck contained a generator-powered automatic milking machine. The idea was to show farmers, in practical terms, just how useful and reliable a Kohler generator could be.

Generators: Diversifying Into an Entirely New Business

Walter's decision to enter the electrical generator business in 1920 helps illuminate his management style.

The use of electricity in factories and the home was still relatively new, and many rural regions were not yet served by utility systems. For farmers and others outside the utility grids, the only way to obtain a source of electricity was by purchasing a generator. However, the generators of the time were awkward and primitive: they charged batteries, and the batteries in turn supplied 32 volts of power.

Walter's good friend, Anton Brotz, who was Kohler Co.'s chief research engineer, was always tinkering with things and was full of new ideas. For

whatever reason, he turned his attention to the problem of supplying electricity in remote locations. And in doing so, he invented the modern gasoline-powered generator. In Brotz's configuration, a four-horse-power engine drove a generator which delivered 110 volts of current directly to the line, eliminating the need for batteries. In addition, unlike battery systems, Brotz's invention supplied power in response to demand, shutting off automatically when there was no demand.

Walter immediately saw the possibilities of this revolutionary device, and he authorized its manufacture, even though Kohler Co. had no experience whatever in the generator business. One reason Walter decided to manufacture and sell generators was to offset some of the seasonality of plumbing products, which sold well when new homes were being constructed in the summer but not so well in the winter.

The new product was called the Kohler Automatic Power & Light, and its sales took off immediately. Walter was both smart and lucky in this regard. Whereas he intended to sell the Kohler Automatic mainly to farmers, that market never panned out to the degree he expected. On the other hand, a host of unforeseen applications did develop — standby power for hospitals, power for small airports, power for entire remote villages in Peru, power for isolated British castles. To this day, in some

Kohler Co. completed its new general office in Kohler Village in 1925. The building was designed by architect Richard Philipp in the Romanesque Revival style, which is characterized by solidity and strength. Standing directly across Highland Drive from The American Club, it remains the worldwide headquarters of Kohler Co.

parts of South America, Asia and Africa, a generator is known generically as a "Kohler."

One of the major early uses was to power the beacons that guided pilots flying night mail for the United States Post Office. The first regular overnight airmail service began on July 1, 1925, between New York and Chicago. The federal government installed revolving beacons, powered by Kohler Automatic generators, every 25 miles along the route to guide the pilots. This market grew rapidly as night airmail service was expanded and beacons were installed to demarcate the air lanes between major cities throughout the eastern United States. Although the use of

beacons for night flying was eventually supplanted by radio navigation, for years this was an important market for Kohler Automatic generators.

Walter's decision to manufacture generators had lasting effects. As we shall see in Chapter Seven, the power systems business (generators and small engines) remains a pillar of Kohler Co. to this day.

How Kohler Became a Full-Line Plumbing Products Company

Even as he developed Kohler Village and diversified into generators, Walter embarked on a major expansion of Kohler Co.'s plumbing products business.

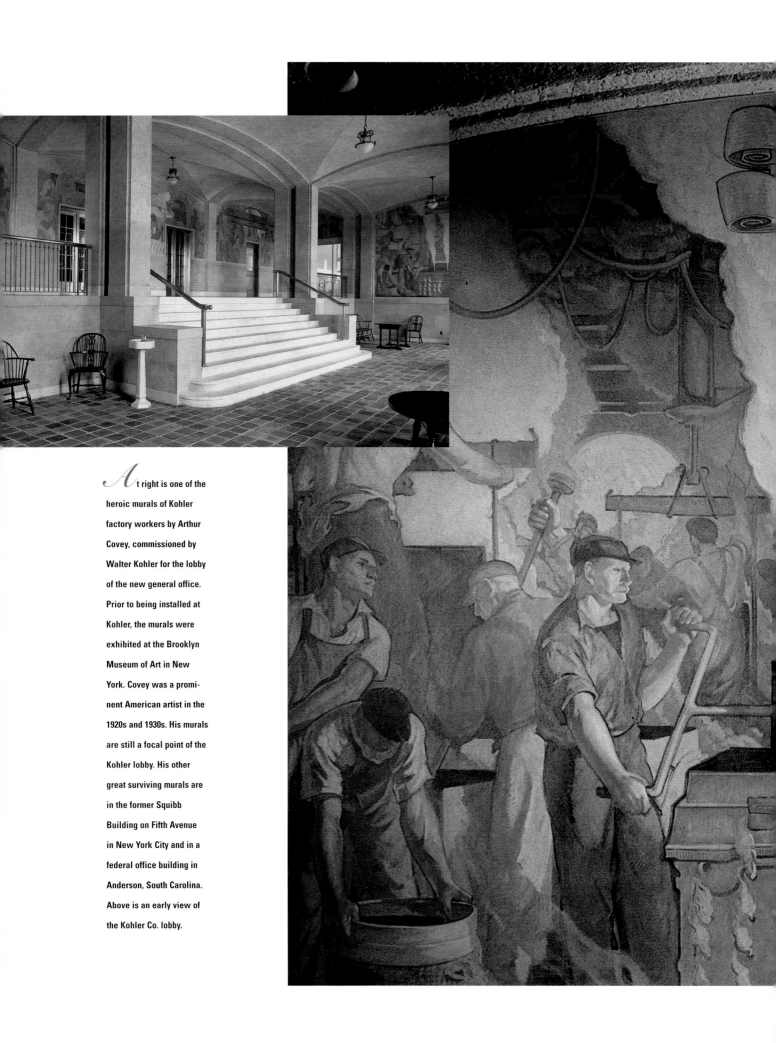

At right is one of the heroic murals of Kohler factory workers by Arthur Covey, commissioned by Walter Kohler for the lobby of the new general office. Prior to being installed at Kohler, the murals were exhibited at the Brooklyn Museum of Art in New York. Covey was a prominent American artist in the 1920s and 1930s. His murals are still a focal point of the Kohler lobby. His other great surviving murals are in the former Squibb Building on Fifth Avenue in New York City and in a federal office building in Anderson, South Carolina. Above is an early view of the Kohler Co. lobby.

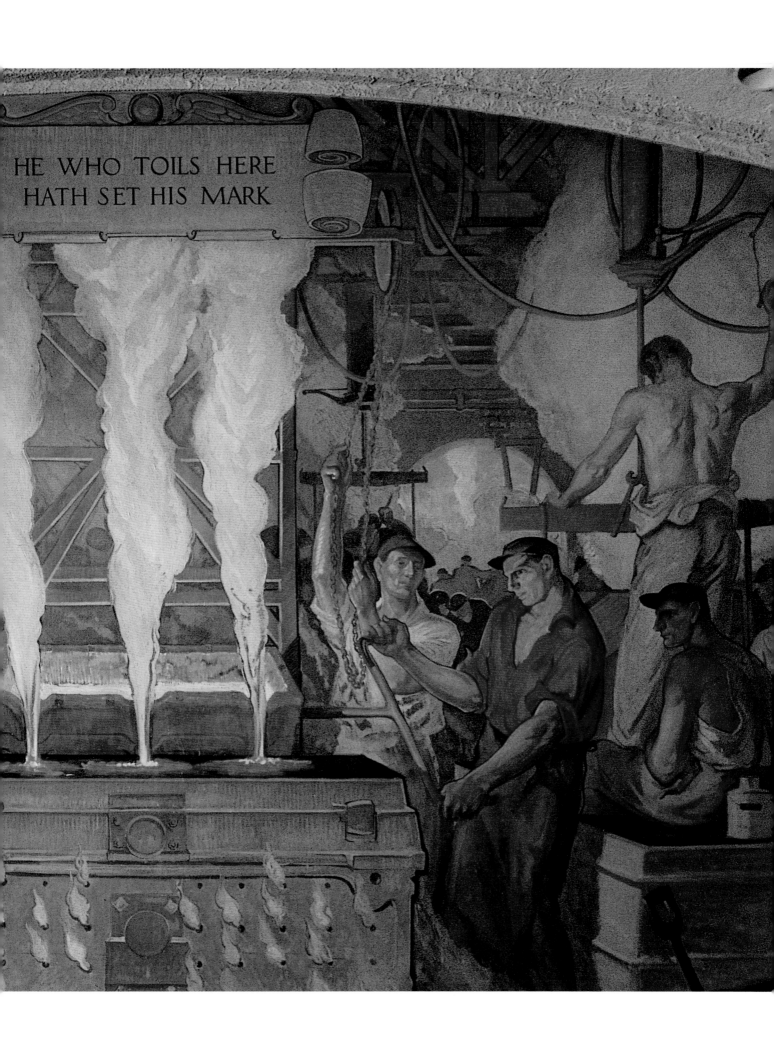

HE WHO TOILS HERE
HATH SET HIS MARK

BIRD'S-EYE VIEW OF KOHLER PLANT, KOHLER, WIS.

POST CARD

SHEBOYGAN
AUG 20
4 PM
1929
WIS.

These three views highlight the rapid development of the Kohler Co. plant and Kohler Village. The postcard at bottom shows the main street of the village in 1912 with the company's early office at left. The card immediately below shows the plant in about 1919. At left are the plant and general office in 1929, as the canceled postmark on the back of the card indicates. The main street is now a broad avenue with trees. Part of The American Club can be seen at the bottom of the picture.

Kohler Company's Plant, Kohler, near Sheboygan, Wis.—5

Kohler Sheboygan Coun

*L*eft, the brass plant was completed in 1926. It signaled Kohler Co.'s entry into the manufacture of faucets and other brass fittings. The pottery, in the background, was completed in 1927. One reason Walter Kohler built these facilities in Kohler Village, rather than elsewhere, was his desire to provide jobs for the people of Sheboygan County. Below is an employee in the brass plant, circa 1940. Opposite is a conveyor line for bathtubs in the foundry in 1933.

By the early 1920s, Kohler had established itself as one of the nation's foremost producers of cast-iron enamelware. However, it did not make two other major types of plumbing products: sanitary pottery (vitreous china fixtures, such as toilets, bidets and lavatories) and brassware (including faucets, drains and showerheads). It purchased brass fittings for its cast-iron tubs and sinks from other suppliers, among them Hoffmann & Billings, Milwaukee Brass and Federal-Huber. On large orders, distributors often made up their own combinations of fixtures and fittings. A popular combination was Kohler enamelware, Maddocks china and Speakman brass fittings, all considered top of the line.

The problem was this: if a cast-iron fixture bore the Kohler trademark, customers often assumed the china fixtures and brass fittings were

Kohler also. As a company memorandum stated, "This sometimes proved embarrassing, as in the Mayflower Hotel, Washington, and the Drake Hotel, Chicago, where the china fixtures became badly crazed." In other cases, faucets leaked, casting doubts on the quality of Kohler enamelware.

On the other hand, many distributors preferred to combine products from various suppliers, and they might be offended if Kohler Co. impinged on that freedom by manufacturing china and brass in addition to cast-iron enamelware.

Never one to throw up his hands in despair, Walter found an answer. He decided to enter the china and brassware businesses. He decided also to tread gingerly with distributors, encouraging but not forcing them to sell Kohler china and brass. A letter to Kohler Co.'s sales force stated, "It is not our intention to disrupt

𝒦ohler Co. was the first plumbing products company to advertise directly to consumers. The painting at right was used in an early ad. Opposite, these advertisements from the 1920s exemplify the refined and distinctive look of Kohler's advertising. The top two ads feature Kohler's pioneering color fixtures, introduced in 1927.

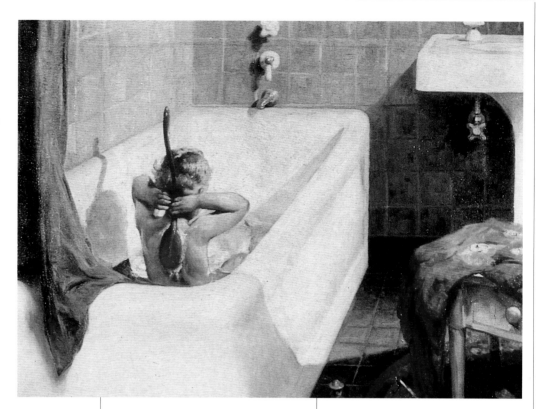

arrangements of long standing which some of our customers may have at present with other sources of supply."

At that time, sanitaryware manufacturing in the United States was concentrated in Trenton, New Jersey, and along the Indiana-Ohio border, close to clay deposits. Thinking independently as always, Walter decided to build a pottery in Kohler and import clay in order to provide jobs for the people of Sheboygan County. In 1925, he purchased the Cochran, Drugan & Co. pottery in Trenton for $150,000. For the next two years, he produced Kohler brand sanitaryware at the Trenton plant. In addition, he sent a group of Kohler employees to Trenton to learn about vitreous china manufacturing technology and train

to be supervisors. In 1927, he sold the Trenton plant to the Pennsylvania Railroad, which tore it down to build a transformer station, and transferred production to the newly completed pottery in Kohler. The new facility, billed as "the world's largest pottery plant under one roof," was staffed by the supervisors. Other employees were hired and trained locally. In this way, Kohler Co. became a leader in the sanitaryware market. It continues to manufacture toilets and other vitreous china products in the same building today.

Having erected a pottery in Kohler Village, the company almost immediately established itself as an industry technology leader, setting new standards for quality and style.

One of Kohler Co.'s major early advances was to introduce the industry's first vitreous china and enameled cast-iron products in colors other than white. These early Kohler colors were mostly pastels, including spring green, horizon blue, lavender, autumn brown and old ivory, all introduced in 1927. Kohler added the industry's first jet black plumbing products in 1928.

"Walter Kohler and his people were able to take a color and apply it to a cast-iron enamel finish and a vitreous china glaze and make both materials look the same — same hue, same depth," Herb Kohler says. "This was true innovation, and it had a real impact." For the first time, customers were able to purchase a suite of bath-

Kohler Fixtures in Lavender: the Imperator Bath, the Belmore Lavatory, the Rockbourne Toilet

For bathrooms *glorious* in color

America discovered the bathroom—and glorified it! And now comes Kohler Colorware, bestowing upon this room an added charm and dignity. Now bathrooms may be glorious in color. With fixtures in beautiful shades of lavender, blue, ivory, brown, green, gray—delicate yet everlastingly permanent . . .

Different bathrooms, you will perceive, may be done in different color scheme, each with its individual charm and character. Tub, lavatory, toilet—all contribute to the harmonious ensemble, for Kohler fixtures in both enamel and vitreous ware are now made in color. Kohler fittings in softly lustrous chromium plate add the final touch of perfection.

Color means Kohler. To appreciate this new beauty you must see Kohler fixtures. Visit a Kohler showroom if you can—for a true aesthetic thrill. And consult your plumber. He will tell you that a bathroom in Kohler Colorware costs little more than one in white . . . Mail the coupon for glimpses of bathrooms in all the Kohler Colors.

KOHLER of KOHLER
Plumbing Fixtures
LOOK FOR THE KOHLER TRADE MARK ON EACH FIXTURE

Kohler Fixtures in "Old Ivory": the Imperator Bath, the Standish Vitreous China Lavatory, the Rockbourne Toilet

Start with color *in the fixtures*

That is the happiest formula for creating the colorful bathrooms which today are so universally desired. Let the fixtures themselves—the tub, lavatory, and toilet—strike the color keynote. The treatment of walls and floor may be as simple and inexpensive as purse or taste may dictate—your bathroom will still be glorious in color.

Kohler Colorware brings this new and gracious beauty within the reach of everyone.

A bathroom in this ware actually costs little more than one in white . . . There are six exquisite colors to choose from—delicate, everlastingly permanent shades of ivory, blue, green, lavender, brown, and gray. With Kohler fittings in rich chromium plate to set off their exclusive beauty . . .

To appreciate these fixtures you must see them. If there is a Kohler showroom near you, be sure to visit it. And ask your plumber about this new ware. It is made, by the way, for kitchens and laundries as well as for bathrooms. The coupon will bring you complete information.

KOHLER of KOHLER
Plumbing Fixtures
LOOK FOR THE KOHLER TRADE MARK ON EACH FIXTURE

The Shops, Kohler Village

Kohler Village is developing a finer community life just as surely as the great Kohler factories—where enameled plumbing ware and private electric plants are made—are developing an ever finer sense of craftsmanship.

SUMMER may go and winter come, but the water's always fine in this inviting bathroom with its beautiful Kohler fixtures. . . . Let Kohler Ware help you to realize your ideal bathroom, or the additional bathrooms which your family may need. This fine ware is not expensive; it costs no more than any other that you would care to consider. Ask your plumber to show you Kohler fixtures. Look for the name "Kohler" fused in the immaculately white enamel. May we send you booklet E?

KOHLER CO. *Founded* 1873, KOHLER, WIS.
Shipping Point, Sheboygan, Wis · *Branches in Principal Cities*

KOHLER of KOHLER
Plumbing Fixtures

American Club, Kohler, Wisconsin

The Village of Kohler, a delight to city planners everywhere, surrounds the making of Kohler products—enameled plumbing ware and private electric plants—with an atmosphere which fosters quality

THOSE who know about such things, place Kohler Enameled Plumbing Ware in a rather special and exclusive class. They recognize in its correct and beautiful design, in its snowy purity of color, and in the superb refinement of its enamel, the quiet signs which distinguish the exceptional from the merely good. And yet, Kohler Ware costs no more than other ware of acceptable quality. . . . . When you select plumbing fixtures look for the name "Kohler" in the enamel. May we send you Booklet E?

Kohler Co., *Founded* 1873, Kohler, Wisconsin
Shipping Point, Sheboygan, Wisconsin
BRANCHES IN PRINCIPAL CITIES

KOHLER of KOHLER
Enameled Plumbing Ware

Designed by Ely Jacques Kahn, Architect, New York. Plumbing fixtures, with their metal fittings, designed and executed by Kohler of Kohler

In the Metropolitan Museum of Art

—Exhibition of a modern bath and dressing room

THE new importance of the bathroom as a place of beauty in the modern home could hardly be more strikingly emphasized than it is by this room by Mr. Ely Jacques Kahn in the current Exhibition of American Industrial Art at the Metropolitan Museum, New York.

That the bathroom was chosen as one of the typical rooms to be shown in this internationally important exhibition is in itself an eloquent fact. The manner in which this room unites artistry with logical simplicity demonstrates the wisdom of the choice.

The walls are of glass. The floors are of special yielding rubber. Radiators are recessed behind tiled grilles, and over their warmth

Chromium-plated Kohler fittings in the Cellini pattern enhance the distinguished beauty of the jet black Kohler fixtures

hang the towels. Such thoughtful details throughout illustrate how comfort parallels beauty.

Into this setting are introduced a Kohler bath and lavatory of gleaming black, with chromium-plated fittings—faucets, handles, and escutcheons—also of Kohler make, in the graceful *Cellini* design. These Kohler contributions are in patterns available to all.

Kohler fixtures of modern style and beauty —in lovely color or lustrous white—are made for simplest bathrooms as well as costly ones. Write to Kohler Co., Kohler, Wis., for a free 72-page book, in color, showing fixtures for bathrooms, kitchens, and laundries, with color schemes, floor plans, and prices.

KOHLER Co. *Founded 1873 · Branches in Principal Cities · Shipping Point*, Sheboygan, Wis.

KOHLER of KOHLER
Plumbing Fixtures

room products in a color other than white. In 1929, the Metropolitan Museum of Art in New York recognized this achievement by including Kohler black fixtures and chrome fittings in an exhibition devoted to the artistic qualities of the bath. A museum curator of the time said, "When the general run of American manufacturers are convinced — as the Kohler people are — of the value of art in industry, they will introduce into all the furnishings of the home the fitness of form to function, the same splendid serviceability and convenience which have made the world admit that the American bathroom is a thing of beauty."

Kohler discontinued some colors in the late 1930s and during World War II, then reemphasized its use of color after the war. The colors introduced in the 1920s represented one of two great waves of color from Kohler Co., the other occurring in the 1960s, when the company introduced the plumbing products industry's first vivid "accent" colors, bolder and brighter than the pastels of the 1920s. While the colors of the 1920s were a reasonable commercial success, those of the 1960s were enormously successful, capturing the public's desire for new bathroom designs.

Building a Brassware Plant
In 1925, the same year Kohler Co. acquired the Cochran, Drugan & Co. pottery, Walter Kohler approved a capital investment of $800,000 to

*O*pposite and above, Kohler products were displayed at New York City's Metropolitan Museum of Art in a landmark 1929 exhibition on industrial design. Kohler fixtures were the only plumbing products included in the show.

build a plant in Kohler Village for the manufacture of brass fittings.

Production at the brass plant began in late 1926. However, it soon became apparent that even the ever-optimistic Walter had underestimated the market potential for Kohler brassware. Simply stated, in manufacturing brass, Kohler Co. struck gold. Almost immediately, demand for Kohler brass fittings exceeded the plant's capacity, a condition that continued until 1931, when the full impact of the Great Depression took hold. Brassware sales resumed their growth in the late 1930s, and by 1939 Kohler Co. was again having trouble keeping up with orders, so it built an addition which doubled the size of the original brassware plant. Completed two years later, the facility was immediately converted to military production for World War II, but after the war it provided the basis for significant expansion in the brassware business.

Sales of Kohler brassware were $144,000 in 1926, the first year of production. They climbed to $1.6 million in 1931, $6.2 million in 1941 and $11.7 million in 1948 — and kept right on growing. Entering the brassware business was one of the great decisions Kohler Co. made.

New Products
Having opened a pottery and a brass plant, Kohler Co. began investing in new product development. The late

This Kohler-equipped kitchen, 1928, includes the Kohler Electric Sink, one of the world's first motor-powered dishwashers. The Electric Sink was one of many innovative products introduced by Kohler in the 1920s. It proved, however, to be an idea ahead of its time. Sales did not meet expectations, and it was discontinued during the Depression.

1920s were a period of incredible inventiveness for the company. Some of its new products were quite astonishing.

The Kohler Electric Sink, introduced in 1926, was one of the world's first motor-powered dishwashers, long before dishwashers became commonplace in American homes. A company publication enthused:

KOHLER ANNOUNCES THE
KOHLER ELECTRIC SINK
It must be a rather dull imagination that fails to sense the dramatic significance of that simple statement. The Electric Sink!

The most stubbornly defended fortress of household drudgery taken at last!

However, the Electric Sink turned out to be a great idea whose time had not yet come. Sales never met Walter's expectations, and the product was discontinued in the 1930s. Nonetheless, the Electric Sink did have one component of enduring importance: Duostrainer, the world's first cup strainer and drain control fitting. Originally a Kohler invention, it has since been widely copied and is now a common feature in kitchen sinks.

The Electric Sink was followed in 1928 by the Kohler Electric Clotheswasher as well as by a product combining the two — that is, a unit with a sink, motor-powered dishwasher and motor-powered clotheswasher. The company also began manufacturing cast-iron furnaces and radiators for homes and commercial buildings.

Even though these products are now but distant memories, other Kohler inventions caught on big. For instance, in 1927, Kohler Co. revolutionized the seemingly mundane faucet handle. Traditionally,

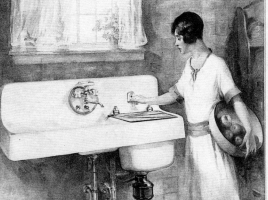

$\mathcal{B}$y 1927, when this advertisement, left, appeared in the *Saturday Evening Post*, the Kohler brand was known nationwide. The unique contrivance above combines a Kohler Electric Sink (on the left side of the unit) for washing dishes, a kitchen sink (in the center) and a large soaking sink (on the right). Utensil and garbage containers are mounted on swing arms under the kitchen sink.

faucets were made with metal bodies and white china handles, but the china handles sometimes broke, cutting fingers and hands. In 1927, one year after opening its brass factory, Kohler introduced a faucet that was all metal, including the handle. Other companies soon followed, and metal handles — made of brass, plated with nickel or chromium — quickly became the industry standard.

A Dispute With Crane Co.
Meanwhile, Walter faced the issue of how best to market Kohler Co.'s products — through independent distributors (wholesalers) or directly to plumbers. Around the turn of the century, realizing (according to an internal memorandum) that "no company can long compete with its own customers," Kohler Co. concluded it had to go one route or the other, and it opted for distributors. They have been vital to Kohler Co.'s success ever since.

As the decade of the 1920s began, Walter reaffirmed that decision, but faced a predicament. In the early part of this century, Kohler Co. sold about 30 percent of its output to a competitor, Crane Co., for distribution through Crane branches. A dispute arose in 1920 when Crane "wanted privileges not available to all," in the words of a Kohler Co. document. Perhaps those asked-for privileges involved price discounts or product exclusivity; we do not know. Whatever

*T*his 1922 photograph of Arthur Maas, a foundry repairman, is from the company magazine, *Kohler of Kohler News*. It is one of several photos, in various issues of the magazine, that showed employees whose eyesight had been preserved in workplace accidents by safety goggles. The message, repeated over and over, was that employees in the factory should wear protective goggles at all times.

they were, Walter refused to budge. As the dispute escalated, he canceled Kohler's arrangement with Crane, lopping off 30 percent of Kohler's sales in one fell swoop. That may seem like a radical solution, but in fact Walter was uneasy about being so dependent on a major competitor. He felt Kohler would be better off in the long run by expanding its relationships with independent distributors, which it did.

A man of great conviction, Walter never backed down one inch from his decision to sell exclusively through distributors — not even when General Robert Wood, chairman of Sears, Roebuck and Co., placed a massive order for 500 boxcars full of Kohler products to be sold through Sears stores. Walter rejected the order out of hand, saying Kohler Co.'s relationship with its distributors was too important to put at risk.

A Workplace Environment Different Than Today's
Walter was concerned about working conditions in the foundry. It was an inherently dangerous place, especially for those who did not pay careful attention to what they were doing, as was true of manufacturing plants everywhere at that time. While working in a factory today is no piece of cake, this was in an era before the development of modern process and safety technologies. The men in the foundry were true heroes for the rugged conditions under which they

labored and the tremendous pride they showed in their work.

Early issues of *Kohler of Kohler News*, the company's employee publication, sometimes had photographs of men wearing goggles with smashed lenses. The message, repeated in the caption for each of these pictures, was that the worker's eyes had been saved by the goggles, and that all the workers should wear them.

Walter viewed the men as his colleagues and considered their work a noble calling. The Kohler family sometimes went out of its way to provide financial support when men were injured or killed. To formalize this support, the company introduced a workers' compensation program in 1909 and a group life and health insurance plan in 1917. The company also organized thrift plans to help employees invest for their future needs.

In the ensuing years, of course, there has been significant improvement in workplace safety nationwide — partly because of better manufacturing methods, but also because of workplace safety laws and because safety awareness is so much greater today than it was a century ago.

A Legion of Talented People

Walter surrounded himself with talented people, many of whom were from hardy immigrant stock, as he was himself. Two of the most important were Anton Brotz, the company's chief inventor, and Anton's younger

*F*rank Brotz, above, and his older brother, Anton, below right, were important members of Walter Kohler's management team. Frank was in charge of production, while Anton invented many of the company's products and technologies.

brother, Frank Brotz, who was in charge of production.

With the personality of an absent-minded professor, absorbed in his work and often oblivious to those around him, Anton was a mechanical genius who pulled off the amazing feat of educating himself in mathematics, physics, chemistry and aeronautics by reading textbooks. In addition to designing much of Kohler Co.'s production equipment and inventing many of its products (including the Kohler Automatic), he utilized the revolutionary technologies of the day in his personal life — building his own automobile, one of the first in Sheboygan County, and his own airplane. Even in the 1920s, there were no rules or regulations about the airworthiness of planes.

Anton Brotz, below, joined Kohler Co. in 1898 as chief research engineer, continuing in that position for 47 years. In addition to working for Kohler and inventing many of its products, he was an aviation pioneer who built his own airplane and owned and managed an airport in Sheboygan. At right, O. A. "Tom" Kroos was a longtime Kohler Co. executive who spent half a century with the company, working right up until his death in 1957 at age 77.

"If you wanted to build your own airplane and risk your neck flying it, that was your business," said Melvin Thompson, who was one of Walter Kohler's pilots. Thompson himself built a plane in 1920 when he was still a teenage farmboy. He later worked in the Kohler Co. shop, one of many individuals with innate mechanical skill who were employed by the company.

In contrast to Anton, Frank Brotz was a tough-as-nails manager who was demanding and precise. He knew how to organize work and command men. "He could have been a four-star general; that's what he was like," said his son, Ralph Brotz. Even though he was an employee and director of

Kohler Co., Frank Brotz believed so strongly in being one's own boss that he organized a plastics company at the depths of the Depression and gave it to his five sons so they would have a business of their own. All five sons spent their careers at that company, Plastics Engineering Company, which has grown and prospered under Brotz family ownership and is today one of the most successful privately owned businesses in Sheboygan County.

O. A. "Tom" Kroos, corporate secretary from 1909 to 1928 and secretary-treasurer from 1928 to 1937, was another key Kohler Co. executive. His brother, Arthur Kroos,

was director of purchasing. Both Kroos brothers eventually became vice presidents and directors, with Tom Kroos serving as executive vice president from 1940 until his death in 1957 at age 77. In those days, senior executives of Kohler Co. seldom retired. Their work was their life, and many of them stayed well into their 70s or even beyond.

Management was strengthened in the mid-1930s with the hiring of Halsten Thorkelson, who had been professor of steam and gas engineering at the University of Wisconsin when Walter Kohler was president of the university's board of regents. As a vice president of Kohler Co., Thorkelson added to the company's overall technical know-how.

In the second half of Walter's 35-year tenure, he turned increasingly to his younger brother, Herbert, for help in managing the company. It was clear that Walter, concerned about management succession, was

*K*ohler Village became a hub of aviation in the upper Midwest after Walter Kohler built an airport there in 1928. Above, Mrs. Nellie Zabel Willhite of Sheboygan was one of many aviators who kept planes at Kohler.

grooming Herbert to be his successor — and that is exactly what happened. Herbert Kohler became chief executive officer upon Walter's death in 1940, leading the company for the next 28 years.

Aviation Pioneer

Walter had a lifelong interest in technology and inventions, including aviation. In 1928, he purchased a Ryan monoplane, the same model as Charles Lindbergh's *Spirit of St. Louis.* Taking to the air as a passenger, he became the first business executive in Wisconsin (and perhaps the first in the nation) to travel routinely by plane. He was no mere occasional wayfarer in the sky. In one 80-day period, he traveled 104 times by plane, most of them short hops within the state of Wisconsin. Although air travel was still in its infancy and considered to be dangerous, Walter insisted flying was "just the thing for the busy manager" and professed that he usually worked or took "a good sound nap" en route. It was nonetheless his habit to celebrate a safe flight and smooth landing by giving the pilot a cigar.

Kohler Village soon became a center of aviation in the upper Midwest. Anton Brotz had opened an airport in Sheboygan in 1923. When the main building was hit by lightning in the late 1920s, burning to the ground, he closed the airport. Walter Kohler then built an airport in Kohler Village with two runways —

one with a cinder surface for all-weather use, the other with a grass surface. For many years, the Kohler airport was the only one for miles around. It was the pride and joy of Walter Kohler, Anton Brotz and others at Kohler Co. who loved aviation. It also provided great excitement for the residents of the village, including youngsters, because of the barnstorming pilots who showed up each summer to take them aloft. Walter said one reason he built the airport was to give local youngsters an up-close look at aviation, a field with an exciting future, in anticipation that some might choose careers as aircraft mechanics or pilots. The Kohler Co. airport continued in use until 1961, when the government-operated Sheboygan County Memorial Airport was opened.

Governor Kohler

Walter was a dyed-in-the-wool Republican who relished politics. He believed that government, like business, should be run with efficiency, integrity and fairness.

When he was elected governor of Wisconsin in 1928, taking office in January 1929, he had a chance to put his thoughts into action. He streamlined the state bureaucracy by creating a single annuity and investment board to replace seven and by establishing a central bureau of purchases. In addition, he routinely vetoed projects that he viewed as political pork. At the time of Walter's election,

*O*pposite, in 1928 Walter Kohler purchased a sister ship of Lindbergh's *Spirit of St. Louis* and used it for business trips across Wisconsin and to Chicago. He was one of the first executives in the nation to travel routinely by plane. Holding the propeller is one of his pilots, Lt. Werner Bunge. Above, Walter is greeted by children during his 1928 gubernatorial campaign.

*I*n 1928, Walter Kohler was elected governor of Wisconsin on a platform which emphasized that government, like business, should be run with efficiency, integrity and fairness. He served one two-year term, bringing state spending under control by streamlining bureaucracy and vetoing what he considered to be "pork barrel" projects.

the state treasurer said the accumulated state deficit was likely to reach $3.5 million within a year. Not only did Governor Kohler eliminate the deficit; at the end of his two-year term, the state treasury had a *surplus* of $20 million.

Despite his business background, Walter signed 20 bills sought by organized labor. Most notable was a ban on "yellow dog" contracts. These management-imposed employment agreements specified that workers could not belong to a union. Many business owners opposed the new law, but Walter felt workers had an inherent right to join a union, just as they had an inherent right not to join. This same issue of individual worker

choice would arise from a different perspective in 1934 and again in 1954 when unions representing Kohler Co.'s production and maintenance employees sought closed shops with mandatory union membership, demands the company adamantly opposed. Walter had trouble understanding why some people could not get his point — that forcing an employee to join a union was just as un-American, in his view, as barring an employee from joining. The issue was sometimes painted in terms of political liberals (favoring unions) versus political conservatives (opposing unions). Walter rejected that characterization, insisting the issue was purely one of individual freedom of choice. In the mid-1930s, when Kohler's workforce unionized, Walter did nothing to oppose this, saying his employees were free to belong to any organization they wanted. But he did fight tooth and nail against a closed shop.

Also at Walter's urging, the state legislature passed a Children's Code which strengthened adoption laws and fortified protections for dependent children.

Walter continued to run Kohler Co. even while serving as governor. He spent weekdays in the state capital, Madison, and weekends in Kohler Village, but with greater delegation to other senior executives, including his brother Herbert and Tom Kroos. Walter was like that — he had tremendous energy and always

Time For A Change

KOHLER
FOR
GOVERNOR

*A*bove, Governor Walter Kohler speaks at Ripon, Wisconsin, on June 8, 1929, in celebration of the Republican Party's 75th anniversary. He is remembered today as one of the towering figures in the history of Wisconsin business and politics. Right, a campaign worker uses a bicycle in 1928 to distribute literature.

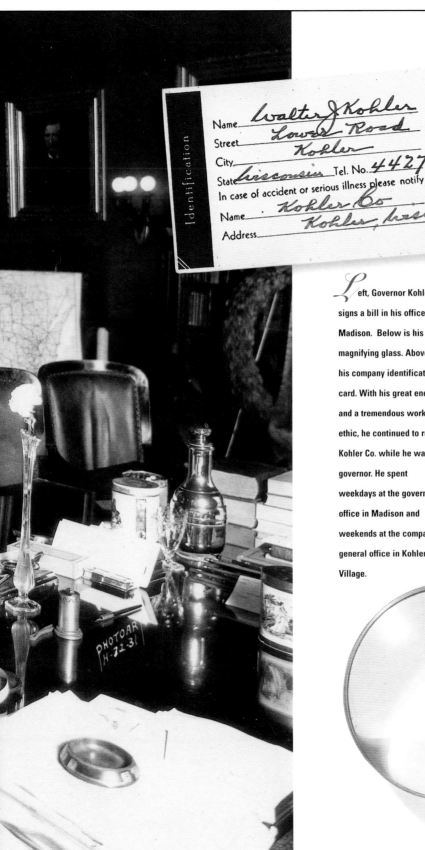

Identification

Name _Walter J Kohler_
Street _Lower Road_
City _Kohler_
State _Wisconsin_ Tel. No. _4427_
In case of accident or serious illness please notify
Name _Kohler Co_
Address _Kohler, Wiss._

*L*eft, Governor Kohler signs a bill in his office in Madison. Below is his magnifying glass. Above is his company identification card. With his great energy and a tremendous work ethic, he continued to run Kohler Co. while he was governor. He spent weekdays at the governor's office in Madison and weekends at the company's general office in Kohler Village.

managed to get his work done, even while holding two jobs at once. (And his plane helped, too, enabling him to travel back and forth quickly.)

Ironically, Walter Kohler, a man known for his exceptional integrity, was indicted and tried as a sitting governor on charges he had exceeded the legal spending limit in his campaign. It was a sensational trial, covered by media from across the state. A central allegation was that Walter had sought to influence voters by providing a free sandwich and beverage to those who toured the Kohler factory during the gubernatorial campaign. Acknowledging the free meals, Walter denied any wrongdoing. "I wouldn't insult the intelligence of any voter in Wisconsin by assuming I could buy his vote for a sandwich," he testified.

The trial had an amusing twist. Walter was an impeccable dresser who nearly always wore a white carnation in his lapel. One of the jurors, a farmer, showed up the first day of the trial in dingy overalls. The farmer's attire improved as the trial continued, and he finally took to wearing a flower in his lapel, just like the governor. Observing the farmer, Walter realized the trial was going well. In fact, he was acquitted unanimously. Walter ran for

In 1934, Federal Labor Union No. 18545 of the AFL struck Kohler Co., seeking to represent its maintenance and production employees. Pickets used ropes to prevent workers from entering the factory. In a government-supervised election, the AFL was defeated by the Kohler Workers' Association.

reelection in 1930, but lost in the Republican primary to Philip La Follette, who won the general election and became governor. Walter ran again in 1932, this time beating La Follette in the primary to become the party's 1932 gubernatorial candidate. By now, however, President Herbert Hoover had fallen from public favor due to the 1929 stock market crash and onset of the Great Depression. Loyal to the core, Walter supported Hoover's 1932 candidacy for reelection, in effect dooming his own campaign. Walter explained, "I'm a Republican and he's a Republican and I'm going to appear with him. It's my duty." In a Democratic landslide, Hoover lost Wisconsin by 350,000 votes. Walter lost the race for governor by 100,000. It was his last bid for elective office.

Kohler Co. in the Depression And the 1934 Strike

The Great Depression was a dire period. Plumbing industry sales in the United States plunged 90 percent by 1932 before beginning a slow recovery. Despite this situation, Kohler Co. kept its employees working full time at full wages well into 1931, building up inventories and avoiding layoffs. Ralph Brotz recalled that his brother, Roman, was hired by Kohler in 1931 to destroy unsold products in warehouses, even as new products continued to be made in the factory.

This build-and-destroy cycle could not continue forever. In 1932, Walter said, "I have always insisted that it is the most important duty of management to provide workmen with as much regular employment as is possible." However, Kohler Co. was now borrowing money to keep afloat and had little choice except to trim production drastically. The work schedule was initially reduced to three days a week in some departments, and then to as few as eight hours a week, but still no one was laid off. By 1933, entire production units — including some pottery kilns — were closed, and the first layoffs occurred.

Meanwhile, squeezed by the Depression, workers across the country were joining unions. And when President Roosevelt signed the National Industrial Recovery Act in 1933, guaranteeing labor the right to organize and bargain collectively, the unions became more vociferous in demanding higher wages and improved working conditions. Lengthy, bitter strikes ensued against General Motors, the textile industry, and many other companies and industries.

At Kohler Co., some employees formed the Kohler Workers' Association, called the KWA. Others formed a local union of the American Federation of Labor. The company, saying it had no problem with unionization, issued a statement that its employees were free to join — or not to join — any organization they wanted. When the AFL claimed the right to represent all Kohler Co. production and maintenance employees and

sought a "closed shop" requiring that all employees join the union, the company rejected those demands. The AFL thereupon called a strike. It began on July 16, 1934, with pickets encircling the plant and blocking anyone from entering or leaving. Eleven days later, a crowd of strikers swept through the village, smashing windows and overturning vehicles. They were confronted by police, and in the battle that followed, two strikers were shot dead and 47 people were wounded. It was the darkest day in the history of Kohler Village, which had, after all, been created as a symbol of the ability of management and labor to get along. Order was restored by the national guard.

The AFL ultimately lost. When the National Labor Relations Board held an election, the KWA received 1,063 votes, the AFL affiliate 643, and the KWA was certified as the employees' bargaining agent. But, as we shall see in Chapter Five, the issue of a union shop did not go away. It would recur 20 years later when the United Auto Workers replaced the KWA as the bargaining agent and struck for six years attempting to get a union shop.

The Passing of an Era

The 1934 strike took a heavy physical and emotional toll on Walter Kohler, who felt he had treated his employees fairly and could not understand why they had turned against him. Nonetheless, he blamed the strike more on outside agitators than on the employees themselves. He was not one to hold grudges, and life went on. The company began to come out of the Depression, and by 1940 sales and earnings were recovering nicely.

On Saturday, April 20, 1940, Walter spent a busy day at the office, working until 7 p.m. with his usual vigor and good cheer. He appeared to be in the best of health. Thus, it came as an utter shock to all who knew him when he died the next morning of a heart attack at age 65. He had headed the company for 35 years, leading it through enormous change and growth.

Ralph Brotz, the son of Frank Brotz, who was Kohler Co.'s production manager, said, "I only saw my father weep once, and that was when Walter Kohler died." Ralph once asked his father what kind of man Walter Kohler was. His father answered, "Son, there was one thing about him. You couldn't work for him very long unless you had high ethics and high purpose." His father also said, "If you had anything good in you, he found a way to get it out."

Lucius P. Chase, who joined Kohler Co. in 1926 as a young attorney and spent his entire career with the company, said at the time of Walter's passing, "If Kohler Co. can survive the death of Walter Kohler, it can survive anything." Interviewed in 1998 at his home in Florida, Chase said simply, "Mr. Walter J. Kohler was the greatest man I ever knew."

*W*alter was a family man who loved children. He is seated here with his wife, Charlotte Schroeder Kohler, surrounded by their grandchildren. Walter is holding Charlotte Nicolette Kohler, and seated directly in front of him is Terry Jodok Kohler. The three boys wearing jackets are, left to right, Walter J. Kohler III, Carl James Kohler Jr. and Conrad Dings Kohler. Seated directly in front of Conrad is Peter Galt Kohler. Standing in the background is Mrs. Julia House, mother of Mrs. John Kohler, holding her grandson (and Walter's and Charlotte's grandson) John Michael "Mike" Kohler Jr.

*T*he beauty of Kohler Village, with its lovely gardens, is shown in this vintage photograph. The village was modeled on the garden communities of Europe, combining comfortable residential areas with a job-providing factory.

mong Walter Kohler's many legacies, none is greater than Kohler Village, which has been described as "one of the prettiest and most peaceful villages anywhere." Located about 50 miles north of Milwaukee on the banks of the Sheboygan River, Kohler is known for its winding, tree-lined streets, spacious parks and attractive homes, as well as for being the site of a luxurious resort hotel, The American Club.

And by the way, this charming village of 1,900 residents also happens to contain a sprawling Kohler Co. industrial headquarters and manufacturing complex with 8,000 employees. The residential areas, all of which are west and south of the complex (itself a "masterpiece of art deco industrial design," according to the travel guidebook *Wisconsin*, by Tracy Will), are shielded from the manufacturing operations by broad avenues and stands of trees. Downwind of the operations, to the southeast, is a large greenbelt set aside originally to absorb emissions from the factory's stacks.

Driving through the residential sections of Kohler, it is virtually impossible to hear the noises of the manufacturing complex or otherwise feel its presence. And that is exactly how Walter planned the village more than 80 years ago.

Championing the American Dream

It might seem easy to assume that Kohler began as a typical "company" town — that is, one in which the corporation owned the homes and rented them to employees. But that was not the case at all.

Ever the idealist, Walter genuinely wanted to improve the lives of his workers. Moreover, he believed that individual homeownership, free of company control or impediment, was essential to the American dream. He

KOHLER
VILLAGE

*A*bove is a 1928 booklet describing the village. At right, Kohler was — and is — a wonderful place to raise children. There were dozens of wholesome activities, like this Maypole dance, to keep youngsters busy.

therefore deeded large tracts of land to the Kohler Improvement Company, which built the houses and sold them to employees at cost. Low-cost mortgage financing was provided by the Kohler Building and Loan Association, owned by the employees themselves. Any employee who bought a home was free to sell it at any time without having to answer to the company.

Today, all the original owners of the early homes in Kohler Village have long since passed away, and their

*A*t The American Club Tap Room, a ham-on-rye sandwich cost a nickel and, following the repeal of Prohibition, a 64-ounce "tulip" of Kingsbury or Jung's beer sold for 40 cents.

1927

Group No 1 · HOUSES at KOHLER · Wisconsin.

*A*bove is a water-color sketch of homes, below a backyard barbecue. Unlike "company" towns, Kohler Co. sold homes to employees at cost, without any restrictions on a homeowner's right to resell.

Brust & Philipp Arch'ts.

*K*ohler Village was designed with winding streets and an abundance of public parks. Below is East Park Lane in 1927.

houses are owned by their descendants or have been sold to newcomers. As a result of this natural progression, the village is no longer dominated by Kohler Co. employees. In fact, well over half its residents do not have any affiliation with the company. They have simply been attracted to a little gem of a community with nice homes, great schools, clean air, wonderful parks and virtually no crime.

The Roots of Kohler Village

Besides being attractive in its own right, Kohler Village is significant historically: it is one of few "garden communities" that survives and flourishes. Garden cities were the brainchild of nineteenth-century European social reformers. By combining affordable housing and job-providing industry, these model towns in the countryside offered workers a chance to live in clean, modern quarters far from urban slums.

John Michael Kohler may have had the concept of a garden city in mind when he built his foundry in the farmlands of Riverside. But he died before he could develop a residential community adjacent to the foundry.

Once the foundry was completed, however, some Kohler Co. employees began building homes on their own. About 40 frame houses had been erected by 1912, when the residents incorporated the village and, by popular vote, named it Kohler. The village was still little more than a rustic hamlet with dirt streets and a small

This photograph of The American Club was taken in the 1920s from the Kohler Co. general office building directly across the street. The American Club provided housing, meals and recreational facilities for single male employees, most of whom were newly arrived immigrants who could not yet afford to buy homes. Below, Walter Kohler, second from left, spoke from a balcony at the facility's dedication in 1918. He said the name American Club had been chosen in hopes that it would encourage patriotism in its residents.

The American Club offered a place for single male employees to live for a modest monthly charge that included a clean room, hearty meals and recreation. Above, board games were a favorite evening pastime. Opposite, American Club residents pose during Christmas dinner.

schoolhouse (and a "pest house" on the school grounds, of all places, in which residents with communicable diseases were quarantined). But the village was beginning to grow helter-skelter, and that concerned Walter Kohler, who worried that Kohler would become just another congested metropolis. So in 1913, he toured Europe with Milwaukee architect Richard Philipp to look at its garden cities and to meet with Sir Ebenezer Howard, the father of the garden city movement.

Returning home, Walter began to plan the long-term development of Kohler Village. The task, as he saw it, involved "the serious business of building a fine American city, with opportunity for homeownership in agreeable surroundings, all tending toward a rational home life."

Recognizing the need for expert assistance, he hired Olmsted Brothers, the nation's preeminent landscape architecture firm, to lay out the overall village, including streets and parks, and to devise a 50-year plan for controlled growth. The firm's founder, Frederic Law Olmsted, had designed New York City's Central Park, the Boston parks system and the U.S. Capitol grounds, and the firm itself

was renowned for its park work nationwide. To design individual houses, Walter retained Philipp, the Milwaukee architect.

The first houses were completed in 1917, and the development of Kohler Village was off and running.

Building the homes was quite an operation. Kohler Co. controlled every step to make sure the job was done efficiently and right. For many years, the company maintained a team of carpenters, masons, electricians and other craftsmen on its payroll. These employees did all the construction, building homes in batches

to keep costs low. Lumber was supplied by a company-owned sawmill located by the railroad tracks. Land on which to build the homes was acquired by purchasing local farms, which continued to be worked by the sellers until the property was needed by Kohler Co. In this way, land was stockpiled in advance of actual requirements.

In addition to buying property for home sites, during the 1920s the company assembled a four-mile-long strip of land from Kohler Village to Lake Michigan for the purpose of digging a canal. Walter Kohler

believed the company needed direct access to the lake, a center of shipping, to bring in raw materials and send out finished products. However, with subsequent improvements in rail service, the canal plan was abandoned.

Dennis Kopf, a retired Kohler Co. employee, recalls that in the late 1940s the company owned 14 working farms in the region, all purchased originally to accumulate land for housing, plant expansion and the canal, as well as to protect against urban encroachment by creating a greenbelt around the village.

In 1965, Kohler Co. gave 650 acres

that had been earmarked for the canal to the state of Wisconsin for the John Michael Kohler State Park, now the Kohler-Andrae State Parks. State Conservation Commissioner Guido Rahr described the land, which included untouched woodlands and dunes along the Lake Michigan shore, as "a priceless property which the state could not have purchased for any amount of cash." Even after that gift, the company today owns sizable tracts of undeveloped land in and around the village.

The American Club

But building individual houses was not enough. Walter also recognized that many Kohler Co. employees were newly arrived immigrants who could not afford to purchase homes. Some of these employees lived in dilapidated apartments in the poorer districts of Sheboygan, in many cases pinching pennies until they could afford to bring their families to America from Europe.

To meet their needs, Walter built The American Club at the center of the village, directly across the street from the foundry. The name American Club was chosen, Walter explained, to help instill in its residents "a love for their adopted country." A handsome Tudor-style red brick structure, this unique "club" provided housing for more than 250 employees of modest means. The company ran The American Club on

a break-even basis, charging $27.50 per month for a private room, laundry service and three wholesome meals a day.

The American Club was like a great ocean liner in the completeness of its facilities. It had a bakery, modern kitchens, a beautifully maintained dining hall with flowers on the tables, a commercial-scale laundry, reading rooms, a card room, a billiard room, a barber shop and even a four-lane bowling alley. Beer was sold in the Tap Room after the repeal of Prohibition in 1933. (Walter respected the European traditions of his employees, including their love of beer.) All the common facilities, including the dining hall, Tap Room and bowling alley, were open to the public, so that The American Club became the social center of the village.

For the men living at The American Club, those early years were a wonderful time of camaraderie and expectation. Many of them had grown up in poverty. One resident said that just being able to take a hot shower each day was a "luxury." In addition to partaking of the many recreational activities at The American Club and in the community, the men were encouraged to enter the mainstream of American life by attending the Kohler evening school, where free classes were offered in such subjects as civics, American history and English grammar.

Walter was a passionate believer in

The American Club was more than a place to live. It helped assimilate its many foreign-born residents into American life, providing opportunities to take English classes, civics classes and other courses. The company even designated an annual Naturalization Day when foreign-born employees were encouraged to file for citizenship. Above is a bedroom, circa 1942. Many of the facility's rooms, such as the Washington Room, right — a reading room honoring George Washington — were named for famous Americans.

*K*ohler Co. employees from all parts of the business — senior executives, office staff and factory workers — bowled in the company league. Here, O. A. Kroos, who became corporate secretary in 1909 and later served as executive vice president, lines up a shot. The men's bowling teams included the Hamptons, the Wilshires and the Gramercys, all named after Kohler plumbing fixtures.

American democracy, and he encouraged all his foreign-born employees to become citizens. The company designated a Naturalization Day each spring. On that day, a company publication noted, "foreign-born members of the Kohler organization who are not citizens, or are not in the process of becoming citizens, are extended a special invitation and are offered the opportunity of taking the initial step toward naturalization." Those signing up were given the day off with full pay, and were taken in company cars to the Sheboygan County

*T*he bowling alleys at The American Club, opened in 1918, were used not only by employees but also by generations of Kohler high school students who learned the sport at Saturday morning sessions.

Court House to fill out their "first papers," an initial step toward citizenship. As many as 80 men and women a year took part, and in this way hundreds of foreign-born Kohler employees were naturalized in the period from 1918 to 1940 with Walter's encouragement.

Life in the Village

Apart from all that was taking place at The American Club, the village itself was a beehive of activity.

Under Walter's direction, Kohler Co. came up with all kinds of good clean fun to keep its employees busy in their spare time. The company

The Kohler Band is pictured in 1916, one year after it was started. Throughout the band's history, members wore uniforms emblazoned with a Kohler patch.

sponsored a Kohler chorus, a Kohler band, sports leagues, drama and civic clubs, and countless other activities for employees, their families and village residents.

This was in the days before television, and people loved to get out of their homes to do things with their neighbors. In the summer, residents streamed into Ravine Park for an outdoor movie each Monday evening, roller-skating each Tuesday, a band concert each Wednesday and an occasional "ice cream social" on Thursdays.

The uniformed Kohler Band, comprised of company employees and high school students, was the pride of the community. The band started in 1915 with 11 members and eventually totaled more than 100. Employees who took part were given time off from their jobs at half pay to attend rehearsals once a week. The band not only performed in Kohler,

but also toured the Midwest and even played one year at the Republican National Convention. But without a doubt, its most shining moment came in 1925, when John Philip Sousa and his band performed in the village before a massive audience. At that concert, the combined bands — Sousa's and the Kohler Band — joined in playing Sousa's great march, "Stars and Stripes Forever," under the legendary bandmaster's direction. It must have been an incredible thrill. (Why Sousa, an uncompromising perfectionist, agreed to let the Kohler band play with his is today unknown. Perhaps it had to do with Walter's powers of persuasion.)

The Kohler Recreation Club organized sports and recreational activities, including a baseball league, bowling league, tennis club, horseshoe-pitching club, gymnastic society, rifle club, jazz orchestra, camera club and many others.

Always a believer in leadership by example, Walter took part in some of these activities himself. He was a member of the company bowling league, participating alongside employees from the factory and the office. With a touch of showmanship, he led the parade of uniformed players through the village each spring to mark the opening of the baseball season. And he always threw out the season's ceremonial first pitch.

Recreation activities in the village were headed for many years by Roy A. Ebben, a teacher and coach in the Kohler school system from 1934 until joining Kohler Co. in 1955 as the company's recreation director, later serving as its personnel director.

One of the grandest annual events in the village was the Quarter Century Club dinner, held for many years in Recreation Hall (which now houses the Kohler Design Center).

*C*ommunity events in Ravine Park, such as this "ice cream social," were popular from the 1920s until the 1950s. Other weekly activities in the park included concerts, outdoor movies and roller-skating.

Compliments of The CIVIC CLUB of Kohler, Wis.

DEDICATION OF NATURE THEATRE

·MUSIC BY SOUSA AND HIS BAND·

OCTO..R 20, 1919

EVENING — 8:00 O'C.....NG BLDG.

Good for Reserve..

if Prese..

Compliments of The CIVIC CLUB of Kohler, Wis.

DEDICATION OF NATURE THEATRE

MUSIC BY SOUSA AND HIS BAND

OCTOBER 20, 1919

AFTERNOON — 2:15 O'CLOCK — NATURE THEATRE

Good for Reserved Section at Afternoon Concert
if Presented Before 2:00 P. M.
In Case of Rain, Concert will be Given in Engineering Building
High Street

*J*ohn Philip Sousa and his world-famous band performed in the Nature Theatre in Ravine Park in 1919 and again in 1925. Each concert was a huge success. For the 1919 performance, streetcars and interurbans brought people from all over the county to Kohler.

Walter established the club in 1924 not only to honor Kohler Co. employees with 25 or more years of service, but also to foster a corporate culture of teamwork and pride in craft. The Quarter Century Club continues today as one of the oldest organizations of its type in American industry. More than 5,000 Kohler employees have belonged to the club since its inception. Of that group, 68 employees have served 50 years or more with the company. Walter was himself the first 50-year employee.

While the Quarter Century Club dinner was limited to club members, the Christmas dinner was open to all employees. Also at Christmas, the company gave each employee a holiday present — a goose for each married man and typically a pocket knife for those who were single.

Festival and Field Day was another popular annual event. Sponsored by the Kohler Recreation Club, it featured vaudeville performers, a horseshoe tournament, a baseball throwing contest and numerous other activities. Equally festive was the Village Fair, at which prizes were awarded in more than 100 categories of baked goods, flowers, vegetables, and sewing and fancy work.

Kohler's youngsters were not overlooked. For those growing up in the village, finding ways to keep busy was never a problem. Piano lessons were offered at the Kohler Music Studio. In fact, pianos were a fixture in many homes. "In Kohler Village, we believe

*A*rchery, croquet, baseball and volleyball were among the many sports sponsored by the Kohler Recreation Club for employees, their families and others in the village. Kohler Village was perhaps unique among small American communities in the enormous range of social, athletic and cultural programs available to its residents. The house above was that of Dr. Kent, the company dentist. It was located on Orchard Road when the street ran to the north and west of the school. The house was later moved to the southeast corner of Valley Road and Pine Tree Road and is now the residence of Oscar Ward, the village president.

*A*bove, children were — and are — a constant sight on the tree-lined streets. At left is a doll buggy parade in Ravine Park. The parade remains a popular annual event today.

Above, the Kohler baseball team won the 1919 league championship. The initials on the uniforms stood for Kohler Recreation Club. At left is the 1908 Kohler basketball team. At right is Sidonia Radtke, a member of the 1930 Kohler Recreation Club Girls' Team. Opposite is a 1933 championship trophy.

The Quarter Century Club was founded in 1924 by Walter Kohler to honor employees with 25 years or more of company service. It was one of the first organizations of its type in the United States and continues today. At right is the 1945 Quarter Century Club dinner, held in the Wisconsin Room of The American Club, at which 75 new members were inducted, the largest incoming class in the organization's history to that time.

in homemade music," *Kohler of Kohler News* observed in 1931. For those who loved winter sports, each year the company built a high-speed toboggan run and an ice-skating rink for public use. It even stationed a nurse at the toboggan run in case anyone was injured! And if you were a high school student and wanted to learn to bowl, Kohler was just the place to be. Bowling lessons and a junior league for high school students were offered each Saturday at The American Club lanes under the tutelage of Harvey Richter, a Kohler Co. employee who is now retired. Richter estimates that nearly 3,000 youngsters took part during the 41 years he ran the program.

Kohler Village had (and still has) cultural amenities not found in communities with a population 50 or 100 times its size. When Herbert V. Kohler Sr. married Ruth De Young, women's editor of the *Chicago Tribune*, in 1937, she became active in the Kohler Woman's Club, the largest in the state of Wisconsin, and initiated its Distinguished Guest Series. This program brought some of the world's most celebrated musicians and writers to Kohler for concerts and lectures that were open to the public at no charge. The performers included, among many others, violinist Jascha Heifetz, opera singers Risë Stevens and Eileen Farrell, author Pearl Buck, Broadway actress Mary Martin (who performed scenes from *Peter Pan* and other favorite stage characterizations), the Boston Pops Orchestra, Hollywood columnist Hedda Hopper, Antarctic explorer Richard Byrd and even Frank "Bring 'Em Back Alive" Buck, the popular animal showman — each performing before a standing-room-only crowd in the little community of Kohler, Wisconsin. The

COMMUNITY DRAMA

Marie C. Kohler

The annual Festival and Field Day offered horseshoe-pitching contests, jazz music and other entertainment. Charlotte Van Wickle, above, sang in 1924. Opposite, two youngsters enjoy a snack in 1927. Near right, amateur theater for village residents was sponsored by the Kohler Civic Club.

Distinguished Guest Series continues today under the sponsorship of Kohler Foundation, Inc.

The Three Sisters

Walter's three sisters, Evangeline, Marie and Lillie, none of whom ever married, were bright and well educated and devoted to the village, especially to its young people. They were revered in the community, although some residents did not know quite what to make of their eccentric personalities. The "Kohler girls," as they were called, wore large, floppy hats and fancy, full-length dresses, and were a familiar sight riding in their chauffeured limousine. For many years, their chauffeur had a little dog which sat next to him up front, adding to the colorful scene.

The sisters helped start the local Girl Scout troop, which met in the Waelderhaus, the "house in the woods," a replica of an Austrian house-barn. (Built in 1931, the Waelderhaus serves as a community building and is open to the public.) To this day, the Girl Scouts in Kohler are called the Elms, legend has it after the initials of the sisters — Evangeline, Lillie and Marie.

Civic-minded to the core, the sisters were constantly giving awards for beautification and public service. "A kid couldn't put up a birdhouse without them coming along and giving him some kind of award," recalls Bundy Lorenz, a longtime village resident, former policeman and retired

*W*alter Kohler poses with, left to right, his sister Evangeline, his sister Lillie, his aunt and stepmother Minnie, his wife Charlotte and his sister Marie. The three Kohler sisters were devoted to the village and to helping the poor and underprivileged throughout the county.

Kohler Co. employee. In fact, there *was* an annual award — sponsored by the Kohler Woman's Club, in which the sisters were active — for the best birdhouse in the village. There were also annual awards for best-kept house, best yard and best garden and in nearly a dozen other "best" categories. It's not surprising, in light of these awards and the spirit of civic pride that pervaded the village, that all the properties in Kohler were beautifully maintained.

The sisters were also instrumental, again through the Kohler Woman's

Club, in the construction of a "demonstration house" each year, furnished with modern appliances and incorporating the latest ideas in home design. The house was open for public viewing for several weeks, after which it was sold and construction was begun on a new demonstration house. People came from miles around to see the Kohler demonstration house. At its peak, this program attracted 30,000 visitors annually to the village.

While the sisters were highly visible in their support of public

causes, they went about their private philanthropy quietly. Many families in need, throughout Sheboygan County, received financial assistance from the three sisters without a word being whispered to anybody. Their niece, Ruth Kohler II, states, "To this day, people come up to me and say,

'Do you know what your aunts did for my family? Do you know what a difference they made in our lives?'"

A New 50-Year Plan

More than 400 homes had been built in the village by 1931, and in the ensuing years the community

continued to be a wonderful place to live, as it is today. However, the construction of new homes virtually came to a halt during the Depression and World War II and even in the years after the war. Just 20 homes were built from 1931 to 1961.

In the late 1960s, the original 50-year plan for controlled development finally ran its course. At that time, Herbert V. Kohler Jr. hired the Frank Lloyd Wright Foundation to devise a new 50-year master plan. Vernon Swaback, a Wright Foundation official who helped prepare the new plan, recalls there was some concern that the village was becoming stagnant. "There were no commercial facilities, not even a supermarket or gas station," he says, "and the number of students in the public school system was decreasing as more residents reached retirement

John Michael Kohler's first wife was Lillie Vollrath, above left. After she died in 1883, he married her sister, Minnie Vollrath, above right. At left is the Waelderhaus, a replica of an Austrian house-barn built in the village in 1931. It was designed by Kaspar Albrecht, an Austrian sculptor and architect who was related to the Kohler family.

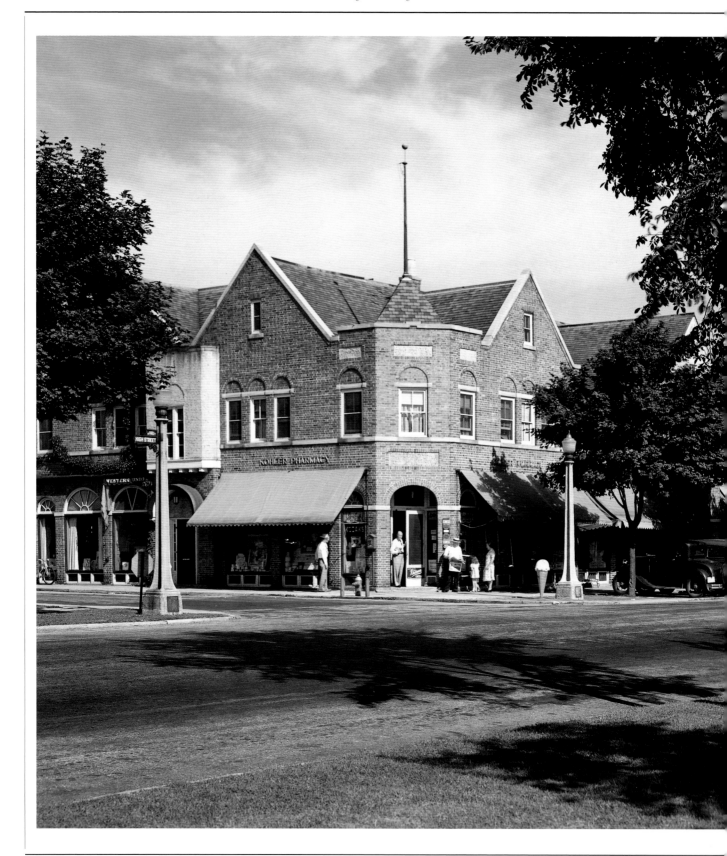

and the population aged." The purpose of the plan, he says, was to "breathe new life" into Kohler Village.

The new 50-year plan called for opening additional land to residential development while maintaining the community's sense of gracious living and natural beauty. It also addressed such issues as commercial facilities, health care and stable job opportunities. In its early years, the village was a self-contained community with an array of commercial facilities, including a drug store and soda fountain, post office, Western Union office, beauty parlor, hardware store, grocery store and butcher shop, and shoe store. In addition, the Kohler Public Garage gas station — located in the building directly south of the current firehouse — had 14 gasoline pumps selling many of the major brands. However, these stores went out of business one by one in the 1950s and early 1960s, no longer able to compete with malls and shopping centers in the county. The gas station lingered into the 1960s.

The new 50-year plan included the development of an upscale commercial center called The Shops at Woodlake, containing a supermarket and retail stores, and the opening of a gas station. Many Kohler Village residents were pleased to see the return of commercial facilities to the village. But that was only the beginning. In mulling over the new 50-year plan, Herbert Kohler Jr. came up with the concept

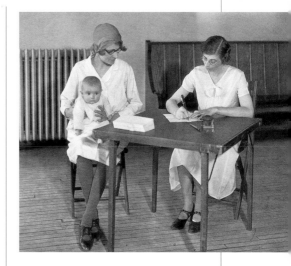

*A*t left, commercial facilities were located in low-rise buildings immediately north of The American Club. The buildings today house Kohler Waters Spa and other facilities. Above, infants and toddlers received free medical exams and vaccinations at annual Children's Health Clinics conducted by the Child Health Committee of the Kohler Woman's Club in cooperation with the Kohler Co. Medical Department.

of "Destination Kohler" — that is, turning The American Club into a premier resort hotel and adding other tourist attractions, such as golf courses. There were many skeptics, but Herb went ahead after convincing the Kohler Co. board of directors that his plan made sense. "Destination Kohler" has, in fact, been a great success, bringing increased prosperity to the village, as we shall see in Chapter Eight.

It's amazing what a community of 1,900 can be: the site of a major industrial plant, a quaint residential village and now, on top of that, a tourist destination. Yet, through careful planning and a single, far-reaching sense of quality — in the architecture, the landscaping, and the maintenance of the buildings and the grounds — it all works.

Not many families can say they started a village with their name on it, sold houses to their employees at cost, still live there themselves and remain devoted to its success. The Kohlers of Kohler, Wisconsin, can.

*H*aueisen's Kohler Pharmacy was one of the stores in the commercial area. Herb Kohler recalls, "The best ice cream sodas in the world came out of that soda fountain."

*H*erbert V. Kohler Sr., left, and his wife, Ruth De Young Kohler, right, were devoted to each other. She was women's editor of the *Chicago Tribune* when they met in 1937. He sent her a bouquet of red roses each day for the next three months until she married him. Their oldest child, Herbert Jr., was born in 1939.

or 68 years following the death of John Michael Kohler, the company continued to be headed by one or another of his sons. The first of these sons was Robert, who became chief executive officer in 1901. When Robert died four years later, he was succeeded by Walter. And when Walter died in 1940, the baton was passed to yet another son, Herbert, the youngest of John Michael's seven children. Herbert was 48 years old when he took charge, leading the company for the next 28 years. He was an astute, tenacious businessman who guided Kohler Co. to dramatic growth in the post-World War II economic boom.

Lengthy Career With the Company

Herbert Vollrath Kohler Sr. was born in the family home in Sheboygan in 1891. He was 11 years younger than the youngest of his "three-quarters" brothers and sisters, and they adored him. (As noted in Chapter Two, when John Michael Kohler's first wife, Lillie Vollrath, died, he married her sister, Minnie Vollrath. Herbert was the only child of that second marriage. He was a "three-quarters" brother because he and his siblings had the same father, and Herbert's mother and the mother of his six siblings were sisters.)

Herbert attended public school in Sheboygan and then Phillips Academy in Andover, Massachusetts, before enrolling at the Sheffield Scientific School of Yale University.

Beginning at age 16, he spent summers as an enameler and molder in the Kohler Co. foundry, work that involved tough physical labor. He graduated from college in 1914 with a bachelor of philosophy degree and immediately joined the company full-time in its engineering department. Except for a two-year leave for active duty in the army from 1917 to 1919, he remained with Kohler Co. for 54 years until his death in 1968.

His army service arose from his membership in the Wisconsin National Guard. He had volunteered for the guard after graduating from

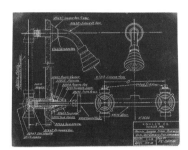

*L*eft, this stylish illustration is from a 1939 Kohler ad. Above is a 1942 blueprint for a shower fitting. During World War II, when the use of brass in consumer products was virtually banned because of military needs, Kohler made "Win-the-War" fittings of cast iron.

*H*erbert V. Kohler Sr. was a captain in an artillery unit, the First Wisconsin Cavalry, during World War I, participating in major battles in France.

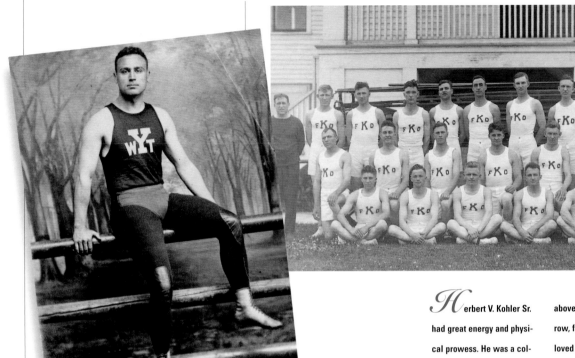

*H*erbert V. Kohler Sr. had great energy and physical prowess. He was a college wrestler at Yale, left, and a member of the Kohler Volunteer Fire Department, above. (He is in the back row, far right.) Opposite, he loved to walk through the factory and talk with employees, including this laboratory visit in 1935.

college, becoming an officer in the First Wisconsin Cavalry, an artillery unit with horse-drawn cannons. In July 1917, three months after the United States entered World War I, his unit was mobilized and he was promoted to captain. The unit subsequently shipped out to Europe, where it took part in major battles late in the war. The men in his company were all volunteers — chiefly from Sheboygan County, including many Kohler Co. employees — and even the horses were Sheboygan County-bred. Herbert's daughter, Ruth, says, "The men were a close-knit group and many of them remained lifelong

friends. My father had deep respect and affection for them and loved to tell about his time in France with them. At Christmas, he experienced the cease-fire during which the Germans and Americans talked to one another and sang carols across enemy lines in the darkness." Nearly two decades after the war, in 1936, Herbert organized a reunion of his comrades at The American Club. The invitation read, "While this is a re-union of the cavalry outfit, it isn't necessary to come on horseback."

Herbert was large and robust and, especially in his younger years, main-

tained a high degree of physical fitness. He had been a member of the Yale track and wrestling teams and, on joining Kohler Co., became a volunteer fireman — but not just any volunteer fireman. He signed up for the crack hook-and-ladder team. The Kohler Volunteer Fire Department at that time had a hook-and-ladder truck that was pulled by six men. It was not until the early 1920s that the department bought its first motor-powered truck. Herbert and five other firemen kept in shape by running to Sheboygan and back each noon, an eight-mile round trip, dragging the hook-and-ladder truck

*R*uth De Young Kohler, Herbert Sr.'s wife, was a journalist and historian. She continued to write after her marriage and was, in addition, president of the Kohler Woman's Club, initiating its Distinguished Guest Series. The portrait at left is owned by the Wisconsin Historical Society. Below left, she appears on stage with comedian Joe E. Brown, who had come to Kohler Village to appear in the Distinguished Guest Series.

behind them. This unbelievable dedication paid off: the Kohler Volunteer Fire Department won the hook-and-ladder race at the Annual Eastern Wisconsin Firemen's Tournament three years in a row, retiring the trophy. Throughout his life, Herbert showed a similar passion in just about everything he did.

Marrying at Age 45

Herbert and his older brother, Walter, got along extremely well, trusting each other implicitly, and it soon became apparent that Walter was grooming Herbert to be his successor. Herbert was elected to the Kohler Co. board of directors in 1921 at age 30, was appointed treasurer the following year and was elected to the newly created post of executive vice president in 1928. In 1937, Walter moved up to chairman and chief executive officer, relinquishing the presidency to Herbert.

A bachelor until 1937, Herbert married that year at age 45. He met his wife-to-be, Ruth De Young, at a women's conference in Chicago. She was 15 years younger than he and was a successful journalist and women's editor of the *Chicago Tribune*, writing about women's issues and covering national political conventions. According to one version of the story, Herbert attended the women's conference to hear his brother, Walter, speak. Sitting in the audience, he was quite taken with De Young, the conference moderator, and leaned over to her assistant, Bess Vydra, and said, "I'm going to marry that girl." He introduced himself that very day and sent her a bouquet of red roses each day for the next three months until, indeed, they were wed. After honeymooning in Europe, the couple returned to Kohler to live in the village. Their romance never lost its sparkle.

Intelligent and sophisticated, yet down to earth, Ruth De Young Kohler became one of the community's most active and well-liked residents. She was not only president of the Kohler Woman's Club, initiating its Distinguished Guest Series, but also continued to write for the *Chicago Tribune* and remained involved in women's rights issues.

Ruth also devoted herself to the heritage of Wisconsin. For the celebration of Wisconsin's 100th anniversary of statehood in 1948, she headed the development of a building filled with exhibits recounting the history of women in the state. She also wrote two books, *The Story of Wisconsin Women* and *Wisconsin's Historic Sites*, published for the centennial. Subsequently, she founded the Women's Auxiliary of the State Historical Society of Wisconsin. In addition, she saved and personally directed the restoration of Wade House, one of the state's finest examples of a nineteenth century stagecoach inn. Wade House was later donated to the State Historical Society of Wisconsin.

Ruth and Herbert had three children: Herbert Jr., born in 1939; Ruth II, in 1941; and Frederic, in 1943. Herbert was especially close to his daughter, Ruth II. When she was a girl, they often painted together and even attended the Banff School of Fine Arts in Canada. She says her father was a talented artist, "a kind of lyrical expressionist."

*H*erbert and Ruth were a handsome couple. They were married in 1937. He was devastated when she died just 16 years later.

*H*erbert Sr. poses with, back row left to right, his sisters Lillie and Evangeline and wife Ruth. In the front row are the children — Herb, Frederic and Ruth II. Years later, at right, Herbert Sr. is photographed with his granddaughters Rachel and Laura, both of whom work for Kohler Co. today.

Ruth II continues her love of art. Since 1972, she has been director of the John Michael Kohler Arts Center in Sheboygan, one of the most innovative and successful arts facilities in the nation. In that position, she conceived and is the driving force behind a unique collaboration between the Arts Center and Kohler Co.: the Arts/Industry residency program. The program — founded in 1974 and believed to be the only one of its kind in the United States — enables artists to spend two to six months in the Kohler Co. factory in Kohler Village, using industrial materials and equipment to create works of art. The artists receive free studio space within the factory, as well as materials, technical assistance, photographic services, housing, transportation and weekly stipends. All of the work produced by artists during their residencies belongs to them. Artists are asked to give one work to the Arts Center, which holds periodic exhibitions of works from the program, and one to the company, which displays them in company facilities and around the village.

Frederic, the youngest of the three Kohler children, was deeply interested in all aspects of Kohler Co. and knew many of its associates, although he himself was employed at the company for only a short time — as an inspector in the enamel shop in his early 20s. He died in 1998.

Frederic loved sports and was the number-one fan of the Kohler Blue Bombers high school basketball team, faithfully attending its games and other high school sports events.

He had a lifelong interest in history and psychology. He was particularly fascinated by the workings of the office of the president of the United States and had the opportunity to visit the White House on a number of occasions. He always supported both the Republican and Democratic parties — and did so with a sense of humor. By being bipartisan, he

explained, he received invitations to White House events regardless of whether a Republican or Democrat sat in the Oval Office.

Frederic was patriotic to the core. Pete Fetterer, Kohler Co.'s retired manager of civic services, who accompanied Frederic on a trip to Ellis Island in New York Harbor, recalls the deep respect that Frederic expressed for the values the island symbolized. Frederic noted that his grandfather, John Michael Kohler, was an immigrant, just like the millions who entered the United States through Ellis Island and who are honored today at the Ellis Island Immigration Museum.

Fetterer says, "Frederic was the kind of a guy you simply cannot forget."

*L*ucius P. Chase **worked at Kohler from 1926 until his retirement in 1971, serving for many years as general counsel. In addition, he was a member of the Kohler board of directors for 47 years, one of the longest tenures in its history.**

Central Role in the Company's History

Herbert V. Kohler Sr. cared deeply about the company and viewed himself as the steward of the Kohler family heritage. During his 28-year tenure as chief executive officer, Kohler Co. expanded into new products, such as small engines, and introduced the industry's first accent-color plumbing products. In addition, he was active in promoting the growth of Kohler Village, personally supporting the building of a school-village theater (Kohler Memorial Hall), a school-village swimming pool and a school athletic field, among other facilities.

Sam H. Davis, a longtime senior executive now retired, says, "Herbert Kohler Sr. was a very forceful personality in the company and the plumbing

SUPPORTING EDUCATION AND THE ARTS

For more than a century, Kohler Co. and the Kohler family have been active in a variety of community causes, especially in the arts. This involvement is carried forward today not only by individual family members, but also by two important

organizations established during the tenure of Herbert V. Kohler Sr.

The first is Kohler Foundation, Inc., created in 1940 by Herbert and his sisters, Evangeline, Marie and Lillie Kohler. The foundation supports various educational and cultural programs, primarily in Wisconsin.

A major program benefits graduates of Sheboygan County's 12 high schools, who are eligible for college scholarships from the foundation based on leadership qualities and academic and artistic achievement. In addition, the foundation manages the Waelderhaus in

The John Michael Kohler Arts Center is housed in a contemporary facility that incorporates John Michael Kohler's Victorian home, left. It offers innovative explorations in the visual and performing arts.

Kohler Village; administers the Distinguished Guest Series of performances in the village by world-renowned musicians, dancers and actors; and provides financial support to Wade House, an 1850s stagecoach inn which is maintained by the Wisconsin Historical Society as a historic site open to the public.

Since the late 1970s, under the direction of Ruth's daughter, Ruth De Young Kohler II, the foundation has been in the forefront of preserving large-scale art environments and entire bodies of work by self-taught artists. An example is Grandview, the dairy farm of the late Nick Engelbert in Hollandale, Wisconsin. From the early 1930s to the 1950s, Engelbert turned his farm into a fantastic fairyland. He made more than 40 extraordinary life-sized concrete characters from fairy tales, myth and history and displayed them on his lawn. In addition, he coated his house with concrete embedded with shells, buttons, beads, and shards of glass and pottery. The sculptures and house fell into disrepair after Engelbert's death. Kohler Foundation purchased the site in 1991, restored it and deeded it to an educational foundation that now oversees the property. As is true of other self-taught artists' sites preserved by the foundation, Nick Engelbert's Grandview is open to the public. Many student groups visit each year, and there is an artist-in-residence program at the location. Across the nation, self-taught artists' environments are gaining recognition as important works of art and an irreplaceable aspect of our cultural heritage. Kohler Foundation has

restored more than half a dozen such sites and continues to acquire, conserve and gift others.

The second major nonprofit organization that Herbert V. Kohler Sr. helped establish is the John Michael Kohler Arts Center in Sheboygan, created in 1967 to encourage and support innovative exploration in all the arts. His daughter, Ruth II, is its director. In 1999, the *Milwaukee Journal Sentinel* described the Arts

*R*uth De Young Kohler II is the Arts Center's director. Known for her arts leadership, she has been honored with the Governor's Award and the Smith College Medal for alumnae of exceptional achievement, among many other distinctions.

Center as "the antithesis of a mecca for the elite," adding, "It's a kid-centered, grownup-friendly, wildly innovative space for art-making as well as for art showing." Housed originally in John Michael Kohler's Victorian home, it now encompasses 99,000 square feet of space, including light-filled exhibition galleries, studios and performance spaces built in 1970 and 1999. The most recent addition features six unusual washrooms made by artists in the

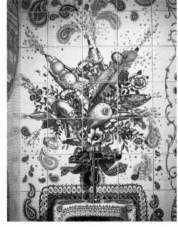

$\mathcal{T}$he Arts Center commissioned artists in its Arts/Industry residency program to create the six washrooms for its 1999 expansion. Some of the wildly imaginative results are shown on this and the facing page. Ann Agee, above, is pictured working in the Arts/Industry studio space of the Kohler Co. plant on a ceramic panel for the washroom she created. Water is the subject of her motifs, including the depiction of super-soaker squirt guns at left.

*T*he washroom created by artist Matt Nolen, above and left, wittily depicts the progression of architecture from ancient Egypt to the present.

Arts/Industry program at Kohler Co.

The Arts Center exhibits contemporary art, emphasizing new genres, installation works, craft, ongoing folk traditions, and the work of self-taught artists and visionaries, and presents performances of theater, music and dance. It receives financial support from nearly 2,000 corporate, individual and government donors, and attracts more than 160,000 adults and children each year.

*T*he children's washroom features colorful tiles painted by 70 three- and four-year-olds.

*J*obs in the iron foundry during the 1940s, 1950s and 1960s involved both skill and hard physical work. Pictured is the molding of cast-iron bathtubs.

products industry." Herbert hired Davis in 1957 to manage a new plant in Spartanburg, South Carolina, giving Davis the freedom, personal encouragement and financial resources to develop the Spartanburg facility into one of the largest plumbing products factories in the nation.

Herbert ran the company with a small group of advisers in whom he had total confidence. Herbert and the key members of his management team lived and breathed the company and were extremely hard workers.

One of the most important members was Lyman C. Conger, a vice president and director of the company who was in charge of labor relations. Conger grew up in Greenbush,

Wisconsin, where his father was a farmer. He graduated from the University of Wisconsin, signing on with Kohler Co. in 1922 as an enamel scaler. He soon transferred to the chemical lab, studying law at night. The day after he passed the bar, he transferred to the company's legal department.

Conger stood five feet, one inch tall. His son, Kenneth W. Conger, describes him as "a tough little guy who could get things done." Conger was resolute and demanding and never backed down from anyone, yet had a wonderful sense of humor and loved to tell amusing stories. Ken Conger adds, "My dad had this unusual trait. When he got really

mad, he would hum the *Ave Maria*, being a good Catholic. We kids would split when he did that. I would see him in meetings when he would hum the *Ave Maria*, and I'd think, 'Oh, somebody's going to get it now!'"

In 1968, after the death of Herbert Kohler, Conger was elected Kohler Co.'s chairman of the board, the only person other than a member of the Kohler family ever to hold that position.

The Kohlers and the Congers lived next to each other in the village and were friends as well as business associates. Even today, the two families remain closely associated: Ken Conger was with the company 30 years, retiring in 1998 as senior vice president-human resources. His

*L*yman Conger spent 50 years at Kohler Co. and was known for his intelligence, toughness and humor. He was in charge of labor negotiations for many years, and served from 1968 to 1972 as Kohler Co. chairman, the only individual other than a member of the Kohler family ever to hold that title.

Kohler ads from the postwar years reflected the public's mood of optimism and a desire to return to normal life. The illustration above is from 1947. At right is an ad that appeared in the *Saturday Evening Post*. It featured the Kohler Delafield cast-iron sink and the Kohler Edgewater chromium-plated brass faucet.

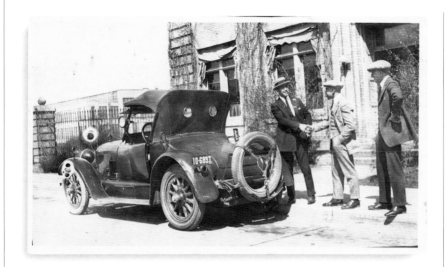

*P*ictured are four longtime employees who were members of Herbert Sr.'s management team. Walter J. Ireland, above, standing next to the car, and also pictured bottom right, was the company's personnel director. Edmund J. Biever, below, top left, was the plant manager. Anton A. Braun, below, top right, was Kohler Co. treasurer. Harry C. Schrader, below, bottom left, was branch manager in Kansas City and then in Chicago.

responsibilities included labor negotiations, the same responsibilities held for many years by his father.

Other members of Herbert Kohler's inner circle were L. L. Smith, executive vice president, who was responsible for advertising and public relations and was an excellent writer, and Lu Chase, vice president and general counsel. Chase, a University of Wisconsin graduate, joined the company in 1926. His intelligence, integrity and wit soon caught the attention of Herbert. When Herbert became president in 1937, Chase was elected to the Kohler Co. board of directors, remaining on the board for 47 years, with four years' leave of absence for military service during World War II. Chase was a highly decorated war hero. First as an army lieutenant colonel and then as a colonel, he helped plan the D-Day assault at Normandy. He himself landed on D-Day with the first waves of troops and continued in action despite being wounded on the Normandy beach. Chase returned to Kohler Co. after the war as a vice president and later as senior vice president, retiring in 1971 at age 69. He was known not only for his work at the company, but also for his involvement in numerous civic and philanthropic causes.

Herbert Sr.'s management team also included Edmund J. Biever, a plant manager and member of the board of directors who spent 37 years with the company; Anton A. Braun,

ARMY **E** NAVY

"for great achievement
in the production
of war equipment."

KOHLER

*K*ohler Co. converted
to military production
during World War II,
receiving a coveted Army-
Navy E Award for excep-
tional performance in
wartime production.

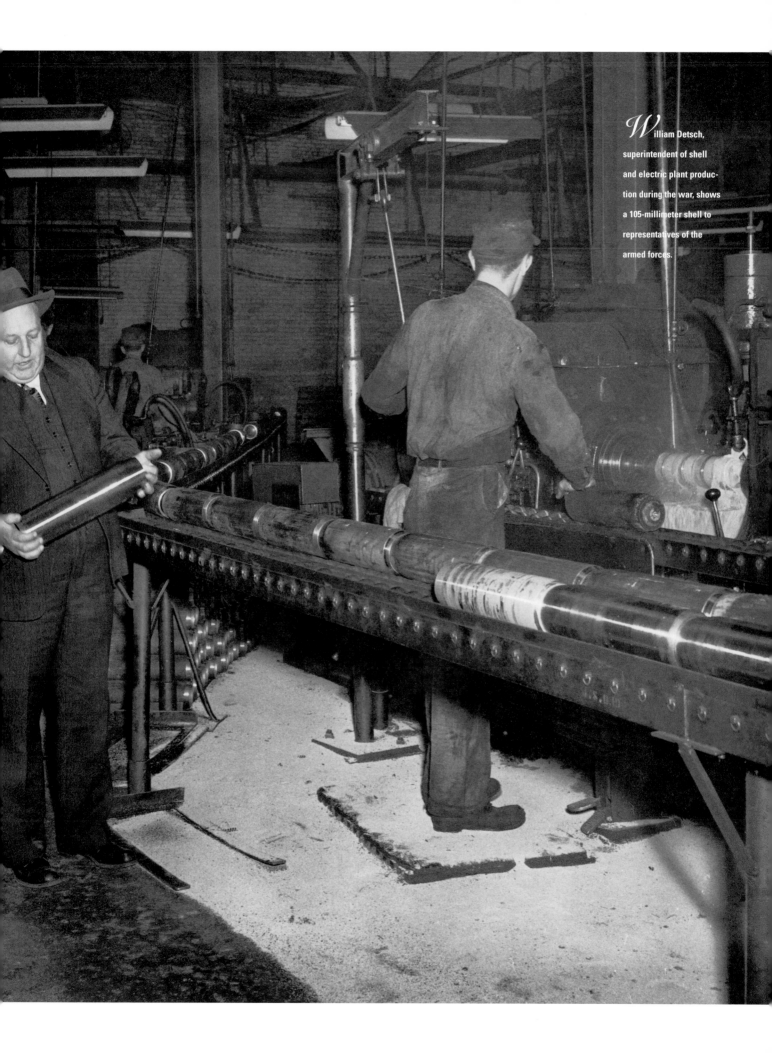

William Detsch, superintendent of shell and electric plant production during the war, shows a 105-millimeter shell to representatives of the armed forces.

another 37-year veteran who was treasurer and a member of the board of directors; Harry C. Schrader, a branch manager (a key sales position), first in Kansas City and then in Chicago, who was with the company 39 years; and Walter J. Ireland, a 55-year veteran who was personnel director of Kohler Co. and treasurer of Kohler Village.

Kohler Co. During World War II

One of the first challenges Herbert Kohler faced on becoming chief executive officer in 1940 was to convert the company to wartime production. Because brass was a vital war material, the manufacture of brass fittings for the bathroom was virtually banned from 1942 through 1944. Showing great ingenuity, Kohler Co. produced special "Win-the-War" fittings made of cast iron. Few other companies produced bathroom fittings of any type, and Kohler Co. gained market share during the war, albeit in a depressed market.

Kohler Co.'s main focus during World War II was to manufacture artillery shells, submarine torpedo tubes, aircraft controls and other military goods. Although most Kohler military products were discontinued after the war, Herbert decided to stay

*M*any women worked in the factory in the early 1940s, replacing men who had gone off to war. The company produced 105-millimeter and three-inch high-explosive shells, forgings for 75-millimeter high-explosive shells, 4.5-inch rocket shells, fuses for artillery and aircraft shells, submarine torpedo tubes, aircraft piston rings, shell rotating bands and engine bearings.

in the precision controls business. In a 1972 interview, Lyman Conger explained, "Herbert felt it was beneficial for morale to make parts to very close tolerances. He believed this craftsmanship would be reflected in the work of people in other areas of the factory."

Over the next three decades, Kohler Co. supplied hydraulic valves and other controls for virtually all types of commercial aircraft manufactured in the United States, from the DC-3 to the Boeing 747. In addition, nearly every jet engine made in the United States had Kohler fuel valves. In the 1960s, the company supplied controls for the Saturn and Atlas rockets used by NASA to send astronauts into space. When Neil Armstrong made his historic lunar walk in 1969, it was said that Kohler Co.'s export markets had "reached the moon."

But profits of the precision controls division began to flag in the 1970s, and the company sold these operations in 1976, ending this unique chapter in Kohler Co. history.

The 1954-1960 Strike

By the early 1950s, as the postwar economic boom continued, Kohler Co.'s business was humming along nicely. Then came the 1954-1960 strike, the longest labor stoppage in American industrial history, according to the *Encyclopaedia Brittanica.*

In 1952, production and maintenance employees at the Kohler factory had voted to affiliate with the United Auto Workers, becoming UAW-CIO Local 833. Two years later, the UAW sought a wage increase, benefit increases, a union shop and strict seniority in promotion and layoffs.

Herbert Kohler expressed a willingness to raise wages and benefits, but was adamant in opposing a union shop and strict seniority, saying they would harm the company's ability to manage its business. In any event, Kohler Co. had long maintained that each employee had a fundamental right to belong to a union or not. In 1929, Governor Walter Kohler had initiated pro-labor legislation outlawing the "yellow dog" contracts used by employers to bar workers from joining unions. In Herbert's view, a worker's freedom *not* to join a union was the other side of the same issue.

Herbert V. Kohler Jr. says, "My father and Walter Reuther [president of the UAW] got locked into positions of principle — Herbert Kohler for freedom of choice, Walter Reuther for the union shop. It's one thing to bargain over wages. You can always compromise on money. But when you throw in a principle or two and both sides take firm stands, it becomes very difficult to compromise."

The strike began on April 5, 1954, when 2,000 UAW pickets blocked the three main entrances to the Kohler

*A*bove is a mass picket line during the 1954-1960 strike, which centered on union demands for a closed shop and strict seniority in promotion. Herbert V. Kohler Sr. refused to give in to those demands, saying that to do so would harm the company's ability to manage its business. He was a villain to the union, as the caricature at left demonstrates, but was a hero to many business executives across the nation.

plant. "Shut down like a drum," a union publication proclaimed. When the Wisconsin Employment Relations Board ordered the union to disband its mass picketing and permit entrance to the factory, the union disputed the board's jurisdiction and refused to do so. The sealing off of the factory by pickets continued for 54 days until it was ended by a court injunction.

With access to the plant restored, some workers returned, and new employees were hired to fill the balance, bringing the facility into full operation. But the strike had already turned violent, and after the plant reopened the disorder continued and even escalated as the union sought to bring the company to its knees. "It was a terrible time," recalls Ken Conger, who was then in his teens. "There was a lot of vandalism, a lot of fights, shotgun shells through windows, threatening phone calls in the middle of the night. Kids traveled in groups to avoid being beaten up."

One of the most explosive incidents, the "clayboat riot," occurred 15 months into the strike. In that era, Kohler Co. imported English ball clay, bringing it down the St. Lawrence River and across the Great Lakes. On July 5, 1955, when a ship carrying clay tried to unload its cargo at the Sheboygan harbor, 500 to 600 pickets converged on the docks and prevented it from doing so, in the process pulling two men from the cab of a truck and roughing them up, rocking

a company car which tried to reach the scene and pelting it with stones, and breaking a gasoline line. The Sheboygan police chief, later explaining why his men did not intervene, claimed that "the entire area was out of control, beyond reach of normal law and order."

There ensued an epic struggle between the company trying to get the clay and the union trying to block the shipment at every turn. Unable to discharge its cargo in Sheboygan, the vessel went to Milwaukee, but authorities there refused to let the clay be unloaded, saying they feared a repeat of the events in Sheboygan. Because of pressure from the union, no other port in Wisconsin seemed likely to accept the shipment. Finally, the vessel went to Montreal, where the cargo was transferred to a train. "And the train came down to Sheboygan and headed for a switching line to the Kohler plant, but pickets blocked the track," says John M. "Mike" Kohler Jr., a grandnephew of Herbert Sr. "The saga finally ended when executives of the railroad, with drawn guns, stood on the engine of the switching train. And the clay got through. It was a very long trip before the clay arrived. But the Kohler Co. hung in."

The company said it would not give in to union tactics of violence and intimidation. The UAW, in turn, accused the company of spying on striking employees and refusing to bargain in good faith. The strike became a national cause célèbre,

with organized labor and American industry lined up on opposing sides. Many business people viewed Herbert Kohler as a hero for standing up to the UAW and resisting a closed shop in an era when the power of organized labor was at its peak. He "became a symbol of embattled individualism to much of the business world," according to the *New York Times*. In 1958, as the strike wore on, the National Association of Manufacturers named him its Man of the Year.

Turning up the heat, the UAW launched a nationwide boycott of Kohler products. However, even as the UAW assigned 15 of its international agents full-time to the promotion of the boycott, the United States Chamber of Commerce organized dinner meetings of business people in major cities to discuss the issues from the viewpoint of Kohler Co. management. And Kohler Co.'s general counsel, Lu Chase, was among the Kohler executives who went on the road, seeking not only management but also labor backing for the company's position. "I had no difficulty getting local plumbers' unions to refuse to join the boycott," he recalled. "At that time, we were building a new engine plant in Kohler with union construction labor. I had a meeting in Miami with the national president of the Journeyman Plumbers. He was impressed by what I told him about Kohler's labor relations and the use of union construction workers in our

plant, and he agreed it would be a mistake for his union to join the boycott."

Herbert V. Kohler Jr. says, "We ended up with about 60 percent to 70 percent of our normal production the first year of the strike, about 90 percent the second year and nearly 100 percent thereafter. However, it was one thing to make products. It was another to sell them, because of the secondary boycott that was generated around the country by the UAW. Thank God for a whole host of home builders who believed earnestly in the cause for which we were fighting — that is, the freedom of an employee to join or not join any organization

The strike that began in 1954 quickly became confrontational, as the union sought to bring the company to its knees and the company sought to maintain operations. Here, picketers close in on employees trying to enter the factory.

he wished. During this strike, many home builders bought Kohler brand plumbing products exclusively. And it was this support which pulled the company through the strike. Nothing else."

Kohler Co. was profitable every year of the strike. However, no one in management was gloating. Bitter, protracted strikes are detrimental to all parties. Nobody escapes their impact. The company's relationship with its unionized employees was severely tested, and it took years for Kohler Co. to shake off charges that it was "anti-union." Many distributors of Kohler products were hurt by the boycott. Above all, the strike was traumatic for people in the village and the county, and not just because of the violence. Many families in the village and the surrounding communities were torn apart, as siblings, cousins, fathers and sons split into pro-company and pro-union factions. Bundy Lorenz, who was born in Kohler in 1927 and has lived there all his life, says his father continued to work, two of his brothers picketed, two other brothers left the company rather than take sides and he himself was a village policeman trying to keep the peace. The Lorenz family members had the strength to remain together on loving terms, but other families did not. Hard feelings lingered in some families long after the strike had ended.

The strike continued for six years,

*A*s the strike continued in 1958, Kohler Co.'s Lyman Conger, above, testified at a U.S. Senate hearing. He said the company was back at full operation despite the strike and had overcome a union boycott of its products. Striking employees returned to work in 1960. Opposite right, company negotiators head for a bargaining session in 1962, the year a new contract was finally signed. Second from left is James L. "Les" Kuplic, Kohler Co. president. In the foreground is George Gallati, assistant director of public relations.

finally grinding to a halt in 1960 when the picketing was disbanded. A new contract was signed two years later, providing wage and benefit increases, but foregoing a union shop. It was not until 1965, however, that the litigation ended. When it did, Kohler executives were dismayed: Kohler Co. was ordered by a federal court to rehire nearly all the former strikers (the company had said it would not rehire those who had engaged in violence and other misconduct) and to pay wages and benefits of $4.5 million lost during the strike.

Out of this titanic struggle came a mutual recognition that management and labor could not continue to clash in this manner. Indeed, except for a two-week strike in 1983, the company's core Wisconsin operations have been free of labor stoppages ever since. "Do we love each other? That's not true," says Charles Conrardy, a onetime Kohler Co. employee who is now a retired UAW international representative. "But we respect each other. And we have learned to work together. You're always going to have something to gripe about or something you want to improve, but I think on the whole we've progressed with the company." He gives Kohler Co. generally high marks for the benefits it provides to its unionized employees in Kohler and also thinks it has done a "fine job" of supporting worthwhile causes throughout

Wisconsin. Perhaps surprisingly, he also credits the company for investing in automation. "You can argue all you want that automation puts people out of work," he comments. "It also creates jobs. In this day and age, if you don't move in that direction, you're not going to stay in business."

Demands for a union shop did not disappear. The UAW kept plugging away at this issue, and in the late 1970s Kohler Co. compromised by agreeing to an agency shop — meaning that employees do not have to join the union, but must pay dues. "We gave ground to avoid another big battle," Ken Conger says.

Despite the ferocity of his conflict with the UAW, Herbert never lost his love for going onto the factory floor and talking with the men. In his later years, Herbert began to chew tobacco, as did many of the workers in the plant. Boot Jack, an especially potent brand, was his favorite. "One of my father's joys was to go up to these rough characters in the factory and offer them a chaw of Boot Jack," Herbert Jr. says. Some of the men found the brand so strong they had to spit it right out. In moments like these, everybody had a good laugh, and Herbert was one of the boys.

Spartanburg Plant: First Expansion Outside Wisconsin
Unlike his brother Walter, an aviation pioneer, Herbert Kohler preferred not to travel by air for reasons that are easy to understand. In addition to having personally survived a plane

In 1958, Kohler Co. opened its first plant outside Wisconsin when it built this pottery in Spartanburg, South Carolina. Sam H. Davis, right, joined Kohler to manage the new facility, developing it into the largest full-line pottery in the United States. In 1971, he was named group vice president-plumbing products and precision controls and later became vice chairman with responsibility for international operations. He retired as an officer in 1996 and as a director in 1999, continuing as director emeritus.

crash in the English Channel, a harrowing experience for even the hardiest traveler, he was badly shaken when a corporate plane of Crane Co., a major competitor, went down, killing that company's senior management team.

Thus, when Herbert and his advisers journeyed to Spartanburg, South Carolina, in the mid-1950s to inspect potential sites for a new Kohler Co. pottery, they made the 2,000-mile round trip by chauffeured car. Spartanburg was attractive to Kohler Co. because of nearby clay deposits for the production of china fixtures, the availability of labor and the growth of southeastern consumer markets.

Although Spartanburg is today a thriving industrial community, home to a huge BMW automobile manufacturing complex and other factories, in the 1950s the local economy was still dominated by textile mills and agriculture. The city fathers were try-ing to attract job-creating industry and they welcomed Herbert and his team, showing them an unusually good construction site — an aban-doned military parade ground. "That parade ground closed the deal," Herbert V. Kohler Jr. says. Within days, Herbert Sr. had selected Spartanburg for Kohler Co.'s initial manufacturing operation outside Wisconsin and its first major new plant since the 1920s. Kohler Co. became one of the first national companies to open a plant in Spartanburg, embarking on a long and mutually productive relationship between community and company. The facility began production in 1958 and, through a series of expansions, soon evolved into the largest full-line sanitary pottery in the United States and a major producer of fiberglass-reinforced plastic plumbing fixtures.

In 1957, as the Spartanburg plant was nearing completion, Herbert hired Sam H. Davis to manage the facility — a decision that, like the choice of Spartanburg itself, would prove important to Kohler Co.'s future. A lanky Oklahoman with an engaging personality, Davis had joined the army in 1940 after high school. He served during the war in the Southwest Pacific, participating in campaigns on New Guinea, Biak, Leyte, Mondoro, Mindanao and

Luzon and winning the silver star for gallantry in action. By war's end, he held the rank of major and com-manded an artillery battalion. After the war, he enrolled at the University of Texas and graduated in 1949 with a degree in ceramic engineering, joining Kohler eight years later to manage Spartanburg. He ran the facility for 13 years and was then

*H*erbert V. Kohler Sr. speaks to visiting distributors at a 1928 luncheon in Roosevelt Park in the village. Kohler Co.'s nationwide network of finan-cially strong distributors has been crucial to the company's success in plumbing products for the past century.

*M*ike Kohler, right, poses with Joe Childress, executive vice president of the National Association of Plumbing-Heating-Cooling Contractors, at a 1982 industry convention. A great-grandson of founder John Michael Kohler, Mike Kohler was active in the company's management for 37 years, retiring in 1997.

tapped for a management position at company headquarters in Kohler Village, becoming one of Kohler Co.'s most capable and esteemed senior executives during the presidency of Herbert V. Kohler Jr.

Today, Kohler Co. has 46 plants with 25,000 employees worldwide. About 8,000 of those employees work in Wisconsin, still the heart of the company's operations. However, it was the Spartanburg plant, as much as any facility, that expanded the company's horizons beyond Wisconsin and re-accelerated its growth. Even though Kohler Co. is dramatically larger today than it was in 1958, Spartanburg remains a core production site, just as it was when it opened its doors.

Why He Was Chosen

One of the interesting aspects of Herbert's presidency is why he was chosen president in the first place and the enduring consequences of that choice in terms of management control of the company.

In deciding on Herbert as his successor, Walter Kohler bypassed his own four sons — John, Walter Jr., Carl and Robert — all of whom worked in the business. John, a graduate of the University of Wisconsin, worked at Kohler Co. for 42 years,

beginning in the factory and becoming Chicago branch manager in the 1920s. He was Kohler Co. treasurer from 1937 to 1947 and, after that, a vice president. Carl, known as "Jimmy," was an MIT graduate and prolific inventor who spent 32 years with the company and held many patents. Walter Jr. was with the company 23 years and, like his father, was elected governor of Wisconsin, serving three consecutive terms. Robert spent 14 years as a director of Kohler Co.

Herbert V. Kohler Jr. says, "Walter Kohler would not have passed the management reins to Herbert Kohler Sr. were it not for the 16-year age difference between them." In other words, Herbert was sufficiently younger than Walter to be his successor, yet older and more experienced than Walter's sons, who were not yet ready to take charge. In addition, as pointed out previously, the two brothers were extremely close and trusted each other absolutely.

Management succession issues in family enterprises often generate sparks. And in the case of Kohler Co., by choosing Herbert as his successor, Walter shifted management control to the Herbert branch and away from his own children. This was a crucial decision with lasting implications. Several of Walter's descendants have held key management positions in the company. In addition to the active involvement of Walter's four sons, his grandson, John Michael "Mike"

James L. "Les" Kuplic, Kohler Co.'s president from 1962 to 1968, was highly respected for his leadership skills and ability to encourage people to develop new ideas. He joined Kohler in 1943 after a career as a professional basketball player.

Kohler Jr., spent 37 years with Kohler Co., serving as a vice president, Spartanburg plant manager and a member of the board of directors. (Mike retired as an executive in 1997 and continues as a director.) To this day, however, the Herbert branch retains majority ownership and control.

For years, the ascendancy of the Herbert branch was an irritant to some of Walter's descendants, but the matter was kept within the family. It finally burst into the open in the early 1960s when Walter Kohler Jr. sued Kohler Co. and his uncle, Herbert Sr., claiming he had been defrauded. Walter Jr. was secretary of Kohler Co. from 1937 to 1942, left for military service and returned as secretary from 1945 to 1947, when he resigned to become president of Vollrath

Company in Sheboygan. In 1953, while serving as Wisconsin governor, Walter Jr. sold his Kohler stock to the company to avoid any appearance of conflict if forced to take sides in the company's negotiations with the UAW. In his suit, he alleged the price he had received was too low. A federal judge dismissed the suit, and that dismissal was upheld by an appellate court in 1963. But the harsh feelings within the family were out in the open for all to see.

In time, the wounds began to heal and relations within the family became generally cordial. Walter Sr.'s grandson, Terry Kohler, was quoted in a 1993 magazine article as saying, "We're not the fuzzy-wuzzy, get-together types. But we get along, and we respect one another."

Changing of the Guard

Ruth De Young Kohler, Herbert's wife, died suddenly in 1953 of a heart attack at age 46. Herbert and Ruth had been married just 16 years. Their daughter, Ruth II, who was 11 at the time of her mother's death, says her father was "desolate," for Ruth had been the love of his life. Nonetheless, he moved on. Ruth II says he "nurtured the children and worked hard to keep the family on an even keel, all the while managing the company and, a year later, coping with the strike."

In 1961, the year after the strike wound down, Herbert reached 70 and turned his attention to identifying and training a successor, eventually selecting James L. "Les" Kuplic. Tall and broad-shouldered, Kuplic was born in Manitowoc, Wisconsin, the

In the 1960s, Armond "Bud" Grube, advertising manager, far left, Charles Pagnucco, director-public relations, advertising, market development and planning, left, and Alfred Ellrodt, manager of market development, right, developed the concept of boldly colored plumbing products. Their idea resulted in an outpouring of new products under the tag line, The Bold Look of Kohler.

son of the chief of police. He attended Beloit College, starring in football, basketball and tennis, and graduated in 1934 with a degree in psychology. After college, he played professional basketball for the Sheboygan Redskins of the National Basketball League, a predecessor of today's National Basketball Association. He began at Kohler Co. in 1943 as a milling machine operator and advanced steadily in the plant. Then, in a rapid rise to the top, he was named production manager in 1961, vice president in 1962 and president later that same year at age 50.

Kuplic was well known and well liked throughout the company. "He was very straightforward and had a marvelous ability to relate to people and command their respect," Mike Kohler says. Kuplic took charge as president, bringing positive change to the company by encouraging employees to pursue new ideas, including the development of accent-color plumbing products and the creation of The Bold Look of Kohler advertising theme. In addition, because he came from the factory and was trusted by both labor and management, he helped negotiate a new labor contract following the lengthy strike. Herbert Kohler pulled back from day-to-day management, giving his full support to Kuplic, and there seemed no doubt that Kuplic would one day succeed Herbert as chief executive officer.

Then tragedy struck. On the morning of July 22, 1968, Les Kuplic — a tall, strapping athlete with no history of heart trouble — died of a heart attack at age 56 while driving to work. Six days later, Herbert Kohler died at age 76. Within less than a week, Kohler Co. had lost its two top executives, and the next prospective CEO within the family, Herbert V. Kohler Jr., was 29 years old and not yet ready to run the business.

Tragedy of this sort was not entirely new to Kohler Co. Nearly seven decades earlier, at the beginning of the twentieth century, John Michael Kohler and two of his sons had died within five years of each other. Difficult as these events were in both cases — that is, in 1900-1905 and in 1968 — the company and its people had the resiliency and determination to keep the business on a strong path of growth.

A company publication noted in 1973, "Adaptability to crises and the strength and ability to rebound and move forward have been characteristic of Kohler Co." This was true in 1900-1905. It would prove true again in 1968.

$\mathcal{K}$ohler Co. has led the plumbing products industry in advertising directly to consumers, not just to the building and plumbing trades. These "Edge of Imagination" advertisements from the 1970s featured striking images of plumbing products in surreal settings. With their unusual imagery, the ads were attention-getting and memorable, reinforcing Kohler's reputation for design leadership. This Bold Look of Kohler logo is from 1967, when bell-bottom pants were the rage.

THE BOLD LOOK OF KOHLER

ON THE WAY TO SAN RAPHAEL...

You never thought you'd see a toilet quite like this. But there it is San Raphael!™ Not a mirage. But a one-piece toilet of ingenious design.
The sleek, low-profile styling conserves space.
The efficient design uses less water than most conventional one-piece toilets—only three and one-half gallons.
Shown in Swiss Chocolate, it's available in a variety of decorator colors.
San Raphael has an oval-shaped bowl. A similar toilet Kohler calls the Rialto™ offers a bowl in the round.

San Raphael, by Kohler. It's really hard to pass up.
For many more kitchen, bath and powder room products see the Yellow Pages for a Kohler showroom or send $2 for a 48-page catalog to Kohler Co., Department HC9, Kohler, WI 53044.

THE BOLD LOOK OF **KOHLER**

Copyright 1983 Kohler Co

THE BOLD LOOK OF **KOHLER**

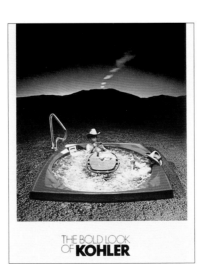

THE BOLD LOOK OF **KOHLER**

THE BOLD LOOK OF **KOHLER**

*H*erb Kohler, a grandson of the founder, has been Kohler Co.'s CEO since 1972. Thirty-three years old when he took charge, he has aggressively expanded the company's business both domestically and internationally.

ith the sudden deaths of Les Kuplic and Herbert V. Kohler Sr. in 1968, the dominant personality and controlling stockholder of the company was now Herbert V. Kohler Jr. He would subsequently become, in the words of one publication, "beyond any question...the most creative and constructive influence on the industry in this era." That same publication also said, "Let's face it: this guy is a one-of-a-kind original."

Demanding, energetic and visionary, and a stickler for quality in every aspect of the company's products and services, Herb Kohler has led Kohler Co. through its greatest growth.

Just 29 years old at the time of his father's death, he was in no rush to assume the presidency, telling one colleague he needed more experience before taking charge and that, in any event, he wanted to continue

in the production side of the business for a while. Herb became vice president-operations, holding that position until 1971, when he moved up to executive vice president. He became chairman and chief executive officer the year after that, adding the presidency in 1974. He continues as CEO today, in the prime of his career.

A Transition Management Team

During the period from 1968 to 1972, when Herb was in charge of production, the company reached within its executive ranks, but outside the Kohler family, for its senior management team. In 1968, Lyman Conger, the company's 66-year-old vice president-industrial relations, was appointed chairman and chief executive officer, and Walter Cleveland, the 52-year-old treasurer, moved up to president.

As discussed earlier, Conger, an attorney, was a longtime Kohler Co. executive known for his brilliance and toughness. He was also one of the memorable raconteurs in Kohler Co. history. "He could go on telling jokes one after another for an hour," Richard A. Wells, retired senior vice president-finance, recollects. Wells adds, "He was a gracious gentleman — a tough person, but very warm. When I became an officer of the company, assistant treasurer in 1969, he took my wife and me to a restaurant to celebrate my election. He picked us up at our house. It was scary to me. Here was the chairman of the

*L*eft to right are Walter Cleveland, Lyman Conger and Herb Kohler in 1970. Following the deaths of Kohler Co.'s two senior executives within days of each other in 1968, Cleveland became president, Conger chairman and Kohler, then 29, vice president-operations.

company picking us up in his car and taking us to dinner. But we had a wonderful time. He was just a warm, friendly, very likable person and a very good executive."

Walter Cleveland was a relative newcomer to Kohler Co. Straight-forward and articulate, he had joined the company in 1959 as a staff accountant, becoming comptroller in 1962 and treasurer in 1963. In an interview shortly before his death in 1997, he said he was surprised when Herbert Jr. approached him in 1968 asking that Cleveland advance from treasurer to president. "I thought Herbert Jr. was going to be president himself," he recalled.

Cleveland said that in accepting the presidency, he viewed himself as a steward and caretaker. "I didn't have any illusions about cutting a big swath," he recalled, "but I did feel I could make a positive contribution until Herbert Jr. was ready."

John Michael "Mike" Kohler Jr., a great-grandson of company founder John Michael Kohler, credits Cleveland with playing an important role in improving the company's profitability. "He was an accountant, and he asked some tough questions about why the plumbing business wasn't more prof-itable," Mike Kohler says. "And he got people looking for ways to make it more profitable. He started ranking distributors by profitability to Kohler, for instance. He also, after a while, underwent a metamorphosis and changed from being a three-piece-suit

*H*erb Kohler is pictured in 1972, the year he became CEO. In 2002, he was named national Entrepreneur of the Year in manufacturing by Ernst & Young LLC, which cited his "persistence and drive" in achieving high levels of quality and leading-edge design.

accountant to someone who wanted to go out and socialize with cus-tomers. He pitched right in and helped strengthen many of our cus-tomer relationships."

Management transitions are often difficult under any circumstances, creating uncertainty among employ-ees. In the case of Kohler Co., with the deaths of Les Kuplic and Herbert Sr. still reverberating through the organization, the transition was espe-cially traumatic and challenging.

Conger and Cleveland immediately issued a statement that there would be no change in management philosophy. And they traveled to each of Kohler Co.'s operations so employees could see the new management team in person. "We toured the plants, visited with employees and let them ask questions," Cleveland recalled. "We wanted to calm people and put their minds at ease about the future of the company."

For the next four years, Conger and Cleveland kept Kohler Co. on a steady pace of growth, increasing revenues at an average rate of about 11 percent a year. Much of this growth was propelled by The Bold Look of Kohler program, which had been initiated during the tenure of Herbert V. Kohler Sr. and Les Kuplic and was, by the late 1960s, proving to be successful in capturing market share.

But Herbert V. Kohler Jr. was not a passive observer. A hands-on executive who is constantly full of ideas for improving the business, he began to make his presence felt even before taking charge as CEO in 1972. "Herb came in and changed the business dramatically, there's no doubt about it," according to Wells. "Even though he was still a vice president, it was pretty clear he was making many of the major decisions. You could just tell by working with him."

To those who had known him when he was younger, it was perhaps surprising that Herb immersed himself in the business with such energy

and enthusiasm. There was a time when many, including Herb Kohler himself, wondered whether he would ever follow in his father's footsteps at Kohler Co.

Rebellious Youth

Herbert Vollrath Kohler Jr. was born in 1939, the oldest of the three children of Herbert and Ruth Kohler. He grew up in Kohler Village and loved fishing, canoeing, horseback riding and other outdoor

*H*erb Kohler was two years old when he and his father sat for this photograph in 1941. Independent-minded and strong-willed like his father, he grew up resisting the idea he would one day lead the company.

The three Kohler children, Herb, Ruth and Frederic, left to right, share a lighter moment with their mother, Ruth De Young Kohler, left, during a radio broadcast in 1949.

activities. Extremely independent-minded even as a youngster, Herb resisted his father's plans for his life, including the hope that Herb might one day head the company. "My father was extraordinarily well intentioned," Herb says, "but he wanted to protect me from failure and establish a career path for me to follow."

Herb's mother died in 1953, when he was 14. A year later, because of the major strike against the company and unrest in the village, Herbert Sr. sent

Herb and Ruth II away to boarding school. Herb enrolled at Phillips Exeter Academy in New Hampshire, but did not last long. Kicked out of Exeter for rules violations, he spent his 1955 spring vacation with Roy Ebben, Kohler Co.'s recreation director and a former teacher, searching for another prep school. He got accepted at the Choate School in Connecticut, where he did well. While at Choate, Herb was offered, at age 17, a chance to go to Antarctica with the explorer, Admiral Richard Byrd, a family friend. (Byrd honored the Kohlers by naming the Kohler Range and Kohler Glacier in Antarctica for Walter Kohler and Mount Kohler, which he mapped in 1939-1941, for young Herb and Ruth II.) "He offered to take me on his last expedition and he wanted to put me in charge of the dogs," Herb recalls. Herb loves adventure and was ready to jump at the opportunity. But his father said no, telling him he had to stay in school. Herb still regrets that he never made the trip. Subsequently, as an adult, he was part of an expedition to the high Arctic, sponsored by the Canadian government and the Admiral Byrd Polar Society, to find a means for the Inuit living there to return to their tradition of self-reliance and get away from government dependence and control.

On graduating from Choate in 1957, Herb enrolled at Yale, from which his father had graduated years earlier. But Herb was a mediocre

*R*oy Ebben joined Kohler in 1955 as recreation director, later becoming personnel director. Before that, he was a teacher and coach in the Kohler school system and was elected to both the Wisconsin Basketball Coaches and Wisconsin Football Coaches halls of fame.

college student who lacked direction. "At the end of my freshman year," he says, "the dean called me in and reviewed my grades. He said, 'Mr. Kohler, they're acceptable, but I don't see any sense of purpose. You can carry on in this school if you wish. But I suggest you consider joining the military for six months and then perhaps a job for six months, and then decide if Yale is right for you.'" Herb continues, "That took a lot of wind out of my sails. But I thought about it and decided to heed his advice." Herb spent the next six months in the Army Reserve, then went to Switzerland to study at the University of Zurich and learn German. "I took heavy courses in math and physics in German and had an awful time, but I made it," he says.

Returning to the United States, he enrolled at Knox College, a small liberal arts school in Galesburg, Illinois — by coincidence, the same city where his grandfather, John Michael Kohler, had lived briefly a century earlier as an immigrant on the way to Minnesota. To this day, Herb savors his rebel image at Knox. Some of his college friends later referred to him, in retrospect, as "the first of the great unwashed." He became a "pre-hippie," he says, who wrote poetry and immersed himself in college theater.

It's true that opposites sometimes attract. Herb started dating the most popular girl on campus, Linda Karger, and they fell in love. Unlike Herb, who would not even consider joining a fraternity, Karger was president of her sorority as well as of the Knox College chapter of Phi Beta Kappa, the national academic honor society. She was, in addition, a director in the college theater. They met when she cast him as a bandit in a play — "type casting," she said. They married in 1961 and raised three children.

Although Herb and Linda divorced in 1984, he still talks about her with admiration and respect. During their marriage, she was active in the Kohler Village community, serving on the Kohler Board of Education and numerous other groups, and was executive director of Kohler Foundation. Daughter Laura describes her as a "regular mom" who has always had time for her children. All three children remain close to both parents.

Herb says that getting married was a "cathartic point" in his life. He suddenly became more serious about his future. "I met my father as he came down the steps of the Twentieth Century Limited in Union Station in Chicago," he recalls. "I extended my hand — to his amazement, he didn't expect me to be there — and said, 'Father, I'm going to get married. And from this day forward, I'm not going to accept another penny from you regardless of your kindness or your interest in helping me out. I have to make it on my own.'"

Herb and Linda moved to South Carolina, where Herb attended summer school at Furman University. He then returned to Yale, this time working hard because, he says, "now for the first time I could do it under my own colors in my own way." He graduated in 1965 with a degree in business administration.

Although Herb did not immediately join Kohler Co., he soon received a phone call from his father, asking him to do so. Herb said no. But Kohler Co. had an emotional pull on him. He recalled the many summers during which he had worked in every division of the company while a student and thought about his deep personal interest in the family heritage. "About three days later I called him back and said, 'Pop, I love the place. It's got a lot of potential and there is one way I would come back and that is if you'd promise not to protect me in any way. Hire me into a position but let me make my own mistakes. Be sure the people who manage me understand that they should manage me like they would manage anybody else.' And he agreed. I'm not sure something like that is really possible. But he promised that and did the best he could to make sure people abided by it."

Herb started as a research and development technician. He then moved on to scheduler, warehouse supervisor and finally to factory sys-

tems manager. Two and a half years after he joined the company full-time, his father passed away following a lengthy illness. Herb was 29 years old. "That's when I discovered there was no one around to protect me," he says. "All those mistakes were mine. I was thrown into an executive role very early and had to sink or swim. And, by God, I paddled like hell!"

Becoming vice president-operations following his father's death, Herb was helped in that role by Elmer Gielow, who had been plant manager but had scaled back his duties and was approaching retirement. At one time, Gielow had been Herb's boss's boss. He was an old-timer who knew manufacturing inside out and commanded great respect throughout the company. "Elmer Gielow was a wonderful consultant, someone who advised me," Herb says. "He was just very helpful."

Relentless Dedication to Change

Kohler Co.'s sales were $111 million when Herbert Sr. died in 1968 and Herb became a vice president. At that time, the company had two main businesses, plumbing products (about two-thirds of sales) and engines and electrical generators (about one-third),

Elmer Gielow, who spent 42 years with Kohler, was production manager from 1962 to 1969. He originated the design of Kohler's first whirlpool. Called Hydro-Whirl, it attached to a bathtub's faucet and mixed air and water to create a whirlpool effect.

and was overwhelmingly a domestic enterprise. Only about five percent of sales came from international markets.

Herb immediately began to put his stamp on the company, investing in the continued growth of plumbing products, increasing international sales and later taking the company into two entirely new businesses: furniture and hospitality. Kohler Co. has been on a nonstop course of growth and change ever since. "We had a hell of a party when sales reached $1 billion" in 1987, Herb recalls. In 1996, sales hit $2 billion, and in 2002, $3 billion.

One of Herb's first priorities was to restructure the company to improve its organizational effectiveness. "Kohler had an organization structure where everything flowed up to the president," Dick Wells says. "There was very little coordination. The people who were making plumbing products didn't talk with the people who were selling plumbing

How Kohler Co. Celebrated
Its 100th Birthday

Not many companies remain family owned for a century, let alone more than a century and a quarter as Kohler is today. Kohler's 1973 centennial was, therefore, a time of grand celebration.

One of the main themes, befitting a birthday bash, was pink champagne. The company bought thousands of bottles of pink champagne from a vineyard and put Kohler labels on them, serving the bubbly at parties for employees, distributors and residents of the village. It also introduced a line of sinks, bathtubs and other plumbing products in a color called pink champagne.

Kohler also launched a new product, the Birthday Bath, a cast-iron bathtub with old-fashioned ball-and-claw legs, but with the tub itself styled in a sleek modern design. At many of the centennial parties, a Birthday Bath was utilized as an oversized ice bucket and, you guessed it, filled with bottles of pink champagne. The Birthday Bath was intended as a commercial product, but it was also a bit of a lark. "We thought we would produce a limited number, sell them and that would be the end of it," said Alfred M. Ellrodt, who was a Kohler vice president.

*K*ohler Co. celebrated its 100th birthday in 1973 with pink champagne and employee picnics. Above, Herb and his son David arrive at a picnic on antique bicycles. "By the turn of the century," Herb says with seeming amazement, "David could reach the pedals and was president of our Kitchen & Bath Group."

*T*he Birthday Bath, introduced in Kohler's centennial year, combined old-fashioned ball-and-claw legs with a sleek modern design. Although Kohler executives doubted the product had great sales potential, the public took a fancy to it, and the Birthday Bath continues as a staple of the Kohler product line to this day.

However, matters worked out differently. With its unique design combining the old and the new, the Birthday Bath captured the public's fancy and has been a staple in the Kohler product line ever since. Still called the Birthday Bath three decades after the birthday, it continues to sell well even today.

The celebration provided an opportunity for Kohler to reinforce its relationships with distributors by honoring their contributions and making them part of the festivities. Gala events for distributors ranged from the homespun (a bratwurst party for more than 1,000 in a Kohler Village park) to the elegant (a black-tie dinner in Milwaukee).

Paying tribute to employees was another priority. The anniversary slogan, "Bold Craftsmen," honoring the creativity and dedication of Kohler employees past and present, was inscribed on practically every piece of literature the company issued that year, from press releases to a 40-page centennial brochure. Moreover, company picnics, which have been held since the early years of the twentieth century, took on a decidedly historic tone in 1973. Many employees showed up in circa-1873 outfits, and the then-new CEO, Herb Kohler, added to the fun by riding about on an antique bicycle with a big back wheel.

"The overall focus of the celebrations was not only on the longevity of the company," recalls Peter J. Fetterer, retired manager of civic services, "but also on showing that Kohler was young and forward-looking." One of the highlights was a futuristic demonstration house built in the village and open for public viewing. Designed in conjunction with *Better Homes & Gardens*, and featured in that magazine's pages, the house had all its utilities, including electricity and water service, in a central core. Such cores, it was theorized, could be pre-manufactured off-site to reduce construction costs. While the idea never caught on commercially, it was interesting and provocative and helped demonstrate Kohler Co.'s commitment to innovative thinking, garnering favorable publicity for the company and its products.

A company publication noted that Kohler Co. was entering its second century with "a promise of leadership, innovation, creativeness and responsiveness to the future" — qualities that remain vital to Kohler's success today.

$\mathcal{A}$ main objective of the centennial observance was to honor the craftsmanship and dedication of employees. This logo was displayed on everything from hard hats to company magazines.

Key executives from the late 1970s into the 1990s included, left to right: Richard Wells, senior vice president-finance; John Lillesand, senior vice president-technical services; and Kenneth Conger, senior vice president-human resources. Kohler honored the three, all University of Wisconsin graduates, in 1998 with a major donation to expand the university's materials science and engineering building.

products, and the same with engines. That's not to say people didn't work hard and we weren't successful. But it was an ineffective organization structure, even if people didn't realize it."

Herb moved rapidly to decentralize operations, establish profit centers and assure coordination among production, marketing and other functions. "First, we tried to understand the existing organization structure," Wells says. "We didn't have organization charts. There was nothing in writing showing who reported to whom." Wells drew up charts and showed them to Herb, who revised them to incorporate his vision of how the company should be structured. "For instance, he defined that we were going to have an engine and generator group. In the late 1960s

and early 1970s, he designed the organization structure basically as it has evolved today."

Herb probed every detail of the business, from the design of new products to the company's financial structure. He had a thirst to know everything and an obsession to make Kohler the best possible company in every conceivable way.

"He had such a command for the various disciplines," according to Wells. "I can recall meetings where Walter Cleveland, who was a CPA, and Bill Krekel [then Kohler Co.'s treasurer], who was a CPA, and myself, a CPA, were discussing financial questions with Herb. And his opinions or approaches often made more sense than ours and resulted in changes in the way we did things

financially." Herb also has an unusual ability to focus on detail and get quickly to the essence of any matter. "If you hand him a piece of paper and there's something wrong, he hones in on that immediately like radar," Wells says.

Talented executives were brought to company headquarters in Kohler, Wisconsin, to join Herb's management team. At the time, Sam H. Davis ran the Kohler plant in Spartanburg, South Carolina, and he and Herb had become good friends when Herb worked on the pottery line at Spartanburg one summer. (Making toilets and other pottery products requires considerable skill. Davis says young Herb was a very hard worker for whom the word neatness had no meaning whatsoever. "More of the clay ended up in his boots than it did in the products," Davis quips.) Davis had graduated from the University of Texas in 1949 with a degree in ceramic engineering, joining Kohler Co. eight years later. In 1971, he was brought to corporate headquarters as group vice president-plumbing products and precision controls and was later vice chairman of the board with responsibility for international operations. He was a key member of Herb's management team for more than 25 years.

John W. Lillesand, assistant secretary, a University of Wisconsin graduate, was appointed vice president-technical services and was instrumental in the continued development

*L*eft, John Lillesand, who died in 1996, was a Kohler executive for more than 20 years. He was both an engineer and an attorney, a rare combination. Right, Ken Conger retired in 1998 as senior vice president-human resources following a 29-year career with the company.

of Kohler Village. "John was both an engineer and a lawyer, and that's a rare combination, particularly back in the 1970s," Herb says. "John was excellent in real estate and construction. When he talked to engineers, he could negotiate very well because of his combined background." Lillesand was also active in many public and private organizations, such as the Sheboygan County Chamber of Commerce. "He was called on frequently by outside groups because he had such a strong intellect," Herb Kohler says. "He could cut to the quick and help people get organized and focused." A large man with a large, gregarious personality to match, Lillesand died in 1996 at age 58. His untimely passing drew an outpouring of tributes, with comments on every-

thing from his commitment to public service to his passion for playing Scrabble (at which he seldom lost).

In 1969, Herb convinced Kenneth W. Conger, a childhood friend who was an East Coast attorney, to return to Kohler Village and join the company as director of industrial relations. Conger's father, Lyman Conger, was then chairman of the board and chief executive officer. In 1980, Ken Conger was elected vice president and a member of the board of directors, overseeing all employee services. His responsibilities included chairing the company's bargaining committee, a position that had been held for many years by his father. Ken Conger became senior vice president in 1994 and retired in 1998.

Herb Kohler notes, "Ken had a major impact on our relationships in the factories in North America, whether they be union or nonunion. He did a remarkable job of medical care cost containment."

He says also, "One of the wonderful story lines in this company's history is that a Kohler and a Conger ran the company in the '40s and '50s and through part of the '60s, and the sons of those two fellows, with the help of quite a number of others, ran it in the '70s, '80s and '90s."

A Big Bet

One of Herb's important early decisions, even before he became CEO, was to install a new state-of-the-art cast-iron production line. The decision was controversial for two

A FAMILY APPROACH TO BUSINESS

Kohler Co. has been built over the past century and a quarter by tens of thousands of individuals who have contributed to its success. Especially striking are the many families whose members have worked at the company for generation after generation with great loyalty.

Few companies in the world have had a family like the Madsons. Nels Madson came to the United States from Denmark, joining Kohler Co. in 1893 as a teamster. He stayed with the company 41 years until his death in 1934 at age 72. His son, Art Sr., spent 46 years with the company in plumbing sales, while another son, Max, was with the company 56 years in the shipping department. Even with those lengthy tenures, no employee in Kohler Co. history can match the employment span of a third son, Jens Madson. Jens started with Kohler in 1904 at age 14 as a mail boy, later joined the payroll department, and subsequently became secretary of the Kohler Home Improvement Association. When he retired in 1966, he had completed 62 years of service, still a record.

But that is only the beginning. By 1925, Nels and his three sons, as well as two nephews and two sons-in-law, were all working at Kohler Co. Subsequently, two grandsons, Ralph Madson and Art Madson Jr., came on board and had lengthy tenures. And today, Nels' great-grandson, Dan Madson, who joined Kohler in 1966, keeps up the family tradition as an associate in the casting finishing department.

Other families, such as the Wirtz family, the Kroos family and the Brotz family, have also made major contributions generation after generation. It is often said that people drive the success of a business. Kohler, with the loyalty and work ethic of its employees, can prove it.

*I*n 1999, Joyce Schelk became the 68th employee in Kohler Co. history to achieve 50 years or more of service with the company. She joined Kohler in 1949 as a packer and then moved to die cast as an x-ray technician in an inspection area where her father once worked. On her retirement in November 1999, Herb Kohler presented her with 50 red roses — one for each year of service — and a gold necklace and pendant.

Few families have contributed as much to a company for such a lengthy period as the Madsons have to Kohler. The tradition began in 1893 when Nels Madson arrived from Denmark and joined Kohler as a teamster. By 1925, when this photo was taken, Nels (front row, center) and seven other members of his family were employed at Kohler. Front row, left to right, are son Jens Madson, Nels Madson and son Max Madson; center row, nephews Rasmus Nelson and Fred Nelson; and back row, son-in-law Math Mischo, son-in-law Paul Balke and son Art Madson. There has always been at least one Madson at Kohler without interruption since 1893. Great grandson Dan Madson carries on the tradition today as an associate in casting finishing.

$\mathcal{R}$ichard Wells, left, who retired in 1999, was senior vice president-finance. Natalie Black, right, is general counsel, senior vice president of communications and corporate secretary. Her responsibilities include law, internal audit and corporate communications.

reasons: the cost, and widespread doubts about the future of cast iron as a material for the bathroom. New materials, including acrylics, were gaining popularity, and many thought that cast iron would soon be obsolete.

Herb is a risk-taker, but not a reckless one. He mulls over ideas at length, examining every possible angle before reaching a conclusion. He tends to internalize this process — that is, he thinks through a plan in detail in his own mind before discussing it widely with others. He then announces a decision, and many in the company wonder where it came from because they didn't even know he was thinking about the matter. For this reason, people sometimes perceive that he makes snap judgments, which in fact he doesn't.

In contrast to his measured process of analyzing ideas, once he reaches a decision he moves ahead full-throttle to implement his plan.

Convinced of the need for new cast-iron production capacity, Herb took his idea to the Kohler Co. board of directors, which gave its approval. "I was confident we had a good future in cast-iron products, but we needed to modernize our facilities," he declares.

The investment was $8 million. Although modest by today's standards, the amount was substantial for Kohler Co. at the time. "And this was a rather serious decision," Herb says, "because it forced the company to sell public debentures to finance the investment." Kohler Co. had never before tapped the public financing markets, and has never again since.

In issuing public securities, Kohler Co. was suddenly required to disclose its financial results for all the world to see. This drove Herb crazy. He prefers to keep results strictly private so as not to reveal sensitive data to competitors. "Even more important," he says, "private ownership and privacy of results help focus our people on implementing big ideas and achieving excellent long-term performance."

The debentures were repaid by mid-1978 and the company reverted to financial privacy. "Herb repaid those debentures as quickly as possible," says William J. Drew, retired corporate secretary. "He couldn't do it fast enough."

Herb's bet on cast iron paid off handsomely. Because of the investment made in the early 1970s, and the continuing investments made since that time, no other company in America today can match Kohler Co.'s technical skills or low costs in manufacturing cast-iron products. Kohler makes tubs from acrylics and fiberglass, as do other manufacturers, but cast-iron bathtubs, lavatories and kitchen sinks remain core product lines.

Role of the Board of Directors

Herb's decision to go to the board of directors for approval of that investment, rather than wield his clout and proceed without meaningful board input, highlights the vital role of the board at Kohler Co.

Beginning in the mid-1970s, Herb strengthened the board by adding outside directors — that is, directors who are not Kohler Co. executives or members of the Kohler family. Two of the first were Catherine Cleary, chairman and CEO of First Wisconsin Trust Company, now retired, and Lawrence Appley, president of the American Management Association, who died in 1997. Both were prominent in the business world and were much sought-after to serve on corporate boards.

Cleary says she accepted Herb's invitation because she knew the Kohler family and was fascinated at the idea of seeing the company from the inside. "At board meetings, I didn't ask many questions at first," she says, "because I was still learning about the company. After a couple of meetings,

Herb took me aside and said, 'Why don't you ask more questions?' I think his real interest was in giving his associates a greater understanding of an outsider's view."

Natalie A. Black, Herb's wife, who is general counsel, senior vice president of communications and corporate secretary, and is herself a board member, notes that the role of the board of directors at a private company is sometimes different than at a public company. In both cases, the board represents shareholders. However, in private companies, unlike public companies, the board members and shareholders are often the same individuals. "Kohler has gone a different route with a more independent board, which is atypical of a private company," she states.

*T*op, a worker spreads enamel powder on a red-hot cast-iron bathtub. Coating the metal uniformly with enamel requires a high degree of skill. As indicated by the lower photograph, Kohler Co. has invested significantly in factory automation to keep its manufacturing operations competitive.

"Our board includes directors who are not major shareholders and tends to be more like the board of a public company."

Herb takes all major decisions to the board. Black cites the example of the Global Power Group, which was floundering in the early 1980s. The group's management sought Herb's authorization for a major investment program to revive the business. Herb agreed and asked the board for approval. The board did not authorize the investment at first, debating the matter vigorously before finally giving its blessing. In two other cases, the board rejected Herb's plans to acquire small, high-end plumbing products companies. Speaking of one of these companies, Sherle Wagner,

Herb says, "I really wanted Sherle. I must have gone to the board three or four times seeking approval." However, the board never did give its approval, and the proposed transaction was cancelled.

To some degree, the board is a counterbalance to Herb's dominant personality. By asking the board to approve major corporate actions, Herb must think through each proposal in detail and be able to lay out his case clearly — and be prepared to accommodate viewpoints other than his own.

The Flying Reverend

In addition to restructuring the company, investing in cast iron and broadening the membership of the

board of directors, Herb made other changes. One which seems logical enough — but which provoked several people to write him letters of protest, saying he was dishonoring the memory of his father — was to resurrect the corporate aviation department. Unlike his father, who preferred not to fly and would not allow the company to own a plane, Herb loves aviation and earned a pilot's license in his 20s. He still takes the controls on occasion, although only with an experienced pilot at his side.

On reestablishing its aviation department in 1969, Kohler Co. leased a twin-engine Navajo seating eight passengers and hired a corporate pilot, Stan Kuck, who is an

*S*tan Kuck not only taught Herb Kohler to fly, but also became the company's pilot after Herb reestablished the corporate aviation department in 1969. He is pictured with the twin-engine Navajo leased by the company that year. Kuck subsequently was director of the aviation department, retiring in 1995. He and his wife continue to live in Kohler Village, and he remains an avid aviator.

ordained minister in the United Church of Christ as well as an aviator. "I always loved flying with Stan because we said 'he was right there next to God,'" Natalie Black says. "We always figured that was the safest way to travel." Kuck himself has a sense of humor about the matter and says he was always more concerned about flying the plane and paying attention to the controls than he was about counting on the Lord.

Kuck continued as a Kohler Co. pilot and director of the aviation department for nearly 30 years until his retirement in 1995.

A Reverse Stock Split and Strengthened Family Control

Another of Herb Kohler's early priorities was to maintain the company's private ownership. Although Kohler Co. has been family controlled from its beginning, in the late 1960s two of Herb's cousins let some Kohler stock get into public hands. One cousin sold 3,850 shares publicly through Marshall Company, a Wisconsin brokerage firm. The other cousin pledged 4,000 shares for a loan, then defaulted, and that stock ended up being owned by a subsidiary of ITT Corp.

Marshall Company, the brokerage firm, began to make a market in Kohler shares, creating demand, and by 1978 the number of stockholders was more than 400 and rising. Herb was concerned. If the number reached 500, Kohler Co. would, by

law, be considered a publicly owned business and would be required to comply with a host of securities regulations and disclose detailed financial results. Kohler Co. had just finished paying off its public debentures, and Herb did not want to go back down the road of having to release annual financial results for all to see.

He acted decisively. In 1978, Kohler Co. took the unusual step of declaring a 1-for-20 reverse stock split. Under the terms of the split, those owning fractional shares were given two choices: sell their stock to the company, or come up with enough cash to round up to full shares. The post-split stock sold at more than $8,000 a share, and most fractional shareholders chose to sell. As a result, the number of shareholders was reduced to less than 200.

Herb was pleased. Commenting on the reverse split, he wrote, "Adoption of this proposal permits the Company to continue free of certain unnecessary regulatory burdens (and I mean unnecessary), free from exposing proprietary data to competitors, and free of what could be a long

The *Wall Street Journal* provided this account of Kohler Co.'s 1-for-20 reverse stock split in December 1978. The purpose of the split was to keep ownership of the company private.

Kohler Co. Planning 1-for-20 Reverse Split To Maintain Privacy

* * *

Firm Seeks to Slash Number Of Holders to Avert Need To Disclose Certain Data

A WALL STREET JOURNAL News Roundup

KOHLER, Wis.—Kohler Co., a privately held maker of plumbing fixtures, engines and generators, values its privacy above all. Thus, it's offering shareholders a 1-for-20 reverse stock split, to insure that its shareholder total doesn't cross the magic 500 mark, necessitating disclosure of detailed financial information to the Securities and Exchange Commission.

The company, which says it believes it's the largest plumbing manufacturer in the U.S., has 423 shareholders, with the Kohler family thought to own more than 70% of shares outstanding.

If shareholders, at a meeting on Tuesday, approve the plan by a two-thirds majority and if every holder of fewer than 20 shares accepted cash, the company said that 254 shareholders would be eliminated.

Kohler is offering cash payments of $412.50 for each odd share, well above what's considered to be its fair market value of $396 a share, the company said. Holders of odd shares also may elect to purchase additional shares up to 20, and exchange them in the split.

Company officials explained that filing reports with the SEC would "greatly increase" Kohler's vulnerability "through identification of target products by competitors."

James E. Stiner, Kohler's public-affairs director, added that the company wants to continue to be "free of new and unnecessary regulatory burdens," and if data were filed with the SEC, it would become "available to

term concern for the most noxious practice in the American economic system — the corporate takeover. Adoption permits employees to continue to focus on developing products and services that give other people a more 'gracious living'; to do so aggressively and independently within a structure of policy, law, and ethics."

When Kohler Co. first announced its reverse split, ITT sought an injunction to block the transaction, apparently feeling its Kohler shares would become less liquid if the split took place. A court turned down ITT's request, and ITT did not pursue further legal action. Six years later, ITT sold its Kohler stock to the company, and those shares were removed from the market.

However, the shares distributed through Marshall Company remained in public hands, although reduced in number from the original 3,850 by the reverse split. They represented less than two percent of Kohler Co.'s total shares. For many years, Kohler Co. stock had the second-highest price of any common stock in America, exceeded only by Berkshire Hathaway, renowned for its lofty stock value. However, when Berkshire Hathaway split its stock in 1996, the price of Berkshire Hathaway was reduced to a mere $35,000 per share, and Kohler, trading at more than $100,000 per share, became the new king of the hill.

Kohler Co. stock continued as the most expensive per share in America

until 1998, when the company cashed out the publicly owned shares through its recapitalization plan. Natalie Black, the company's general counsel, says that for more than two decades Kohler Co. had been seeking a method to maintain its private ownership into future generations. "Over that period, we had a cast of colorful characters — lawyers, investment bankers, others — come through here advising how we might do this," she says. "Each of these individuals had a particular point of view, including some who thought we should sell the company." However, Herb Kohler had no interest in selling outright or even taking part of the company public. "None of the plans really provided for the kind of multi-generational concept of stewardship we were looking for," Black says.

Finally, in the mid-1990s, Black and an outside law firm developed the recapitalization plan. The plan was approved in 1998 by a majority

of shareholders, although some objected to the buyout price and filed suit in a Sheboygan court, seeking a higher price. The case involved novel issues of law; no Wisconsin court had previously decided how to value a company in a dissenters' rights case. Black notes that businesses can be valued in many ways, such as discounted cash flow, fair market value and enterprise value, each with the potential for a dramatically different price than the others. Because of this uncertainty, Kohler Co. took a significant risk in proceeding with its recap not knowing the ultimate cost. Herb Kohler says the recap was not quite a "bet-the-business" decision, yet close. He was willing to proceed, he says, because of his strong desire to preserve Kohler Co.'s private structure.

Just before the dissenters' rights case was scheduled to go to trial, the two sides reached a settlement at a price both found reasonable.

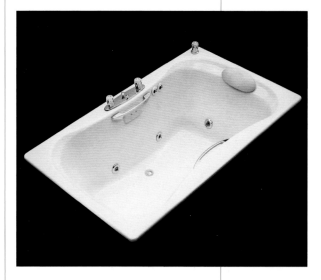

*H*erb Kohler is actively involved in product design review and has designed over 200 new products himself, such as the Infinity, left, one of the industry's first two-person whirlpool baths. It featured body-contour styling, a master console with all controls at one location and six adjustable jets.

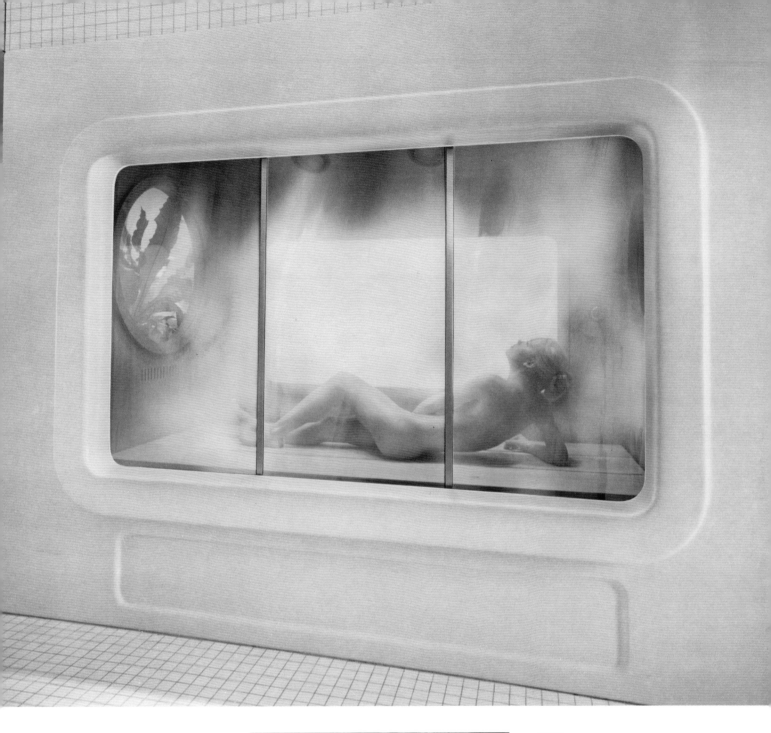

The Environment was an enclosure that the user could program to simulate the effects of sun, steam, gentle rain or warm breezes. Introduced in 1977, it won a special award from the American Society of Interior Designers for bringing "innovation to the field of interior space."

In this way, the matter was resolved without the uncertainties of a court decision.

Profusion of New Products
In 1972, summarizing his business philosophy, Herb Kohler said, "I believe in producing a quality product consistently, selling it honestly, competing vigorously." He said also, "I believe in the long term. I don't believe in looking for the short-term buck."

The chapters that follow highlight some of the new products and services introduced by Kohler Co. in each of its core businesses during Herb's tenure as CEO. Indeed, one of the remarkable accomplishments of Kohler Co. since the early 1970s has been its ability to stay at the forefront in each of its business segments, introducing new products and services that respond to the public's wants and meet or exceed its expectations.

Herb not only charts the company's strategic direction, as do many CEOs, but also involves himself in

product technology and design decisions to a degree that is uncommon among CEOs. He insists that each new product enhance the Kohler brand and personally reviews most new plumbing and power systems products, giving final approval.

He has even designed many products himself. Most notable were the Environment, introduced in 1977, a two-person enclosure that showers its occupants with artificial sun, rain, wind and steam, and the Infinity, one of the first two-person whirlpool baths in the United States. He holds more than 200 design and utility patents.

Working Hard, Playing Hard
Herb is not only an astute, demanding businessman, but is also quite a character, doing things that the CEOs of most other large companies would never be caught dead doing. In January 1997, when the Green Bay Packers, beloved throughout Wisconsin, were about to play for the National Football Conference championship of the National Football League, hundreds of Kohler Co. associates held a noontime pep rally in front of the factory. Herb dyed his beard green, one of the Packers' team colors, and joined the crowd, whooping it up just like one of the guys. He lingered to chat with employees and have his picture taken with anyone who wanted. An outdoorsman to the core, he didn't bother to wear an overcoat even though the

temperature was near zero. In fact, he almost never wears an overcoat. His wife, Natalie Black, says, "He has a closet full of them. He just won't wear them, except for this wonderful old bear coat he's had for who knows how long. On occasion, if it gets very, very, very cold, he will get out the bear coat. But it's the only one I've ever seen him wear."

Herb works hard and plays hard. He enjoys venturesome family vacations, such as bare-boat sailing in the Caribbean and South Pacific, raft trips down class four and five rapids, and stalking the mountain gorilla in Africa. Vacations turn his mind loose to dream and create. As a result, he often returns to work full of ideas for new products and new services. In his spare time, he likes to ride and drive horses as well as hunt and fish, and has become an avid golfer since building the Blackwolf Run and Whistling Straits venues.

In 1989, Kohler Co. bought 1,400 acres of undeveloped land in southwestern Wisconsin on a 300-foot bluff overlooking the Mississippi River. The property was in bankruptcy and for sale. Herb instantly fell in love with it. "He had searched for land for some time and knew of this special area," says John D. Green, former director of corporate landscape and Kohler Shops. "He and I flew to the property in March 1989. It was a warm spring day. The snows were melting. We walked about two-and-a-half miles across the property, and we were on a

*I*n January 1997, days before the Green Bay Packers played in the National Football Conference championship game, Herb Kohler dyed his beard green, one of the Packers' team colors, for a pep rally of Kohler Co. employees.

bluff overlooking the river. We didn't say a word to each other. We just sat on the rocks. And within a couple of minutes, two eagles flew over our heads. I knew at that moment he was going to buy the property." In fact, the company bought it less than a week later. Herb envisions the sensitive development of the land over the long term, while permanently preserving a deep valley filled with 70-year-old oaks and used by bald eagles as a roost in winter. In the short term, the company has turned the entire property into a nature preserve, reintroducing native vegetation. Herb goes there several times a year to hike and to hunt deer and turkey.

"This is just my sense," Green says, "but I think he longed for a place where he could reconvene with nature, which, if you will, is his recharge." While serving that purpose, the land is also a valuable asset for the company's future.

*H*erb Kohler works hard and plays hard. One magazine said of him, "He is a man who intensely enjoys what he is doing — be it designing a new whirlpool bath; developing a strategy for a new business in France; leading a multi-billion-dollar corporation; or riding his horse through the pine."

The Kohler name is synonymous with quality in power products. The company is a leading supplier of generator sets ranging in size from five kilowatts to two megawatts (2,000 kilowatts), as well as small engines ranging from four horsepower to 26 horsepower.

ohler Co.'s first diversification beyond plumbing products was into power systems after World War I. Indeed, in some parts of the world, Kohler is better known for its power products than it is for its plumbing products. In a 1972 interview, Lyman Conger, then Kohler Co. chairman, said, "Years ago I went to Kodiak Island in Alaska for some bear hunting. And if somebody asked where I was from, I would say, 'Kohler, Wisconsin, where we make all the plumbing fixtures.' I didn't quite come across at first. After a while, I would say, 'We make generators too.' And they'd say, 'Oh, you're from the place where they make Kohler electric plants.'"

To this day, in some areas of Latin America and Asia, the name Kohler is virtually synonymous with generators and small engines. And in the United States, the Kohler brand is widely known as the Cadillac of the power products industry.

The company's Global Power Group encompasses:

- Electrical generators ranging from small units that provide backup power for the home to large industrial power plants for factories;
- Automatic transfer switches and switchgear to manage electricity safely and reliably;
- Small engines that power riding lawn and garden tractors and other consumer, commercial, industrial and construction equipment;
- The rental of generators for sporting events, concerts and other

special events, as well as for use in commercial and industrial facilities and for emergencies and natural disasters; and

- Event services, encompassing event planning, staging, lighting and other services in addition to power generation and distribution.

The business is led by George R. Tiedens, group president, who joined Kohler Co. in 1982. Tiedens is hard-driving and outspoken, and has a wonderfully quirky sense of humor. Speaking of his previous employer, Onan Corporation, where he was vice president-manufacturing for engines and generators, Tiedens says, "I worked for the competition, and Herb Kohler kept calling, offering a job. I ignored him for as long as I could, but he didn't let up and finally I thought I'd give it a shot. This was my first opportunity to work for a private company, and I thought I'd stay two or three years and move on. But here it is 21 years later and I'm still at Kohler. And the business is doing okay."

Doing okay? When Tiedens joined Kohler in 1982, its power business was behind the competitive eight ball, suffering from a lack of investment and a dearth of new products. That situation has since changed dramatically. Herb Kohler says, "George Tiedens has built and driven our power business globally for two decades, from sales of $120 million in 1982 to nearly $600 million in 2002."

Herb has set his sights on further

*B*elow, in 1988, Kohler Co. leapfrogged the competition by introducing the industry's first overhead camshaft small engines, which are quieter, more efficient and more environmentally friendly than traditional side-valve engines. Opposite, Kohler entered the generator rental business in 1996.

growth. In fact, achieving continued increases in the sales and profitability of this core business — by keeping on the leading edge of power systems technology, developing new products in response to market needs and expanding geographically — is a key element of his corporate strategy.

From American Farms to European Castles

Kohler got into the power business eight decades ago in a radical diversification from plumbing products. Even though the company had no background in generators or small engines, three factors enabled it to leap feet-first into this then-new industry: 1) its familiarity with agricultural markets and a resulting ability to identify an emerging demand for electricity on farms; 2) its expertise in cast iron, from which its early generators were made; and 3) the ingenuity of Anton Brotz, then Kohler Co.'s chief research engineer, who designed the company's first power product, the Kohler Automatic Power & Light generator set.

The Kohler Automatic was introduced in 1920, when electricity was still a relatively new form of power. Many remote locations, such as farms and small towns off the beaten path, were not yet hooked into utility power grids. While generators existed, they were inefficient and difficult to operate: the generators of the time charged storage batteries, which in turn supplied 32 volts of power.

The Kohler Automatic was the first modern generator as we know the product today. Driven by a four-cycle gasoline engine manufactured by the company, it furnished 110 volts of current directly to the line and turned itself on and off automatically in response to electricity demand.

The product was an immediate hit. When the Kohler Automatic was exhibited for the first time — at the National Tractor Show in Kansas City — the editor of *Motor Age* wrote, "The only [generator] plant that attracted wide attention was the Kohler." During the 1920s, thousands of the devices were sold to supply electricity for farms, hospitals, aircraft directional beacons, city parks, European castles and other locations and uses in the United States and abroad.

Residents of Puerto Maldonado, a Peruvian village, enjoyed the benefits of electricity for the first time with a Kohler. To their cheers and applause, Don Bruno Paulsen, provincial mayor, turned on the lights in a dramatic ceremony in the public square. "The installation of lighting equipment using one of your plants of 1500 watts was started on our Patriotic Holiday of 1927 with great success," the mayor advised.

Kohler salesmen often went to extraordinary lengths to promote the new product. W. C. Green, a salesman in Atlanta, drove what he called "the Kohler Automatic demonstrator car." Within the car he installed a Kohler

*M*any Kohler salesmen traveled their assigned territories in trucks like this, selling and servicing Kohler generators.

*A*t right is a 1926 ad for the Kohler Automatic Power & Light. The product was called the "Automatic" because it was the world's first portable electric generator that turned on and off automatically in response to power demand.

Following the introduction of the Kohler Automatic, Kohler Co. established a national marketing organization for its generator business. Above, the staff of the San Francisco office poses in 1926.

$\mathcal{A}$dmiral Richard
Byrd took Kohler genera-
tors on his expeditions to
the South Pole in the 1920s
and 1930s. His use of
Kohler electric generators
in the harsh Antarctic
environment helped
establish their reputation
for superior quality and
reliable performance.
Below, Walter Kohler
greets Admiral Byrd in
Sheboygan.

generator to supply electricity for the fan, the car jack and 20 light bulbs mounted in the vehicle's ceiling, in effect turning the car into a glowing beacon at night. "The car is striking in appearance, creates favorable attention, and is practical and effective," according to a company publication in 1925.

A tremendous publicity coup was achieved when Admiral Richard Byrd chose Kohler generators for his first two expeditions to Antarctica, betting his life on their reliability. He took five Kohler power plants on his first expedition in 1928-1929, using them to furnish electricity for everything from the lights on his schooner to the equipment at expedition headquarters.

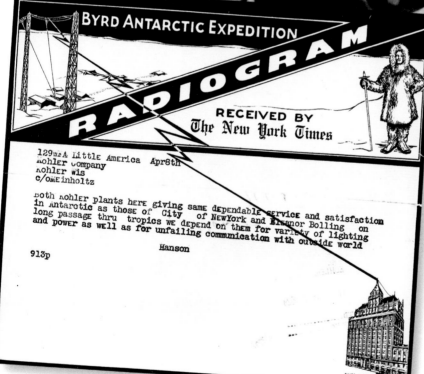

*A*bove is a member of the Byrd expedition team on Antarctica. At left is a 1930 radiogram from the team and below is one of the Kohler generators it used.

*A*dmiral Byrd sits in the cockpit of his Curtiss-Wright aircraft, 1933. Chief pilot Harold June sticks his head out a window. Byrd became a friend of the Kohlers and was the godfather of Herbert V. Kohler Jr.

Byrd again specified Kohler for his second expedition in 1933-1935. Several months into that journey, members of his party dug through snow and ice to uncover the first expedition's headquarters, where the admiral had left two Kohler generators. A radio operator dried the spark plugs of one of the generators and flipped the switch, and the generator sprang to life as if brand-new. Kohler Co. built an entire advertising campaign around Byrd's use of its products. The association with Byrd helped solidify the reputation of Kohler generators for reliability even in the harshest environments.

During World War II, in contrast

to the curtailment of production of plumbing products, Kohler increased its production of electric plants to meet the needs of the armed forces. Thousands of Kohler generator sets were shipped to troops in the European, African, Italian and Pacific theaters, as well as in Alaska and Central and South America.

Congratulating the company for its wartime production, Admiral Ben Moreell, chief of the Navy Bureau of Yards and Docks, said, "The settling of a large section of airstrip in the Aleutians threatened to halt all air operations at the field unless speedy repairs were effected. Your electric plants enabled the Seabees to work

*A*bove, Kohler Co. ran a series of magazine ads in the 1920s extolling the benefits of its generators. Opposite, a technician tests Kohler generator sets in 1933.

nights as well as days to complete the task. It is because your generators play such a vital part in the work of constructing and maintaining the advance bases for our offensives that the Navy counts on you for maximum production."

Entering the Small Engine Business

After World War II, Kohler Co. diversified into small engines. Although the company had originally manufactured the engines that drove its generators, it had switched to Briggs & Stratton engines in the 1930s. In the years following the war, however, Briggs & Stratton couldn't keep up with Kohler Co.'s demand. At the recommendation of Arthur G. Kroos Jr., a salesman in Kohler Co.'s generator division and later the general manager of its engine division, Kohler resumed making engines to supply its own needs. Kroos recalls, "I went to L. L.

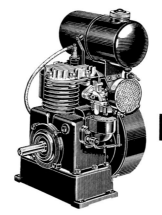

*A*fter World War II, Kohler broadened its power business to include the manufacture of small engines, sold primarily to manufacturers of riding lawnmowers and other equipment. Because of the Kohler reputation for durability and reliability, some consumers will buy a lawn and garden product only if it is powered by a Kohler engine.

Smith" — a Kohler Co. vice president — "and we approached Herbert Kohler Sr. with the idea. He said, 'You're a couple of engineers. Do it.'" The company initially produced engines in the corner of a Kohler Co. warehouse, eventually taking over the entire building.

Having resumed engine production for its own needs, Kohler began selling small four-cycle engines to other manufacturers for installation

*B*y 1950, when this photograph was taken, Kohler was expanding rapidly in the generator business, adding diesel-powered units and larger-capacity plants.

in their products, including golf carts, tillers and riding tractors. This business was a huge success. By 1963, Kohler was supplying engines for nearly half the lawn and garden tractors built each year in the United States, as well as for a host of other outdoor power equipment.

Engines for agricultural pumps were a key international market. Andrew Apostolopoulos, a Kohler distributor in Athens, Greece, said,

Dan Wahlen, who worked in power systems engineering and development for 25 years, retiring as director-generator division engineering in 1992, and Alvin P. Fenton, a research engineer from 1963 to 1988. They, together with others, invented new technologies such as the automatic compression release (which offers the ability to pull-start an engine without much resistance) in 1967 and the automatic choke assembly in 1976, helping to establish Kohler's reputation for easy-start engines.

Not satisfied simply to make engines in the United States, in 1964 Kohler established a subsidiary, Kohler de Mexico, S.A. de C.V. (Komex), to manufacture engines in Mexico — Kohler Co.'s first plant of any kind outside the U.S. That facility now makes engines for export to Asia, as well as for the Mexican market, and has increased its capacity tenfold since its opening.

Also in the 1960s, the company acquired a plant near Toronto, Ontario, and converted it to the manufacture of two-cycle engines for snowmobiles. This venture was successful for a time and even led to the production of engines for championship race cars. However, Kohler eventually closed the facility because of the volatility of the snowmobile engine business. "We'd build these engines in the spring and summer, and ship them in the summer and fall," Herb Kohler says. "But then, if there was little or no snow that winter,

*A*rthur G. Kroos Jr. spent 45 years with Kohler Co. and was general manager of the engine division. He helped take the company into the small engine business after World War II. His father, Arthur G. Kroos Sr., spent 60 years with Kohler and was a vice president and director. His uncle, O. A. "Tom" Kroos, spent 58 years with the company and was executive vice president and a member of the board.

"Your factory turns out products that really contribute to the prosperity and well-being of the world. Kohler engines have enabled our farmers to irrigate and improve their arid land. It is a blessing for a farmer to own a small and inexpensive pumping set with which he can pump water to meet the irrigation needs of the small plot he owns."

Two of the inventive geniuses who helped make Kohler's engines the cream of the industry crop were

the snowmobile business would go to the dogs." When that happened, sales of Kohler engines would plummet for a year or two until the snowmobile market rebounded.

Kohler Co. did not then, and does not now, sell engines directly to the public, selling them instead to original equipment manufacturers and through a worldwide distribution network. Even as a component of these other manufacturers' products, however, Kohler engines retain their brand identity because of the Kohler reputation for quality and durability. In fact, manufacturers of riding lawn and garden tractors and other equipment often differentiate their products by stressing that they are powered by reliable Kohler engines. "There are many American consumers who will not buy a lawn and garden product unless it has a Kohler engine," George Tiedens states. "Not the majority, but a lot of them. Because they've had excellent experience with a product powered by a Kohler."

Continued Growth in Generators

The postwar years were a boom period also for the generator business. In the 1950s, Kohler began manufacturing diesel-powered units to go with the gasoline models it had pioneered in the 1920s. Moreover, it kept building bigger and bigger units in response to market demand. In the early 1950s, it introduced its first 100 kilowatt unit, followed by its first 170

kilowatt unit in 1963 and a 230 kilowatt unit in 1966. Five new models ranging from 300 to 500 kilowatts were introduced in the early 1970s. Today, the company's product line goes up to 2,000 kilowatts (two megawatts).

The postwar growth of the generator market was propelled, in part, by demand for generators to provide emergency standby power. As hospitals, commercial buildings, factories, government installations and other

*G*eorge Tiedens has led Kohler's power business since the mid-1980s, dramatically improving its performance.

facilities invested in computers, electronic elevator controls and other sophisticated electronic equipment, they needed an assured source of electricity that would take over in the event of a utility blackout. Today, standby power systems are indispensable. The world is so dependent on computers and electricity that we couldn't get by without them.

Another market took root in the

*S*implicity celebrated its 75th anniversary in 1997 with a parade of 800 tractors through downtown Port Washington, Wisconsin, earning *Guinness Book* recognition for the "world's largest tractor parade." All the tractors in this photo are powered by Kohler engines.

1960s — generators for motor homes and recreational vehicles, for the family that enjoyed traveling and wanted home cooking and air conditioning along the way. Responding to this market's needs, Kohler pioneered the concept of the modular acoustic enclosure: the generator was installed as a completely sealed unit in a sound-deadening enclosure for maximum silencing.

*S*ears, Roebuck and Co., a leading retailer, uses Kohler engines in many of its lawn and garden products, such as this Craftsman mower. Kohler has been supplying engines for Craftsman mowers and tractors since 1988.

The company also became a leading supplier of generators for houseboats, yachts, sailboats and other vessels. As the nation became more affluent, Americans bought expensive boats in record numbers and equipped them with all kinds of electrical and electronic devices, including radar, air conditioning and refrigerators — powered, you guessed it, by onboard generators.

Downturn and Turnaround

Kohler's power business kept going great guns — until the late 1970s. During the late 1960s and early 1970s, Kohler invested heavily in its plumbing products business but did not invest significantly in power products. Lack of investment does not necessarily hurt a business in the short run, but in the long run

the impact can be devastating.

A specific problem in the engine business was Kohler Co.'s failure to embrace newer materials, including aluminum. "In fact, we began making engines from aluminum right after

World War II," Herb Kohler says. "However, they were perceived as lacking durability because they didn't dissipate the heat very well. The irony is that we really were on the right track with aluminum, but we didn't have confidence in the material. So we switched to cast iron in 1951 and made only cast iron until the 1970s even though the cast-iron engine was quite a bit more expensive to make than the aluminum engine. At about the same time we were getting out of the aluminum engine, Briggs & Stratton came out with its first aluminum engine, and they stayed with aluminum and we stayed with cast iron. Just because of that funny little move, Briggs & Stratton had lower production costs and began taking market share from us."

Kohler's generator business began to falter also, due not only to inadequate investment in new products but

*T*his John Deere lawn and garden tractor is powered by a Kohler 15-horsepower overhead valve engine. In 2002, Kohler became the first engine supplier to attain "partner" status, the highest level in the John Deere Achieving Excellence Program.

Kohler's innovative overhead camshaft 18-horsepower engine captured the 1998 New Product Award in a competition sponsored by the National Society of Professional Engineers. Leading the teams that designed and built the new engine were, left to right, Cameron Litt, product manager-twin cylinder engines; Todd Gerhardt, manager-new product design; and Jerry Reineking, supervisor of design engineering.

also to the erosion of its distribution network.

The power business was headed in the 1970s by William S. Hatten, a talented and experienced manufacturing executive who joined the company from Clayton Mark & Co., an Illinois manufacturer of equipment for the oil industry. Hatten worked long and hard to get the power business back on track and was widely respected for his many accomplishments. Under his leadership, Kohler improved its manufacturing processes, resumed its production of aluminum engines, and introduced

a number of new products and technologies, such as the automatic choke assembly.

Despite Hatten's efforts, the competitive position and financial performance of the Global Power Group began to erode, worsening after he retired in 1980. By the early 1980s, Kohler's power business had reached a fork in the road: Kohler Co. faced the unavoidable choice of either getting out of the business or making the necessary investments to revitalize it. There was great controversy within the company as to which route to follow. Herb Kohler wanted

to invest and revitalize, but many members of the company's board of directors disagreed, insisting that any further investments would be like throwing money away. After intense debate, Herb prevailed. "This was a leap of faith because the business was doing so poorly," Natalie Black says.

Given a go-ahead to invest in new products, the management of the Global Power Group began by addressing the problems of the engine division. Within the division, the revitalization plan came to be known as the "fingernail" strategy. "We took a classic approach right out of Harvard Business School," says Richard W. Shoemaker, president-Kohler Engines. "Our goal was to hang on by our fingernails with our old products, market them aggressively and use the cash to develop new products." He adds, "At one point in the mid- and late '80s, we were putting over 10 percent of our revenues into engineering."

New engines introduced in 1987 were a success, helping recapture market share. Building on that progress, the company began to seek technology breakthroughs. Herb Kohler says, "Mind you, our power systems business was born in 1920 because of a breakthrough in technology and we continue to make breakthroughs today." Indeed, since the late 1980s, the small gasoline engine has undergone a technological revolution sparked by Kohler Co.

In 1988, Kohler leapfrogged the

$\mathcal{R}$ichard Shoemaker, left, is president-Kohler Engines. He poses with George Tiedens, group president-global power, behind an OHC 18 horse-power utility engine. Since the late 1980s, Kohler's engine business has achieved rapid advances in small engine technology.

competition by introducing the industry's first overhead-valve small engines. Overhead-valve engines are quieter, more efficient and more environmentally friendly than traditional side-valve engines. Although automobile manufacturers have used overhead-valve designs in high-performance engines for a number of years, up to that time manufacturers of small engines (4 to 29 horsepower) had not. "The trick is to produce that technology at an effective price

point," Tiedens notes. "And we were able to do it. Our competition in the engine industry includes some of the strongest companies in Japan and America — Honda, Kawasaki, Briggs & Stratton and Tecumseh. Honda is a company that lives on technology. To establish ourselves as a technology leader against the likes of Honda and Briggs & Stratton is not an easy matter. But we have done that."

More recently, Kohler introduced the OHC 18 horsepower utility engine for lawn and garden tractors, compactors, pressure washers and similar products. The OHC 18 defines the leading edge of small engine technology. It is manufactured with lost-foam casting technology, which reduces the number of parts and eliminates the need for machining. Additionally, it incorporates several advanced automotive-style design concepts, including a belt-driver overhead cam system, and is made primarily from phenolic (plastic) and powdered-metal components. Benefits include lower maintenance costs, reduced emissions and quieter operation. In a nationwide competition sponsored by the National Society of Professional Engineers, the judges unanimously selected the OHC 18 as the best new product of 1998 in the large company category. For perspective, the winner in 1997 was the Boeing 777 airplane.

In 2000, Kohler Co. unveiled its Aegis liquid-cooled engines, representing the next wave of small engine

Kohler standby generators begin providing electricity within seconds of a power outage. They are controlled by high-tech switchgear systems that sense when the voltage from the normal power source drops to a preset minimum and automatically signal the generators to start. When multiple generators are installed, the switchgear systems synchronize, parallel and match the electrical power from the various generators to the size of the load requirement. When the original power source is restored, the switchgear systems retransfer the load to normal power and shut down the generators.

WEATHERPROOFING.

No one can shut down your business faster than Mother Nature.

Yet, having the single-source dependability of a Kohler power system on your side means assembly lines keep moving, production schedules remain on track and communication lines stay open.

With generator sets from 5 to 1600 kilowatts, transfer switches from 25 to 4000 amperes, and a broad line of precision-engineered switchgear, each quality Kohler product is backed by Kohler's extensive warranty coverage and global network of factory-trained dealers and distributors.

So team up with the dependable single-source power system that can handle anything Mother Nature decides to dish out.

For more information on the complete line of Kohler emergency/standby system products, as well as solutions to your specific electrical needs, write or phone Kohler Co., Generator Division, Dept. WP, Kohler, Wisconsin 53044, U.S.A., 1-800-544-2444, Fax: 414-459-1646.

KOHLER
POWER SYSTEMS

© Kohler Co. 9/93

Circle No. 126 on inquiry card

technology. These engines are based on the heavy-duty oil cooler technology used in larger off-road applications. "The liquid-cooling technology [of Kohler Aegis engines] results in impressive reductions in oil and cylinder head temperatures," *SAE Off-Highway Engineering* magazine reported. These lower temperatures, together with a unique heavy-duty air filtering system, contribute to greater operating reliability and longer engine life. "Along with our popular Kohler Command series, we can now offer our lawn and garden customers a choice — air cooled or liquid cooled," according to Cameron Litt, product manager for Kohler engines. "Each configuration has its own

*A*bove, the Los Angeles International Airport is one of many facilities that rely on Kohler generators for standby electricity in the event of a power failure. Standby generators are essential in the modern era of computers and other electronic equipment. Right, the Aegis liquid-cooled engine, introduced in 2000, helped extend Kohler's leadership in small engine technology.

distinct set of advantages and applications, and we are pleased that we can meet the needs of customers with two bona fide engine choices."

With the growing success of its new products, Kohler's engine business has achieved a dramatic turnaround.

Revitalizing the Generator Business

Once the recovery of the engine business was underway, Kohler management turned its attention to the generator division. Tiedens had joined Kohler in 1982 to head the engine business, subsequently becoming group president-global power, with responsibility for both engines and generators.

Speaking of generator operations, Tiedens says, "When I moved to this office in 1986, I'd look out the window at a dying apple tree and think, 'This business is not going to make it either.' I sometimes wondered what I was doing here." Despite his concern, the generator division has recovered robustly through hard work and investments in new products.

Kohler's two largest domestic competitors in generators are Caterpillar and Cummins Engine. Although Kohler had fallen to a weak number three in the early 1980s, it has since begun to close the gap. However, Tiedens doesn't want to talk too much about recent market share gains. "I like to sneak up on people," he confides.

This unit is part of the backup generator system at Los Angeles International Airport, the fourth busiest airport in the world based on number of passengers and second worldwide in tons of air cargo handled.

In explaining Kohler's success, Tiedens says, "Beginning in 1986 we spent about a year rebuilding our distribution network. That, and taking our product line above 750 kilowatts, provided the impetus for putting Kohler generators back on the map."

As in small engines, there has been an outpouring of new Kohler generator sets incorporating advanced features. In 1996, the company introduced its first variable-speed generators, which run only as fast as required by power demand. The result: lower operating costs, reduced emissions and improved acoustics versus traditional fixed-speed units. In 1999, Kohler launched a new line of fuel-efficient, four-stroke, diesel-powered generators, ranging from 450 to 2000 kilowatts. Other advances have included generators fueled by natural gas, and sophisticated new electronic monitoring and control systems. With these systems, a company with remote locations — such as a retailer with hundreds of stores nationwide — can monitor and test all its standby generators from a single location.

*M*odern Kohler generators can power entire factories. Upper left is a two-megawatt generator set.

Although overall electricity usage continues to grow at a slow rate in North America, dynamic market changes are fueling demand for generators. One change is the trend toward distributed (or decentralized) power — that is, industrial and commercial companies using generator sets to produce electricity onsite. This trend is based on cost savings and a philosophy that the most reliable power is the closest power. The trend takes many forms. Some companies are generating their own electricity without backup from a utility power grid. Others are generating a portion of their electricity to reduce the amount purchased from the grid during peak price periods. Still others are earning income by generating more electricity than they need and selling the excess into the utility grid.

Kohler Co. has introduced an array of products to capitalize on this trend, including:

- Paralleling switchgear, which contain all the controls and power switching equipment to operate multiple generators in parallel with each other or in parallel with the grid;
- Combined heat and power producing microturbines, which generate electricity and use the exhaust heat to provide hot water, steam or energy for air conditioning; and
- Uninterruptible power supply systems, which deliver electricity during the interval between the onset of a blackout and the startup of standby generators.

As these and other products are launched, Kohler's generator business is evolving from a supplier of emergency standby products to a complete solutions-based organization. "To survive and profit in the evolving distributed generation market," Joseph Weisiger, president-Americas, Power Systems states, "the business will continue to expand into more facets of the power solutions value stream, including aftermarket service."

The telecommunications revolution is another growth factor, since virtually all telecommunications systems worldwide employ backup power to ensure their reliability. As *Wireless Review* magazine puts it, standby generators have become the "guardian angels" of telecommunications, protecting against unexpected power blips.

Looking ahead, a new growth factor is emerging — consumer demand for standby generators. Although generators are currently installed in fewer than one-half of one percent of all U.S. homes, that figure is likely to increase as consumers realize they can have uninterrupted power at an affordable cost. In fact, some architects and general contractors are now pre-wiring new homes for backup power. "It's another way for builders to differentiate themselves," Ron Ford, former sales manager for Kohler Power Systems' residential division, observes. Weisiger believes Kohler is well-positioned to grow in the residential market "because of the quality of our products and consumer awareness of the Kohler brand."

Kohler Rental Power

And then there are all those outdoor concerts and other special events that need a temporary source of electricity. In 1996, zeroing in on this opportunity, Kohler entered the $250 million-a-year generator rental market by forming Kohler Rental Power.

Rental generators not only meet temporary needs, but are popular, as well, with corporations that prefer to rent rather than buy. In addition, they are often used at construction sites. Kohler Co.'s competitive position is based on the quality, reliability and environmental excellence of its generators, supported by a nationwide rental service capability. In 1997, *Heavy Equipment News* magazine named Kohler Rental Power one of

*H*erb Kohler and Mrs. Yu-Foo Yee Shoon, a member of the Singapore Parliament, stride to a stage for the opening of Kohler Global Power's Asia-Pacific headquarters and general manufacturing plant in 1997. The brightly colored lions are a national symbol of Singapore, the "Lion City."

*L*eft and above, through its Kohler Rental Power business, Kohler Co. rents generators for special events, utility outages and power shortages. Rental generators ranging in size from 20 kilowatts to 2,000 kilowatts are available 24 hours a day, seven days a week.

the year's top 50 "new products." Ray Hitchcock, the magazine's managing editor, said, "One of the key factors in choosing the Kohler Rental Power program was that the generators are efficient and reliable. That's very important in the construction industry."

New Investments, Global Growth

Kohler is also targeting strong international growth. In 1988, about two percent of its power sales were overseas. Today, the figure is some 35 percent and rising.

Otto R. Kopietzki has helped lead this growth, initially as vice president-international and currently as vice president-sales, Americas. He is especially enthusiastic about the Asian market. "China's need for power will double by the year 2010," he says. "India is just behind. There is an explosion in building factories and housing in that part of the world unlike anything ever seen before. Electric utilities cannot keep up with the demand for power. Somebody has to pick up the slack, and that's where

we come in." Kohler Co. is selling generator sets for Asian factories that must wait as long as two years before being connected to a utility grid.

Tiedens, too, sees international growth as being vital to the Global Power Group's future. For years, Kohler Co. has manufactured generators at a plant near Kohler Village and engines at plants in Kohler and Mexico City. In 1997, Kohler Co. expanded engine production to a new facility in Hattiesburg, Mississippi, and opened a state-of-the-art generator manufacturing, engineering, training and service complex in Singapore.

Tiedens says his strategy is to manufacture generators and small engines in the Americas, Asia and Europe, and to design products that meet each region's particular needs. "To survive, we must be worldwide," he states.

For a business that was in deep trouble little more than a decade ago, the Global Power Group has come a long way. For many years a jewel in Kohler Co.'s crown, it has been restored to its rightful place and is again contributing importantly to Kohler Co.'s earnings and growth.

*O*tto Kopietzki, a power systems vice president, left, shows Saudi Arabian distributor Arfan Awwa a Kohler generator set slated for shipment to the Middle East. Global expansion is a key element of Kohler Co.'s growth strategy in power products.

*R*ecent years have seen major investments by Kohler in its power business. In 1997, the company broke ground for an engine plant in Hattiesburg, Mississippi. Left to right are Richard Shoemaker, president-Kohler Engines; Herb Kohler, chairman and president; Kirk Fordice, governor of Mississippi; and Ed Morgan, mayor of Hattiesburg. The facility began operation in 1998.

*K*ohler Co. has developed the charming Village of Kohler into a premier resort destination. Pictured is a fireplace at Riverbend, the restored 1923 mansion of Walter J. Kohler.

Creating a hospitality business has been another focus for Herb. The company's Hospitality & Real Estate Group has developed the little village of Kohler, Wisconsin, one hour north of Milwaukee, into a resort known around the world.

With its charming homes and winding, tree-lined streets, the village is straight out of a Currier & Ives print. Without compromising that beauty, Kohler Co. has added two hotels, ten restaurants, four of the world's most acclaimed golf courses, indoor and outdoor tennis courts, conference theaters and meeting rooms, a wildlife sanctuary, hunting and fishing, shopping facilities and other venues.

To many visitors, "Destination Kohler" — as the company calls its resort — is a golfing mecca. Indeed, since opening its first 18-hole course in 1988, Kohler Co. has ascended to the very top of the golfing world. In

Below is a summer view of the Fountain Courtyard at The American Club. Right, it takes a crew of seven an entire month to wrap individual branches on the trees around The American Club with 250,000 tiny white lights for the winter holidays.

At right is the Prairie Courtyard of The American Club. The courtyards offer a tranquil place for guests to relax in a beautiful setting. Below, Rhys Lewis is executive chef of The American Club. He has developed a distinctive midwestern culinary style that showcases locally produced foods, prepared in a simple, classic manner. Kohler Co.'s 10 restaurants and banquet department serve more than 700,000 meals a year.

2002, *Golf Digest* named The American Club and Kohler's four championship courses the number-two golf resort in the nation, just behind Pebble Beach in California. "The American Club has emerged as our No. 2 golf resort," the magazine said, "perhaps for the simple reason its mission seems only to be better today than it was yesterday, when yesterday was just about perfect." That same year, *Forbes* magazine and *The Robb Report* described The American Club as the nation's best golf resort. Subsequently, *Golf Odyssey* lauded Kohler's four courses as "the best 72 holes in the world."

However, *Chicago* magazine declared, "Why should the golfer have all the fun?" The magazine pointed out that other activities, from fine dining to hiking to being pampered at a spa, are among "the many delights" of Kohler Village. And in November 1998, the readers of *Condé Nast Traveler* rated The American Club, an anchor of the resort, as number one for service among mainland U.S. resorts.

The village is brimming with activity even when golf is not in season. Annual events include the Kohler Food & Wine Experience in

*A*lice Edland, group vice president, heads Kohler Co.'s hospitality and real estate business. She joined Kohler in 1980 and assumed her current position in 1997.

domestic and imported chocolate for their creations, which are presented in a 100-foot-long buffet.

How It All Started

Given the dramatic success of Destination Kohler, it is surprising how haphazardly the idea began. "There was no grand scheme at the start," Alice Edland, group vice president-hospitality and real estate, says. Kohler Co.'s hospitality business evolved as the pieces fell into place.

It all began in 1977, when the Frank Lloyd Wright Foundation completed a new 50-year master plan for the village's coordinated growth. Kohler Co. submitted the plan for review by the village planning commission and the village board of trustees, which endorsed its conclusions with some modifications. One modification involved a proposal to build another bridge across the Sheboygan River, an idea rejected by the trustees due to concerns that the bridge might create too much traffic on the village's main street.

"We prepared the new 50-year master plan because the previous 50-year plan had expired and we no longer had a blueprint to carry us into the future," Herb Kohler says. He adds, "The other reason we generated a new master plan was that we owned 3,500 acres of undeveloped land and were misusing this very valuable asset. We had a fiduciary responsibility to the shareholders of the company to make sure this asset

October, the Wisconsin Holiday Market in November, the Women's Wellness Retreat in January, the Teddy Bear Classic in February, the Premier Antique Show in March and the Wisconsin Spring Garden Market in April. On top of that, the In Celebration of Chocolate gala — a candlelight dinner with live music, held each year on the weekend before Thanksgiving — has been described by travel writer Madelyn Miller as an "extravaganza" of cakes, tortes, pastries, candies and specialty items. The chefs at The American Club use more than 600 pounds of the finest

The Shops at Woodlake, above, are a collection of shops, boutiques and restaurants overlooking a lake. Kenneth Steltenpohl, right, is director-group administration and controller of Kohler Co.'s Hospitality & Real Estate Group. James Beley, left, is director-lodging operations.

was being managed appropriately to maximize its long-term value." Most of the 3,500 acres had been acquired years earlier, during the tenure of Walter Kohler, to establish a greenbelt around the village and prevent encroachment by the two cities — Sheboygan and Sheboygan Falls — on either side.

The new 50-year plan called for the construction of an upscale shopping center called The Shops at Woodlake, as well as the release of some acreage for home sites. About 420 homes had been built in the village by 1980. Since then, an additional 182 homes and 112 condominium units have been built under the new 50-year plan.

Increased recreational facilities were another objective of the plan, and this caused Kohler Co. to take its first step into the hospitality business, even though that was not the objective at the time. In 1978, the company set aside 800 wooded acres in the Sheboygan River valley for River Wildlife, a private club consisting of a 500-acre wildlife sanctuary and a 300-acre recreational estate with hiking, fishing, hunting, trap shooting, cross-country skiing and other outdoor activities. Herb Kohler says, "I was determined to protect this very unusual glacial river valley from future development. And the way I

felt I could do this was by creating a membership club which would be strong enough to fight my successors if they tried to develop the land. Someday, someone may try to develop those 800 acres in order to make a lot of money, but if they do try I hope they will be hooted out of town."

River Wildlife features some of the better trout and salmon fishing in the United States in the spring and fall, great pheasant hunting in the fall and early winter, and country gourmet dining at a secluded lodge on a bend in the river.

In 1979, one year after establishing River Wildlife, the company opened Sports Core, a health and racquet center with tennis, racquetball, swimming, weightlifting and a scenic running path. "The idea behind Sports Core," Edland explains,

Aina Henegar, seated, is general manager-River Wildlife and Max Grube is River Wildlife's manager-land management. Grube is the son of the late Bud Grube, Kohler Co.'s long-time advertising manager. Below is the River Wildlife lodge. Left is the Sheboygan River, which has some of the better trout and salmon fishing in the country.

*R*iver Wildlife encompasses 800 wooded acres along the Sheboygan River. "For the outdoors-minded," in the words of one magazine, River Wildlife is "a place to dine, to ride horses, to hunt pheasant and Hungarian partridge, to run bird dogs, to stalk deer, to cross-country ski in winter, to canoe, to fish." At left is the River Wildlife lodge.

Nestled on the shore of Wood Lake, Sports Core is a health, fitness and tennis club for members and for guests of The American Club and The Inn on Woodlake. *USA Today Travel Guide* named Sports Core one of the world's 100 best tennis retreats.

"was to build a recreational club for Kohler employees and county residents." At that time, companies across the United States were establishing exercise facilities for employees to encourage more health-ful lifestyles. While many companies allowed employees to use these facili-ties at no cost, Kohler Co. took a different approach. Citing the adage that people seldom appreciate any-thing they get for free, Herb declares, "I said we can't put another financial burden on the company. I also said employees will take advantage of the facility only if they have their own money at stake." To encourage employee membership, Kohler Co. developed a fee structure that allows associates who join Sports Core and use the facility regularly to receive a discount of up to 50 percent from the normal membership rate. "Not only have we avoided a heavy burden to overhead," Herb states, "but we have stimulated a high level of associate use."

Then there was the issue of what to do with The American Club. It was this decision that ultimately triggered Kohler Co.'s entry into the hospitality business. Built in 1918 across the street from the Kohler manufacturing complex, The American Club had long since outlived its original purpose of housing immigrant employees. It was an aging beauty in need of repair, and many thought the time had come to tear it down.

Believing otherwise, Herb hired three consultants to study, from different perspectives, whether The American Club might be turned into an elegant village inn. All three concluded that the idea lacked merit — that the region did not have a sufficient population base to support such a facility and that, in any event, no one would want to stay at an inn across the street from a factory.

After reviewing the consultants' findings, Herb saw three options: raze The American Club to create more green space; convert it to an office building; or refurbish it to create a

*B*uilt in 1918 to house single male Kohler Co. employees, by the 1970s The American Club had outlived its original purpose. Its renovation into a luxury resort hotel was begun in 1978. That same year, the building was placed on the National Register of Historic Places, ensuring it can never be torn down.

luxurious village inn. He concluded that an inn was the best alternative despite the consultants' advice. A veteran traveler who has stayed at many superb hostelries, Herb had a gut feeling that a village inn could succeed in Kohler by providing the highest level of accommodations and service. Herb's wife, Natalie Black, Kohler Co.'s general counsel, senior vice president of communications and corporate secretary, remarks, "The American Club is a classic case of a wonderful intuitive hunch that was right."

Herb took his plan to the Kohler Co. board of directors, which greeted it with skepticism. In fact, virtually no one on the board or within Kohler Co. management understood his vision of what The American Club might become. How, then, did Herb win the board's approval? He says he laid out his case along the following lines: "Look, we have some very difficult alternatives. We can tear the building down and put up something else in its place. But keep in mind that The American Club is the centerpiece of this community. It is a significant landmark and stands at the very heart of the village. And because of its size and nature, there are very few purposes to which it can be put other than an inn."

Herb continues, "Now the issue was whether this old-line manufacturer could jump into a service business and run it as well as or better than it does its manufacturing. And could it make an inn work in the context where it physically sits opposite the factory? I suggested that if we became expert in a service business it would have an influence on our manufacturing business. Serving people in a high level of quality is a very difficult proposition, especially when you have to do it 24 hours a day. We would have to hire employees locally. Some of these employees would never have stayed in a hotel, let alone have worked in one. And we would have to go through continuous, rigorous training to bring these employees up to a level of service that represents the standard of this company. But if we could do that in an inn, it should have considerable rub-off on our other businesses."

After debating his proposal at a series of meetings, the board gave its approval. Renovation of The American Club began in 1978. That same year, the building was placed on the National Register of Historic Places, ensuring that it can never be torn down. There was no turning back.

The three-year renovation retained the original character of the structure while refurbishing the interior to provide superb accommodations for guests. Many of the common areas, such as reading rooms and dining

When the snows arrive, Kohler Village becomes a sparkling winter wonderland offering many activities, from sleigh rides, left, to cross-country skiing and annual events such as the Women's Wellness Retreat in January and the Teddy Bear Classic in February.

facilities, were preserved and restored. At the same time, the single and double rooms that had once housed immigrant workers were gutted to make way for 50 luxury rooms. Kohler Co. also built a 60-room addition, bringing the facility's total to 110 rooms.

When The American Club was reopened in 1981, it became clear that Kohler Co. had a growth opportunity in the hospitality business. Two expansions of the building followed, and today The American Club is a full-fledged luxury resort hotel with 236 guest rooms.

"Despite accusations to the con-

trary," Herb professes, "I built the hospitality business with zero vision." He pauses and leans back, letting forth a huge, infectious laugh. "No vision at all," he insists. "We had one little success built on another little success. And suddenly the combination of those successes and the demand for golf became synergistic. When we combined River Wildlife with Sports Core and The American Club, we had a resort. But did I set out to do that? Hell no!"

Although The American Club did not turn a profit for several years, Herb kept the matter in perspective. His first priority was to achieve

consistently high quality. By reaching that objective, he reasoned, profits would follow. Indeed, Susan Green, who headed Kohler Co.'s hospitality business from 1983 to 1996, says, "Hospitality has a dual function: image and profitability. The two are equal. The image must jibe with the Kohler Co. mission statement, which says we are going to enhance gracious living. And we must be top of the line. If we can't be top of the line, we don't do it." Green says also, "Everybody can be excellent once in

*G*uest rooms at The American Club showcase Kohler Co. products. Each bathroom features a whirlpool bath and other Kohler fixtures. Some guests request a different room each night just to try different fixtures. Above is a public reception area and library off The American Club's lobby.

a while. Consistency is the killer."

Through training and persistent effort, the service level at The American Club improved steadily until the hotel became world class. A milestone was reached in 1986, when the hotel received the highest rating, Five Diamonds, of the American Automobile Association (AAA), given to less than one-half of one percent of the hotels and restaurants evaluated by the AAA. To this day, The American Club remains the only resort hotel in the Midwest to carry a Five Diamond rating.

Golf Lover's Paradise

The American Club hotel started out, in the words of Sue Green, as "a little village inn." She adds, "There was no thought of a resort."

Five Diamond Award

Then came golf.

"I was not a golfer," Herb says. "But obviously in the summertime, many people who stay with us have an interest in playing golf. We accommodated that interest for about three years by making special arrangements with a private country club and with a public course about 15 miles away."

By 1983, The American Club had achieved an occupancy rate of about 85 percent each summer without golf, so there was not a pressing need to attract more guests by building a

course in Kohler. "But our people kept coming to me," Herb says, "and telling me of the difficulty of the relationships with these two golf courses. And there was more and more interest in golf among our guests. So we started to think about building our own course."

Soon, Herb was searching for a golf course designer. With the assistance of Robert Milbourne, a Kohler Co. vice president, he interviewed a number of candidates before choosing one of the most prominent designers in the nation. Herb asked the designer to stake out an 18-hole course on land next to River Wildlife. "The upshot," Herb says, "was I didn't like what he laid out, even though I didn't know anything about golf. I just didn't like his notions about how

The American Club is the only resort hotel in the Midwest to receive the highest rating, Five Diamonds, from the American Automobile Association (AAA). Opposite page is the Founder's Room. At left is the Appley Theatre, named for the late Lawrence A. Appley, longtime president of the American Management Association and a Kohler Co. director.

*P*ete Dye, left, and Herb Kohler, right, worked closely together — battling over Dye's desire to fell a grove of trees, but otherwise agreeing in their vision — to create four championship golf courses. Far left is the par three 13th hole, Tall Timber, of the River Course at Blackwolf Run.

to use the land. And I came more and more to realize how important it was not to have a manicured environment in the midst of River Wildlife. It had to be sort of a rough-hewn type of course, not pretty planted flowers."

The first designer was let go, and the search was resumed. This time, Herb zeroed in on Pete Dye, described by *PGA Magazine* as "the most loved, hated, and imitated golf-course architect of the past fifty years." Dye's courses are renowned for being a challenge to duffer and pro alike.

Herb and Pete hit it off immediately and have been working together ever since. Both are outspoken and strong-willed and are relentless perfectionists.

In his 1995 book, *Bury Me in a Pot Bunker,* Dye describes his elation on first seeing the land where the Kohler Co. course was to be built. "The

acreage outside Kohler," he writes, "had formerly been used as a hunting area and was distinguished by wooded, rolling hills, wetlands, and little streams and creeks that zigzagged around and through the property. There was a certain feel to the area that told me a great golf course could be built there."

John Green, who was then Kohler Co.'s director of corporate landscape, says, "It was evident from the start that Pete's vision was lined up with Herb's. Herb wanted to fit a golf course into the middle of a wildlife preserve without destroying that preserve. Pete shared that objective." Green adds, "It was fascinating to watch the chemistry between them. They had some major wars over the design of the golf course, but they're still great friends. Two very intense people."

The biggest fight involved Herb's desire to save a stand of elm trees and

*T*he par three 15th hole of Meadow Valleys at Blackwolf Run is called Mercy. In 2000, the low-handicap readers of *Golf Digest* ranked Sheboygan County, Wisconsin, as the seventh best golf destination in the world, even though it has far fewer courses than any other destination on the magazine's top 10 list. Speaking of the greater Sheboygan region, the *Chicago Tribune* said, "The likelihood of turning this vast rural farmland into a golf mecca is about the same as making a toilet a work of art. Herbert Kohler can now say he has done both."

Pete's desire to fell the trees. Leaving the trees in place would have required a 200-yard walk from the 16th green to the 17th tee. Felling the trees would have reduced that walk to about 40 yards. Despite this perceived benefit, preserving the trees was important to Herb "because they are a special part of our her-itage," according to Green.

Dye completed all the other holes before arranging to meet with Herb at the golf course to resolve the matter of the trees. As Dye tells the story, referring colorfully to Herb, "Trees' best friend finally told me he would meet me on the 17th at high noon and a decision would be made so we could complete the golf course."

However, as the morning pro-gressed, Herb got tied up at his office and phoned Dye to postpone the meeting until 5 p.m. When Herb failed to appear at five, Dye took the matter into his own hands: he sum-marily directed his crew to cut the trees, stack the logs into large piles

and set them on fire. Dye also instructed the crew to surround each fire with mounds of earth to prevent the flames from spreading — and then Dye got out of town as fast as he could. At 6:20 p.m., Herb finally left his office and headed for the golf course. Expecting to be greeted by Dye, he was confronted instead by six

piles of blazing logs. There was not a person in sight. Herb still gets emotional when he talks about the loss of those trees. "The entire grove was gone, totally wiped out," he laments. "Seventy- to eighty-year-old elms. Trees that even the Dutch elm disease hadn't killed. I was shocked."

Herb returned to his office and tried to locate Dye, but was told that Dye had left for the airport to catch a flight home. Phoning the airport, Herb was told that the plane had just taken off. When Herb finally reached Dye by phone that evening, he let loose a verbal fusillade. "I said, 'Pete Dye, there are about three gentlemen who would love to put their name on this golf course,'" Herb recalls. "And I named Tom Fazio, Jack Nicklaus and Robert Trent Jones. 'Which one do you suggest I pick? Because you're not coming back.'"

As the conversation progressed, Herb calmed down slightly. "I said, 'Pete Dye, the only way you and I are ever going to survive is if you get back here in 24 hours and we have a long discussion about how we're going to make decisions around this place. And when it comes to trees, it's going to be a mutual decision.'" Dye did return. At their face-to-face meeting, according to Dye, "Herb had a chance to vent his anger at me, and the incident ended up bringing us closer together."

Herb adds wryly, "If you play the hole today, it's a great hole. And it's a short green-to-tee walk."

Best New Course of the Year

Herb named the new course Blackwolf Run in tribute to Black Wolf, a nineteenth-century leader of the Winnebago tribe. The Winnebagos are one of the prominent Native American groups in Wisconsin. In 1929, they had honored Governor Walter Kohler by making him a chief. It was pure Herb Kohler to select a name that embraced the history both of the region and the company.

Opening in 1988, Blackwolf Run was an immediate smash hit with the golfing public and was named the nation's best new public course of the year by *Golf Digest* magazine.

"After we built 18 holes, we had no thought of going to 27 or 36 holes, none whatsoever," Herb insists. "But old Pete kept talking to me about this land out to the west that could contain more holes. And I really liked what he had done on the first 18. So Pete was able to persuade me in 1989 to go forward with the third nine. The third nine was of a character that was different from the first 18, yet it was able to flow with that 18. It made the whole thing more interesting."

In 1990, another nine holes were built, bringing the total to 36. At that time, Blackwolf Run was reconfigured to create the 18-hole River Course and the 18-hole Meadow Valleys Course. This required some rearranging of the holes. For instance, the first four holes of the original nine were

*L*eft, the par four ninth hole of the River Course at Blackwolf Run is called Cathedral Spires. A description reads, "A mid iron just left of the tall trees will follow the terrain back to the right. A longer club hit 30 to 40 yards left of the trees gives you a good opening to the green. But a shot 15 yards left will flirt with the deep pot bunkers in the middle." Above, the clubhouse at Blackwolf Run is set low to the ground so as not to intrude on the landscape.

joined with five brand-new holes to form the front nine of the River Course. "And *Golf Digest* came out with an article saying how awful we were, we had ruined this masterpiece to which they had given their highest award in 1988," Herb says. "Here we were chopping up the first nine of the original course and tacking on another nine, and tacking another nine onto that. They couldn't believe it. Now mind you, they didn't come to see what they were writing about. They were strictly responding to the fact that we would dare touch something to which they had given their highest award. Two years later they wrote an article of apology."

Once the brouhaha had subsided, it was clear that Blackwolf Run was better than ever. In building the original 18 holes, Herb had challenged his people to create a course that would rank among the top 100 public golf courses in the nation. They met that challenge and then some. *Golf Magazine's Top 100 Courses You Can Play*, published in 1999, says the River Course "must be considered the nation's finest public-access course of modern times." Among all public-access courses regardless of vintage, the book ranks the River Course number three in the nation, just behind Pebble Beach in California and Pinehurst No. 2 in North Carolina, both created in the early twentieth century.

There are more than 16,000 public, private and resort golf courses in

*G*reg Norman of Australia, left, congratulates fellow countryman Steve Elkington following the latter's victory, 2 and 1, in the semifinals of the 1997 international leg of the Andersen Consulting World Championship of Golf. The international championship was held at Blackwolf Run. Ernie Els, playing in the same tournament, said, "This is a great match-play course. There is a fine line between hitting a good shot and being in trouble. You can't panic."

North America, of which 6,000 are ranked by another influential publication, *Golf Digest*. River Course is one of just 12 to receive that magazine's highest rating, five stars, while Meadow Valleys Course is right behind at four and one-half stars.

One *Golf Digest* subscriber called River Course "most challenging, most scenic, most variety of hazards, obstacles, best service," while Meadow Valleys has been described as "incredibly beautiful, subtle, devilish."

"I have seen heaven," one golfer told *Golf Digest*, "and it is named Blackwolf Run."

There's nothing a golfer likes more than playing a fabulous course where the top pros compete. Blackwolf Run has hosted a regional championship of the Andersen Consulting World Championship of Golf three times — the United States Championship in 1995 and the International Championship in 1996 and 1997. Some of the world's greatest golfers played at Blackwolf Run in these tournaments, including Greg Norman, Nick Price, Steve Elkington and Ernie Els.

Golf has turned out to be a good business for Kohler Co. not only from a financial viewpoint, but also in terms of the high level of visibility it affords the company and its products. Indeed, in 2001 *Executive Golfer* magazine described Herb Kohler as "the predominant personality our game of golf needs today."

Golf has also brought Kohler Co. some unusual attention. On the *Jenny Jones Show*, a nationally syndicated television talk show, the theme on February 15, 1995, was sexual fantasies. A woman in the audience stood up and said, "This is for Michael, my husband. I'd like to make love to him on the fifth tee of the River Course at Blackwolf Run in Kohler, Wisconsin. It's a beautiful hole. It's just real high up and you look over the whole valley and the golf course. It's gorgeous." The audience roared with approval.

Thirty-Six More Holes

By the late 1980s, having himself taken up golf, Herb fully understood the allure (and frustration) of the sport. Moreover, Blackwolf Run was completely booked for just about the entire golf season. John Green reports, "In 1992, he said to me, 'I want you to look for land for another golf course.' I said, 'Herb, you've got all the land in the world right here in Kohler. Why would you want more land?'"

It turned out that Herb intended to build an Irish links course that hearkened back to golf's origins, and the land in Kohler did not suit this approach. Links courses are typically located along the shores of bodies of

water where the winds are gusty. In addition, they usually have fescue grass which lies down flat, allowing the ball to roll farther than on a Bermuda-grass course. "So you're out there with the elements whipping at you every which way, and you're playing a bounce and run game, and that's the true joy and challenge of it," Herb says.

Herb finally selected a piece of land not far from Kohler Village. When problems arose in acquiring all the individual parcels required to build a course at that location, John Green recommended a site on a bluff along two miles of Lake Michigan shoreline. The Lake Michigan prop-

erty had once been home to an army base and was later owned by a utility which dropped its plans to build a nuclear power plant there.

Herb toured the Lake Michigan site with Pete Dye. They both saw its possibilities, even though the land was flat and was covered with dilapidated military buildings and debris. Kohler Co. acquired the 560-acre parcel in 1995, whereupon Dye applied his magical touch to create a landscape reminiscent of the rugged Irish coast. To pull off this feat, he brought in 13,126 truckloads of sand — approximately 800,000 cubic yards — to fashion dunes and hills as well as fescue grass fairways.

Whistling Straits, as this newest golf venture is called, is located nine miles from The American Club (guests can travel back and forth by shuttle bus) and consists of two 18-hole courses — the Straits Course, a links walking-only course, which opened in 1998, and the Irish Course, which opened in 2000. Adding to the unique experience, Scottish Blackface ewes, like those seen in the Irish countryside, roam and graze the roughs of Whistling Straits.

In April 2002, the Straits Course was ranked for the first time by *Golf Digest.* It immediately received the magazine's highest accolade, five stars — one of only 12 public and resort

golf courses in North America to carry that top designation. At this writing, the Irish Course is yet to be rated by *Golf Digest*.

Combined, Kohler Co.'s four courses — the Straits Course and River Course, both among the dozen five-star courses in North America; the Meadow Valleys Course at four and one-half stars; and the Irish Course, widely considered to be among the finest in the nation, although not yet rated — seduce golfers with a links paradise unparalleled virtually anywhere else in the world. In fact, Kohler is the *only* venue in North America to have two five-star courses.

Five Memorable Days of Golf
The Straits Course opened for play on Monday, July 6, 1998. The date was chosen because it followed by one day the scheduled final round of the U.S. Women's Open Championship, being held at Kohler's Blackwolf Run venue.

The Women's Open was a huge success, attracting 124,000 spectators, the most in the tournament's 53-year history. "Never have I seen this many people on a golf course," said golfer Annika Sorenstam. Blackwolf Run challenged the golfers; not a single one broke par. Adding to the drama, regulation play ended in a tie between rookie pro Se Ri Pak and

*O*pposite is the par three third hole, O'Man, of the Straits Course at Whistling Straits. Above, Blackwolf Run hosted the 1998 U.S. Women's Open Championship. Not a single golfer beat par. Left to right, Jane Geddes, Meg Mallon and Nancy Lopez waved white towels in mock surrender as they approached the 18th green on day two of the tournament. This was Lopez's last appearance in a U.S. Women's Open.

*S*e Ri Pak, left, won the 1998 U. S. Women's Open Championship in dramatic fashion: 72 holes of regulation play followed by an 18-hole playoff followed by two holes of "sudden death." Above, Jennie Chuasiriporn (wearing a visor) was the tournament runner-up.

amateur Jenny Chuasiriporn, both just 20 years old.

The tie forced an 18-hole playoff on Monday, heightening the excitement of the tournament, but running afoul of Monday's planned 10 a.m. opening ceremonies at Whistling Straits. Given the circumstances, the only option was to advance the ceremonies to 7 a.m. and get the participants back to Blackwolf Run as quickly as possible for the Women's Open playoff.

Herb was like a proud new papa at the Whistling Straits dedication. The inaugural festivities were a fund-raiser for The First Tee, which makes the game of golf and its values accessible to economically disadvantaged youngsters. Foursomes paid $30,000 each, and the event raised a total of $500,000 for the nonprofit group. In brief remarks, Herb praised Pete Dye for having "truly outdone himself." Herb also said, "The course offers a succession of spectacular views, each more remarkable than the last." A shotgun was then fired to signal that the new course was open for play. In addition to Herb, golfers who took part that morning included:

- Former U.S. President George Bush;
- PGA of America CEO Jim Awtrey;
- PGA Tour Commissioner Tim Finchem;
- LPGA Commissioner Jim Ritts;
- United States Golf Association President F. Morgan "Buzz" Taylor Jr.;

- United States Golf Association immediate past President Judy Bell;
- Pop singer Amy Grant; and
- Course designer Pete Dye.

As the golfers finished their rounds, they were whisked back to Kohler Village to witness the final holes of the Women's Open playoff at Blackwolf Run. All the golfers got back in time for some of the playoff. And then came a bonus: when the 18-hole playoff ended in a tie, Pak and Chuasiriporn played two more holes of sudden death. Pak finally won with a birdie on the tournament's 92nd hole.

*T*he inaugural day of play at Whistling Straits was a fund-raiser for The First Tee, a nonprofit group. Left to right are PGA of America CEO Jim Awtrey, PGA Tour Commissioner Tim Finchem, former President George Bush, Herb Kohler, course designer Pete Dye, United States Golf Association past President Judy Bell and LPGA Commissioner Jim Ritts.

The dramatic finish at Blackwolf Run, in combination with the ceremonies at Whistling Straits, proved to be one of the memorable extravaganzas in recent golf history. Readers of GOLFonline, the web site of *GOLF Magazine*, voted the lengthy battle between Pak and Chuasiriporn as the number-one golf event of 1998. The *Washington Post* said, "For golf aficionados, it doesn't get much better," and the New Orleans *Times-Picayune* declared that the Women's Open at Blackwolf Run "underscores all that is good about the women's game."

Golf writer Bob Bubka took part in all the festivities. He not only watched and wrote about the

Women's Open, but also played on the initial day at Whistling Straits — with the benefit of some personal tutoring by Pete Dye, who, according to Bubka, advised him on the "proper way" to attack the new course. Bubka wrote, "When it was finally over, there was just one complaint on my part: Why did it have to end so soon?"

Whistling Straits To Host the PGA Championship

Since its opening, Whistling Straits has received many rave reviews. No accolade is more telling, however, than its selection as the site of the 2004 PGA Championship, one of the four tournaments in golf's grand slam. The PGA Championship is played at some of the nation's best

The Whistling Straits clubhouse resembles an Irish farmstead. During construction, Herb Kohler told the workers to turn the rough unfinished side of the stones outward to impart a raw appearance. *GOLF Magazine* said the clubhouse is "elegantly spare" and "looks as if it's been standing there for 300 years." At left is the par three seventh hole, Shipwreck, of the Straits Course.

courses. In announcing the selection for 2004, PGA President Will Mann said, "Whistling Straits will provide the perfect test for the world's best golfers. It has already proven itself worthy of a major championship and will be held in esteem for generations to come."

Kohler Waters Spa: Soothing the Body and Relaxing the Mind

In 2000, the company continued its development of Destination Kohler with the opening of Kohler Waters Spa. The 16,000-square-foot facility offers a host of water treatments, a pool for relaxation, pools for hot and cool dips, and steam rooms, saunas and eight-foot cascading waterfall. *Chicago* magazine says the spa features "more than 70 services, including massage therapies, body wraps, and facial treatments, in a setting worthy of imperial Rome."

Alice Edland notes, "We expect the reputation of this spa will resonate on a national level. Our goal is to become as well recognized for our spa as we are for our golf." The spa broadens Destination Kohler's year-round appeal and adds a refreshing new amenity for guests.

Riverbend: A Unique Private Club

The newest facility is Riverbend, opened in 2001 in Walter Kohler's former mansion near the Sheboygan River. Built in 1923, Riverbend was

*K*ohler Waters Spa provides innovative bathing products and soothing water treatments. Men's and women's lounge rooms include hot and cold plunge pools, saunas and steam rooms.

*A*t the center of Kohler Waters Spa is a tiled pool with an eight-foot cascading wall of water. Kohler Waters Spa was opened in 2000. In 2002 and 2003, it was rated one of the top 40 spas in North America and the Caribbean by the readers of *Condé Nast Traveler.*

described in the 1930s as one of the 40 most beautiful mansions in the United States. Kohler Co. purchased the home in 1985 from the National Trust for Historic Preservation, which had acquired it from Walter's descendants.

Beginning in the late 1990s, the company refurbished the historic mansion with a sensitivity to the past and turned it into an exclusive private club offering individual and corporate membership programs. Herb Kohler refers to Riverbend, the most upscale of all the Destination Kohler facilities, as "the cherry on the Kohler cake."

Riverbend is a quiet retreat

where members can relax, socialize and enjoy all the amenities of Destination Kohler. It features 31 luxurious guest rooms, two dining rooms, solarium, living room, rathskeller, billiard room, meeting rooms, spa with treatment areas, indoor-outdoor year-round swimming pool, steam, sauna, whirlpool and exercise equipment. Members with golf privileges receive preferential guaranteed tee times at Blackwolf Run and Whistling Straits.

Another Destination Site?
Looking ahead, Kohler Co. eventually expects to add more rooms to The Inn on Woodlake, a mid-priced hotel by a spring-fed lake. The company opened the inn in 1994 and more than doubled its size in 1999 to 121 rooms. "Beyond taking The Inn on Woodlake to 180 rooms, we do not plan any significant new lodging in the village," Edland states.

Herb adds that, having built four championship golf courses, there will

be no further expansion of golf in the Kohler area.

Thus, the construction of major facilities for Destination Kohler is essentially complete. By limiting any further expansion, Kohler Co. will preserve the charm and small-town scale that make Kohler Village so special. Future investments, according to Herb, will focus on enhancing the experience of guests by adding more entertainment.

Then comes a surprise.

"Eventually, having refined our skills, we'll go out and develop another destination site," Herb reveals. Destination Kohler, it seems, is only the first step in building the company's Hospitality & Real Estate Group. The location of Kohler Co.'s next resort site remains to be seen. However, one point is certain: Herb never stops dreaming up new ways to expand Kohler Co. and stay on the leading edge in each of its businesses.

*R*iverbend is the most elegant of Destination Kohler's facilities. It is located in Walter J. Kohler's 1923 mansion, which was meticulously restored to create a private club with 31 guest rooms. Pictured opposite bottom is a 1930s gathering of 4-H groups at Riverbend.

*B*aker craftspeople make antique reproductions and other fine furniture. Pictured is Lloyd Van Dornik, now retired. Baker is known for its distinctive handiwork, having mastered and sometimes revived Old World practices. The company has been part of Kohler since 1986.

9. Fine Interiors: Baker, McGuire and Ann Sacks

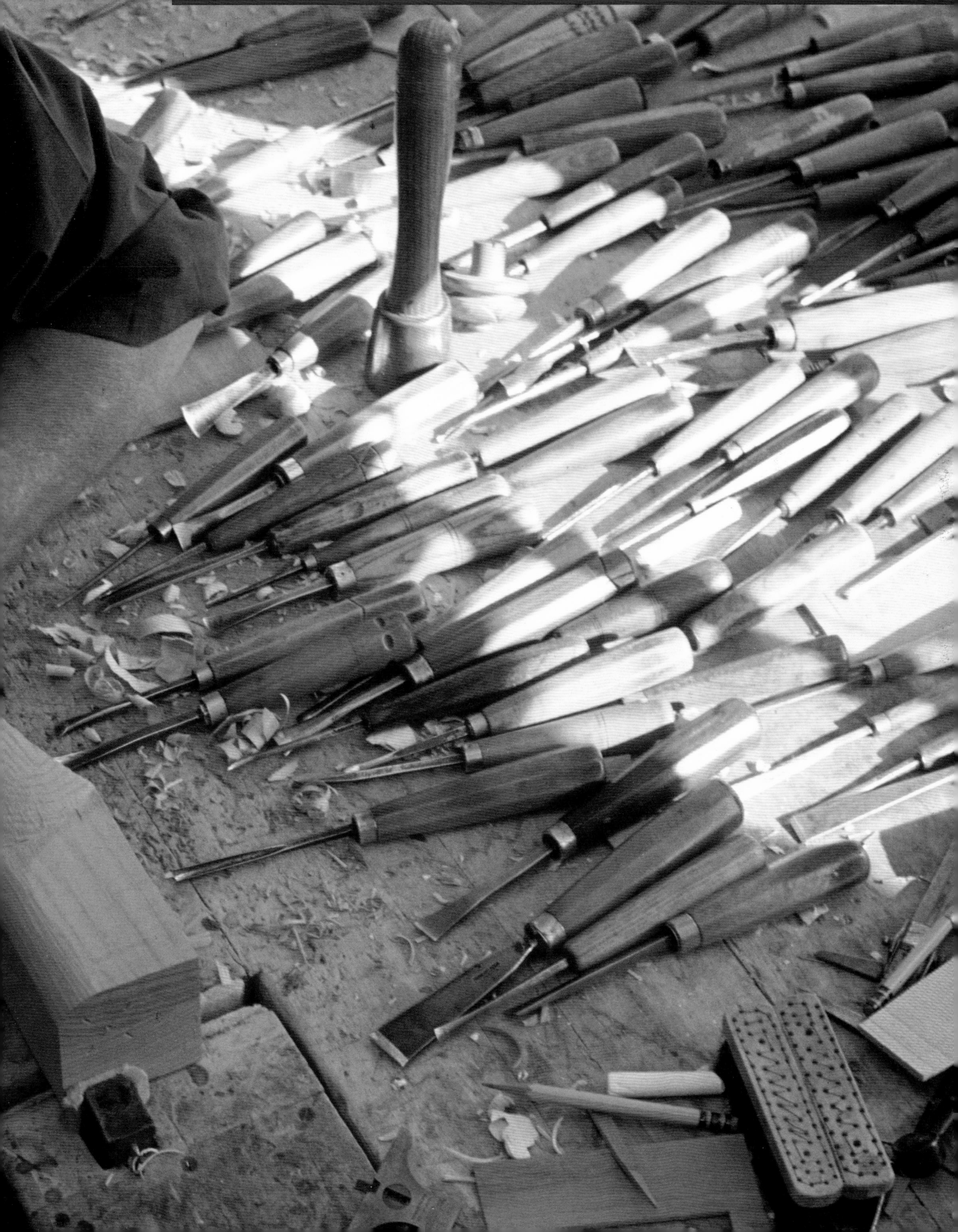

A n unusual and dramatic series of events surrounded Kohler Co.'s entry into the furniture manufacturing and distribution business.

In 1986, Kohler attempted to acquire Henredon Furniture Industries, which was publicly owned. The management of Henredon had put the company up for sale, and Kohler led the bidding through the first two rounds.

Kohler executives thought they had a deal and were waiting to send a negotiating team to finalize the terms. "But we didn't hear, didn't hear, and I just knew something had happened," says Natalie A. Black, general counsel, senior vice president of communications and corporate secretary. So she phoned Henredon's president. The president's secretary, not recognizing Black's voice, asked if she was with Masco Corporation, which happens to be one of Kohler's largest competitors in plumbing products. "That's how I learned Masco was in the picture," she says. "It was the first time we realized another plumbing products company was looking at the furniture business."

Or as Herb Kohler puts it, "Suddenly these two plumbing giants found themselves bidding against each other for a furniture company, which was crazy. Because neither of us had publicly expressed any interest in the furniture industry, and all of a sudden our primary competitor for Henredon was our primary competitor in plumbing products."

He adds, "I was fascinated and sat there trying to figure out what they were doing and even more why the two of us were doing it at the same time. We had our own strategy, but it was hard to believe they had a similar strategy."

Furniture companies were then in great demand, and the prices being paid were escalating rapidly. Black notes that many acquisition-minded corporations were attracted to the industry by favorable demographics, including the prospect that the "baby boomers" were coming into their prime earning years and would be purchasing expensive home furnishings.

Masco eventually acquired Henredon for $58 per share, or a total price of about $300 million. That came to 27 times Henredon's prior-year earnings — at a time when the overall stock market (as measured by the Standard & Poor's 500 Index) was trading at a mere 10 times earnings, indicating just how high-pitched the bidding for furniture companies had become.

Stymied in its attempt to acquire Henredon, Kohler sought to buy Drexel Heritage Furnishing Inc. Again, it was outbid by Masco.

Unwilling to pay what it considered to be excessive prices, but still wanting to be in the furniture business, Kohler looked across the furniture industry for a leading manufacturer with a reputation for high quality. In late 1986, it purchased

*S*ince joining Kohler, Baker Furniture has continued to manufacture high-quality reproductions, such as the mahogany and giltwood cabinet, opposite, and has led the industry in commissioning modern designs, such as the Tufted Classic Side Chair, below, by Thomas Pheasant.

Baker Knapp & Tubbs from North American Philips Corporation, a reluctant seller. "Baker was not on the market. We had to pry it out," Herb insists. "We approached North American Philips and made an offer. Then we hammered away until we convinced them they would never see a price like ours again." Although the price/earnings ratio that Kohler paid for Baker was comparable to the ratio that Masco had paid for Henredon and Drexel Heritage, Herb felt that Kohler Co. was getting better value because of Baker's long-standing quality leadership and reputation for innovative design. *House Beautiful* magazine has called Baker "perhaps America's most venerated producer of high-quality furniture."

Four years later, in 1990, Kohler Co. acquired McGuire Furniture Company, which makes quality rattan furniture. Both companies are leaders in the high end of their market segments. McGuire's products, which are relatively informal, complement those of Baker, which are more formal.

After purchasing Baker and McGuire, Kohler Co. made a niche acquisition — Dapha, Ltd., a custom upholsterer. The three companies, together with Ann Sacks, a leader in decorative tile, stone and specialty plumbing fixtures, today form Kohler Co.'s Interiors Group.

Meanwhile, Masco kept right on buying furniture companies at a breakneck pace, leaving Kohler in its dust. All told, Masco invested approx-

ictured above is a Baker reproduction of an eighteenth century Venetian secretary. Italian painted and lacquered furniture reached its artistic peak in the 1700s. Right, Diem Nguyen is an associate at the Baker Furniture plant in Holland, Michigan.

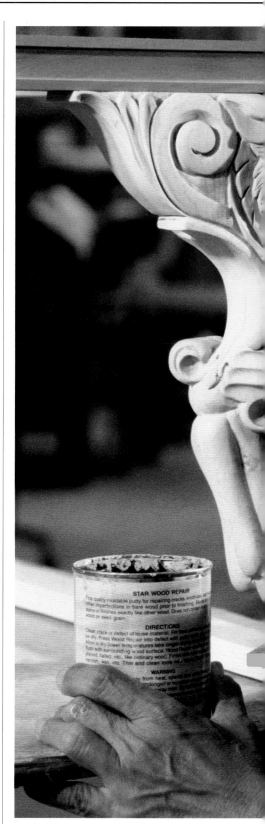

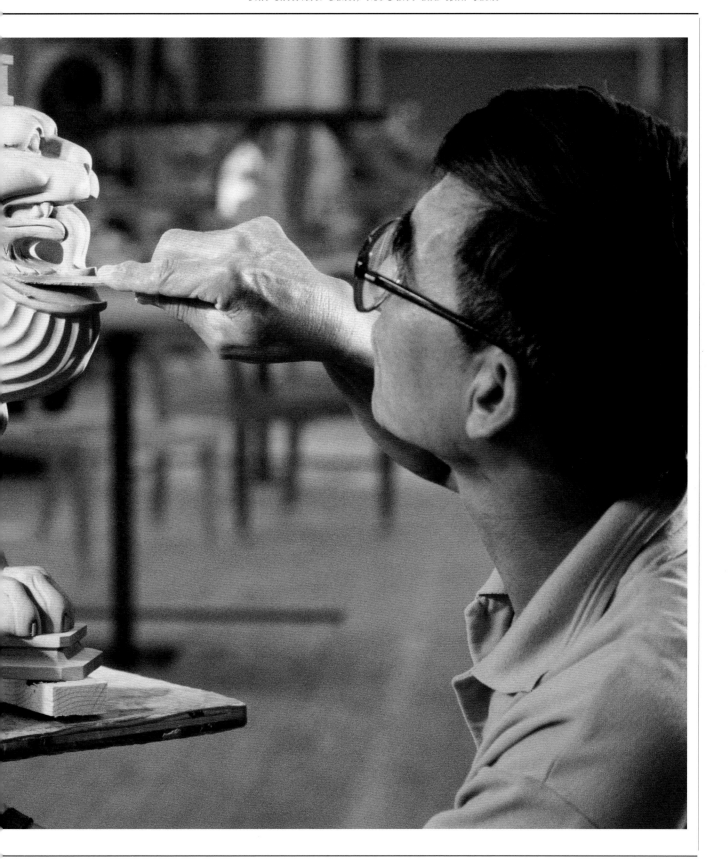

Natalie A. Black is Kohler Co.'s general counsel, senior vice president of communications and corporate secretary, and was the first president of its Interiors Group from 1986 to 2000. She joined Kohler Co. in 1981 after having been an attorney with Quarles & Brady, a Milwaukee law firm. She holds an A.B. degree in economics and mathematics from Stanford University and is a magna cum laude graduate of Marquette University Law School.

bought we bought carefully."

Kohler Co. suffered in the furniture segment in the early 1990s, as did many other industry participants. "However, we had made smaller acquisitions and had less capital at risk," Black points out. "As a result, we were able to get through those difficult times and nurture the companies we had acquired. Today, we are developing a healthy, viable, long-term furniture business."

Most importantly, after acquiring two of the industry's premier brands — Baker and McGuire — Kohler Co. developed an effective strategy for increasing their value by investing in new designs, new products, new production capacity and new distribution capabilities. Black, more than any other individual, devised the strategy and was willing to take the risks to make it work. "Natalie loves this business and really wants it to be successful," Rachel Kohler, group president-interiors, observes. "She has defended the investments and has supported the bold strokes."

Rachel says the businesses in the Interiors Group are distinguished by:
• Best of class brand in their category;
• Products that establish design trends for the category;
• Product purchase decisions that are aided by a design professional; and
• Controlled product presentations and sales through company-owned stores and showrooms to meet the needs of exacting customers.

imately $2 billion in furniture company acquisitions, buying Lexington, Universal and Berkline in addition to Henredon and Drexel.

However, there is a kicker to this story. Although the demographics looked great, those demographics had to translate into higher profits to justify the prices being paid for furniture companies in the 1980s. To the contrary, in the early 1990s the furniture industry went into an earnings

decline, and many of the acquirers ended up taking baths. Masco got out of the furniture business in 1996, selling its home furnishings group for $1 billion and writing off a $650 million loss on its investment.

"Many big companies went into the furniture business," Herb Kohler says, "and virtually none of them is in the business today. We're about the only one left. We're alive because we didn't rush in pell-mell and what we

"For Kohler," she adds, "participation in this luxury arena is important because it supports the company's position as a design leader in the whole home. In addition, the challenge of constantly serving a demanding community of design professionals and affluent consumers provides a cutting-edge perspective on design ideas and consumer expectations. This perspective benefits all of Kohler's businesses."

Baker, McGuire and Ann Sacks are interesting businesses in their own right. Each was founded by an entrepreneur who succeeded by emphasizing the finest quality and design, which parallels the history of Kohler Co.

Baker Furniture Company

Baker Furniture began in 1890 in Allegan, Michigan, as a manufacturer of window sash and doors, then started producing low-priced oak furniture for mass markets. It was not until the 1930s, at the depths of the Great Depression, that it abruptly changed direction to become a high-end manufacturer.

This unlikely change was driven by Hollis Baker, who inherited the company from his father. Believing there was a market for quality even in the worst economic times, he hired European craftsmen and began producing some of the most elegant furniture in America. His strategy was a tremendous gamble in the middle of the Depression, but it saved the com-

pany, and Baker has concentrated on quality ever since.

"Hollis was a real connoisseur," says Roderick Kreitzer, Baker's president from 1989 to 1994. Hollis Baker traveled frequently to Europe to buy antiques, and he even opened a company museum near the corporate headquarters in Grand Rapids, Michigan, to display several hundred of the choicest examples. "He might buy a chair simply because he thought the front leg was good, and maybe some day his designers would develop a chair incorporating that leg," Kreitzer recalls.

When Hollis Baker died in 1966, his son, Hollis Baker Jr., inherited the company. Three years later, Hollis Jr. sold the business to Magnavox Company, an electronics manufacturer that was diversifying into home furnishings.

How Baker Furniture Became Baker Knapp & Tubbs

A decade after the founding of Baker Furniture, Knapp & Tubbs was established in Chicago to distribute fine furniture from various manufacturers, including Baker. Knapp & Tubbs became a force in the Chicago furniture market and was one of the first tenants of the Chicago Merchandise Mart when that massive facility opened in 1930. After World War II, Knapp & Tubbs grew nationally by opening showrooms in Los Angeles, New York, Dallas, Miami and nearly a dozen other cities.

*H*ollis Baker Sr. led Baker Furniture from 1925 until his death in 1966. The American Furniture Hall of Fame calls him a "renaissance man" who "learned more about the history of furniture design and construction than anyone else of his era." Through his design excellence and quality standards, the Hall of Fame says, he "raised the performance levels of the entire industry."

Magnavox acquired Knapp & Tubbs in 1972, three years after having purchased Baker Furniture, and merged the two to form Baker Knapp & Tubbs. This strategy gave Baker greater control over its distribution, a competitive advantage in an industry where distribution channels are highly fragmented. Two years later, Magnavox was itself acquired by North American Philips Corporation. Baker Knapp & Tubbs, included in the transaction, grew steadily during the next 12 years as part of Philips.

Kohler Co.'s Purchase of Baker
Baker's journey of changing ownership finally came to an end in 1986.

*R*od Kreitzer joined Baker in 1957 and was its president from 1989 until he retired in 1994. "Baker is top of the line in furniture," he notes, "and that's why Herb Kohler bought it. Herb came in with new ideas and provided the capital that allowed us to grow faster, while maintaining our absolute commitment to product design and quality."

That year, Philips decided to concentrate on electronics and negotiated the sale of Baker Knapp & Tubbs to Kohler Co., although a last-minute hitch arose: the status of the Baker Museum of Furniture Research, established years earlier by Hollis Baker Sr.

Herb Kohler did not know about the museum, which Philips had excluded from the sale. On the other hand, many Baker employees felt great pride in the museum as a design resource and did not want it to be split from their company. So Kreitzer took Herb aside at a home furnishings opening at the Bloomingdale's department store in New York and told him of the facility.

Herb has a passion for corporate history as well as for good design, and there was no way he was going to let that museum elude him. "I believe quite strongly in understanding your roots," he explains. "And here was a collection that was the roots of Baker. It was the wellspring from which a number of Baker's product lines had come and would continue to come."

Herb wanted the museum. Philips resisted at first, then relented, and the museum became part of the sale. As a result, Kohler Co. now owns a superb collection of antique English and Continental furniture as well as Oriental and modern pieces. It is a source of design ideas not only for furniture, but also for plumbing products.

Much has been written about acquirers who buy businesses and wield a sharp ax, slashing employment and closing plants. Herb Kohler is a builder, not a slasher. He seeks to improve a business, not cut it to shreds. In particular, Kohler Co. has a track record of identifying an acquired company's competitive advantages and leveraging those advantages to increase revenues and earnings.

In analyzing Baker Furniture, Natalie Black — who led the Interiors Group as its president from 1986 to 2000, in addition to being Kohler Co. general counsel — saw two main competitive advantages: the company's design heritage and its distribution. By capitalizing on these

*S*ir Humphry Wakefield is an English baronet who works closely with Baker Furniture in selecting furniture for reproduction in its Stately Homes Collection. He is one of the leading authorities on English antiques and architecture, and he lives at Chillingham Castle, which he is restoring. The historic castle has been continuously owned by the Earls Grey and their relations since the 1200s.

*L*os Angeles designer Barbara Barry is renowned for her sleek, sophisticated furnishings that are reminiscent of Hollywood's golden age of the 1930s. She works with Kohler Co. in designing furniture for Baker, products for the powder room and dressing room for Kallista, and tile and bathroom accessories for Ann Sacks.

*C*ornelia Pelzer, who retired in 2000 as director of reproductions at the Historic Charleston Foundation, worked closely with Baker Furniture for many years. Baker holds a license from the foundation to reproduce fine furniture from many of the great homes of the South Carolina port city. Baker pays royalties to the foundation, a nonprofit group, which uses the money in its work of preserving the city's historical and architectural heritage.

*T*his dining room setting features Baker's Double Pedestal Dining Table and Shield Back Side and Arm Chairs from the Historic Charleston Collection, and Baker's Sunburst Mirror from the Special Selections Collection.

strengths, Kohler Co. has built Baker into a business that is significantly larger and more valuable today than it was at the time of acquisition.

Leveraging Baker's Design Heritage

In terms of design heritage, Baker is an "upscale trend setter," in the words of the *Wall Street Journal.* It has a long tradition of making fine antique reproductions and high-end traditional and modern furniture.

Two of the company's important design relationships are with the Historic Charleston Foundation and Sir Humphry Wakefield, an English baronet who is a world-renowned authority on antiques and architecture. Through Historic Charleston, a nonprofit group, Baker has entrée to many of the magnificent private homes in the South Carolina port city. Baker reproduces furniture from these homes in its Historic Charleston Collection, paying royalties to the foundation, which uses the money to preserve the city's history and architecture. Sir Humphry consults with Baker on its Stately Homes Collection — reproductions of great antiques from private homes in England, Ireland and Scotland.

These and other traditional collections continue to sell well. Rachel Kohler cites a recent study showing that half the furniture bought by young millionaires, including those in the technology and e-commerce fields, is in traditional styles. "To them

it's new," she points out.

Consequently, in leveraging its design heritage, Baker has continued to develop its traditional collections, while broadening its product line by forging relationships with high-profile contemporary designers, including Barbara Barry in Los Angeles and Michael Vanderbyl in San Francisco.

Barry is one of the most important interior designers to emerge in the past decade. Her style, according to one home furnishings writer, is "classic but contemporary, glamorous but simple." She is best known for her interior designs that embrace the elegance and glamour of the golden age of Hollywood. The Barbara Barry Collection for Baker Furniture takes inspiration from the same sophisticated 1930s Hollywood look. "My goal," Barry has said, "is to design a sofa that recedes into the background and a room that will feel just as good in 20 years' time.... I look at the classics, pare them down to their essentials, and evoke a spirit that will never go out of style."

The *San Francisco Chronicle* has described Vanderbyl as "an internationally heralded authority on design," pointing out that he works in a wide variety of arenas, including graphics, interiors, textiles and fashion, as well as furniture design. His Archetype Collection for Baker Furniture blends familiar forms with minimalist interpretation. Comfort is paramount in each of his creations for the collection.

The Barbara Barry Collection and Archetype Collection have both been successful in the marketplace, helping drive Baker Furniture's growth. Their value to Baker extends beyond pure dollars and cents, however. Rachel Kohler notes that these collections have put Baker on the map as a company with innovative ideas. Baker is now a resource within Kohler Co., providing design concepts for Kohler plumbing products, such as Revival faucets, and in turn feeding off the latest designs of the Kitchen & Bath Group. In addition, Barbara Barry has broadened her relationship with Kohler to include products for the Kallista and Ann Sacks brands. Building on the success of its relationships with Barbara Barry and Michael Vanderbyl, Baker has developed relationships with a select group of other top designers, including Bill Sofield of New York and Thomas Pheasant of Washington, D.C.

In 2001, Baker identified an opportunity to provide a "complete look" to the customer, offering not only furniture, but also lighting, textiles, throws, bedding, vases, trays and rugs. The Haven Furniture Collection by Barbara Barry is the first Baker collection to embrace this concept.

Because it is on the leading edge of the furniture business, Baker is increasingly winning attention in influential interior design and architecture magazines, reinforcing the Kohler image of being a trendsetter in design and taste. "We know what

𝒰nder Kohler Co.'s ownership, Baker has broadened its market presence by introducing Milling Road furniture in the Baker tradition of quality, but at lower prices. Pictured is a Milling Road West Indies bedroom setting.

Rachel Kohler joined Kohler Co. in 1992 after having worked in investment banking at First Boston Corporation and management consulting at Booz, Allen & Hamilton. She began as Kohler Co.'s director-corporate planning and development before transferring to the Interiors Group, which she now heads as group president. She has directed the group in the expansion of its production capacity, the broadening of its distribution channels and the relationships it has formed with leading contemporary designers.

ity, including the construction of factories in Hildebran, North Carolina, and Semarang, Indonesia. With these investments, Baker now has six plants — three in North Carolina, two in Michigan and one in Indonesia.

Baker was one of the first U.S. companies to produce high-quality furniture in Asia. Its Indonesian factory, called PT Port Rush, began operation in 1998 and makes finished furniture for the United States and other markets. The facility also supplies parts to Baker's U.S. factories. "There are many highly skilled wood carvers in Indonesia," Rachel Kohler says. "We opened our PT Port Rush plant to draw on that expertise."

Simultaneous to its investment in Indonesia, Baker struck forth ahead of most competitors to source its Milling Road product in Italy, China and Colombia. Rachel says many manufacturers believed that consumers would never accept upper-end furniture produced outside the United States. "In fact," she adds, "the quality has been excellent, contributing to the success of the Milling Road brand."

Rachel is a Princeton University graduate who worked initially in investment banking at First Boston Corporation. She then earned her M.B.A. at the University of Chicago Graduate School of Business, after which she worked in management consulting at Booz, Allen & Hamilton. She joined Kohler Co. in 1992 as director-corporate planning

'good' looks like" is the way Rachel Kohler puts it.

Milling Road: Building a New Brand

Another strategy in acquiring Baker Furniture was to develop a mid-priced furniture line to complement the upscale Baker collections. Herb Kohler personally pushed this idea, which is similar to the Kohler Co. strategy of developing a mid-priced plumbing products line under the Sterling brand name.

Thus was born Milling Road, a

Baker division that makes moderately priced furniture known for its fine craftsmanship, good taste and subtlety of detail. Milling Road is the casual face of Baker. "Nobody does casual elegance better than Milling Road," one design editor observed. The division has been a big winner, expanding rapidly to sales of about $40 million a year.

Focusing on Alternative Production

To support Baker's growth, Kohler has invested in new production capac-

and development, transferring to the company's furniture business later that same year as vice president-showroom operations. She was elected to the Kohler Co. board of directors in 1999 and was promoted to group president-interiors in 2000.

Rachel, who can be as strong willed and outspoken as her father, says she loves running her own business within Kohler. She also loves the fact that Herb's office is in Kohler and hers is in Chicago. "I think the distance keeps us both sane," she states.

House Beautiful has called Baker "perhaps America's most venerated producer of high-quality furniture." Baker controls much of its own distribution through its BKT unit, which sells Baker furniture and more than 15 other high-end brands. Pictured is the BKT showroom in New York.

New Distribution Channels

Rachel has led Baker not only in forging relationships with leading contemporary designers, but also in expanding its distribution business, BKT Showrooms & Stores. BKT has showrooms across the United States and in Europe, and is one of the largest wholesale distributors of fine home furnishings in the world. It represents more than 15 manufacturers, including Baker and McGuire, and about 300 accessory companies. "We deal in high-end products where people want a selection," she

*A*lthough BKT Showrooms & Stores has traditionally sold furniture only to the trade, it is now broadening its distribution by opening retail stores in selected cities under the Baker name. Pictured is the retail store in Pittsburgh.

says. "They want to go to a showroom that is sophisticated, is cutting edge and offers the best of the best."

In the 1990s, BKT embarked on a multi-phase strategy to broaden its distribution channels. It not only upgraded its showrooms, which sell to design professionals, but also opened

its first retail stores. By mid-2002, BKT had established retail stores in eight locations, including the Georgetown district of Washington, D.C., the Tribeca area of New York and La Marais, an elegant historic district of Paris. Rachel says the opportunity to sell directly to the public is based on

"the affluence and sophistication of today's consumers."

As in most industries, distribution is critical to the success of any furniture company, yet distribution methods are in flux, reflecting competition from new channels such as the Internet and discount retailers. "As

furniture and accessories from Baker, Milling Road, McGuire and other manufacturers. BKT identifies the most successful approaches — number of square feet, products presented within that space, advertising, etc. — and offers them as a turnkey program to independent dealers who sell Baker products, thereby supporting their marketing efforts. These dealers remain an important element of Baker's distribution strategy. "Showrooms, stores and dealers — we want all our channels to be synchronized for maximum success," Rachel says.

One of Rachel's goals is to stay in the furniture industry vanguard by experimenting with new distribution methods and developing new channels. She notes that other business units within Kohler Co. face similar distribution challenges. "Our success can be leveraged throughout the company," she states.

McGuire Furniture: A High Level of Elegance and Customer Service

McGuire Furniture was founded in 1948 in San Francisco by John and Elinor McGuire, who single-handedly created the market for high-quality rattan furniture in the United States. "Until the McGuires came along, rattan was considered a material for cheap, casual furniture," says Christopher Berg, the company's president from 1993 to 1999. "They treated rattan like a fine wood and

markets evolve, the whole concept of wanting to control more of our own distribution and ensure the proper presentation of our brands is very important," Rachel states.

BKT's retail stores allow the company to experiment with various methods of displaying and marketing

finished it accordingly, bringing elegance and European design references to their products."

The McGuires developed a unique process for using wet rawhide strips to lash each piece of furniture at its joints. When dry, the rawhide tightens to form a strong, permanent binding. Artisans then spend hours transforming the frames by hand staining, glazing and painting several coats of colored lacquers. McGuire furniture is so highly prized that some of the early designs are in the Smithsonian Collection of the Cooper-Hewitt Museum in New York.

The McGuires sold their company and retired in the 1980s, whereupon it changed ownership three times in three years. When Kohler acquired McGuire Furniture in 1990, it was a historically successful business, with an impeccable brand reputation, that was in the midst of some turmoil due to all the ownership changes.

Kohler set about revitalizing the company by updating and expanding its product line. Early classic pieces designed by John and Elinor McGuire and Eleanor Forbes sell well to this day. While continuing to market these pieces, McGuire Furniture began working with some of the world's foremost designers to create new products — the same formula that has been applied so effectively at Baker Furniture.

In 1996, McGuire formed a relationship with Orlando Diaz-Azcuy, a well-known architect and interior designer, to create the Vendôme Collection and the Moiré Collection, inspired by his Cuban heritage and the landscape of his native home. Diaz-Azcuy has been described by *Interior Design* magazine as "a modernist who has frequently explored the deluxe side of minimalism." His work for McGuire encompasses

elegant tables, chairs and other furniture, including McGuire's first upholstered chairs.

The company engaged San Francisco architect Richard Hannum to create the Huxley Series, which features a unique combination of woods, steel and bamboo. And it selected New York architect Adam

Tihany to create the Grand Café Collection, McGuire's first products targeted specifically to the hospitality market. Tihany has designed many of the nation's best-known restaurants, including Le Cirque 2000 and Jean Georges in New York and Spago in Las Vegas and Chicago, and has been described as "the master of illusion"

*I*n the decade after World War II, John and Elinor McGuire created a market for high-quality rattan furniture. Kohler acquired McGuire Furniture Company in 1990. At right is a McGuire room setting.

because of his stunning visual effects. *Nation's Restaurant News* said his "trend-setting dining environments often rival their restaurants' edible offerings in evoking guests' aesthetic appreciation." The chairs and bar-stools in the Grand Café Collection, made from McGuire's signature material, rattan, are comfortable and functional and are distinguished by their design detail.

In 2000, McGuire turned to Michael Vanderbyl, the San Francisco designer responsible for Baker's successful Archetype Collection, to create the first McGuire collection available at retail. Called Archetype for McGuire, the collection combines teak and aluminum in furniture that can be used indoors and out-doors. The aluminum is powder-coated with a lustrous platinum finish and is heat resistant, making the products at once sophisticated for any décor and practical for outdoor use in any climate.

Additionally, in 1997, McGuire entered the lighting market, adding a collection of chic, sophisticated table lamps of hand-crafted, copper repoussé. In 1998, this line grew with the addition of new creations, includ-ing a floor lamp.

Propelled by these and other new products and designs, McGuire doubled its sales from 1995 to 2000.

*M*any of McGuire's products make innovative use of bamboo and rattan. The Faubourg Collection bedroom, above, features a queen bed with a geometric pattern of bamboo veneer marquetry and an oval commode with intricate bamboo veneer patterns.

**Expanding McGuire's
Production Capacity**

As McGuire's sales have increased, Kohler has invested in new production capacity and addressed concerns about McGuire's dependence on a single supplier. For its first half century, McGuire sourced all its product from factories in the Philippines, which had access to local rattan. "While this

*T*he pieces in this setting, designed by Orlando Diaz-Azcuy for McGuire, include the Cambay Woven Sectional and Ventana Cocktail Table.

was a wonderful relationship and the quality was terrific, there was sole source risk," Berg says. "Herb Kohler felt very strongly that we needed to get closer to our raw material sources and have our own manufacturing facility in the Far East if we were to continue to grow and control our own destiny."

Rattan is a solid vine, found deep in the jungle, that grows for years to reach its enormous length and thickness. Because the world's most extensive stands are found on the Indonesian island of Sumatra, McGuire decided to build a factory there. Indonesian law did not allow 100 percent foreign ownership of produc-

tion facilities, so the company formed a partnership, PT Artcraft, with a respected Sumatran businessman.

"We identified this opportunity in the fall of 1994 and put together a joint venture proposal for submission to the Indonesian government," Berg relates. "At the same time, we looked for a factory manager and were very fortunate to find an Irish expatriate named Sean O'Driscoll." O'Driscoll was hired in January 1995, and the company retained an architect and recruited employees while awaiting government approval. That approval came in April 1995. Construction began the next month and advanced on a fast track. The factory was completed in 1996 and the first products were shipped in October of that year.

"One of our decisions which worked out very well was to hire as many local people as possible," Berg says. "Although this meant hiring people who didn't have experience or skill in the furniture industry, the pool of applicants was greater and we were able to train employees in our production methods." The facility manufactures furniture frames that are shipped to McGuire in San Francisco for finishing to order. In addition, it has a growing business of making products for four- and five-star hotels and restaurants worldwide.

Berg concludes, "Our products work nicely with Baker. They're of the same quality level. They have the same design integrity. They are sold through showrooms, as are Baker's.

*C*hristopher Berg headed McGuire Furniture from 1993 to 1999. He came to the company from Esprit International with a mandate to update McGuire's product line, boost sales and develop new production capacity. He was successful in these efforts, with the result that McGuire's sales doubled from 1995 to 2000. He is today a consultant to Kohler Co.'s Interiors Group.

And McGuire, like Baker, is a top brand franchise. I think Herb and Natalie picked two of the gems of the furniture industry and have created a wonderful business for Kohler."

Ann Sacks: Tile, Stone and Distinctive Plumbing Products

The Interiors Group's Ann Sacks business is a trendsetter in tile and stone as well as in high-end plumbing products. Ann Sacks, its founder, is a tiny, energetic woman with a sparkling personality. She is widely credited with having popularized the use of tile and stone as design elements in the home and, because of her leadership role, is sometimes called the

"Queen of Tile." Sacks retired in 2003 after having built the firm into the internationally recognized leader in luxury tile and stone.

"A fairly classic entrepreneurial process led me to start my business," Sacks relates. She became enamored of tile on a family vacation to a Mexican resort when she was a child. In 1980, after having married and had children and having pursued a career as a teacher and social worker, she spotted some hand-painted Mexican tiles being sold as trivets in a gift store. Those trivets rekindled her interest, and she began her company the following year out of her Portland, Oregon, home.

"I ran tiny black-and-white ads," she says, "and found a responsive market." She turned her home into a showroom, covering every floor and wall with tiles — "even the top of my dining room table," she says. In a key step that helped build the business, she offered to integrate colored tile with a customer's other surfaces, including plumbing, carpeting, laminates, paint and fabrics, and she recruited a local craftsman to produce these tiles. This led to the creation of her custom colored tile line, the Ann Sacks Collection, which went on to become the most successful tile program in the country.

By the mid-1980s, she was also offering limestone, marble and granite. At that time, stone was viewed primarily as a commodity. Believing there should be a value-added approach to such a beautiful material, she came up with the idea of designing and distributing stone countertops through Kohler, even though she had no business relationship with Kohler and did not know anyone at the company. She was attracted to Kohler, she says, by the design and quality of its products. "I worked with some of my granite and marble suppliers to find colors that coordinated well with Kohler products," she says, "and I put together a little board with all these colors." Board in hand, she went to an industry design show with the specific purpose of introducing herself to Kohler Co. Through persistence, she was able to arrange a

The Ann Sacks product line encompasses numerous tile and stone patterns, palettes and textures. This floor features Authenticated Antique Belgian Java Stone. Quarried in Belgium in the mid-1800s, the stone was reclaimed from wealthy merchants' homes in Java and used for many years as ballast in old merchant sailing ships. Peppered with ancient fossils and burnished to a rich patina, it has a homogenous black crystalline mass that gives a feeling of stature and elegance.

meeting at 2 a.m. in the hotel lobby with a Kohler Co. marketing executive, Tim Mullally. After looking at her colored stone and learning about her business, Mullally suggested that Kohler Co. might be interested in buying her company, which it did in 1989.

The Ann Sacks firm has been enormously successful as part of Kohler: revenues have advanced from $1.5 million in 1989 to approximately $40 million in 2002. Sacks says this growth has been driven by new products, new showrooms and steady gains in market share. The Ann Sacks product line covers a wide price and style range, and includes art tile, glass, glazed tile, metal, mosaics, slate and other products. About one-third of the company's products are imported, including antique materials like old terra cotta. Sacks personally oversaw the development of new designs. Moreover, the firm is always on the lookout for small digs that unearth unusual stone.

"People associate us with innovation," she says. "While most of the market is very traditional, we've had a bit of a buzz which has enabled us to get attention. We were the first to do glass, the first to do metal. I'm at heart very modern — modern in a warm and sleek manner."

Sacks says that in developing the business her relationships with suppliers were a vital strength. The firm continues to work with many of her original suppliers, including manufacturers, quarries and manufacturers' representatives in Europe, and has formed exclusive relationships with more than 30 artists who design tile. The company has production facilities in Portland and is building a roller hearth kiln in Italy. "Italy is the dominant force in the firing of ceramics and the fabrication of stone," Sacks says. The new kiln will enable the company to produce higher quality products faster and at less cost.

As of 2003, the Ann Sacks firm had 18 company-owned showrooms across the United States and also marketed its products through approximately 20 independent dealers. Each showroom is open to both the public and design trade. In some cases, stores are co-located with BKT showrooms to generate traffic.

The popularity of tile and stone is being driven by the beauty and variety of products and ease of maintenance. Ann Sacks showroom personnel work closely with customers to explore their preferences and explain the many choices available to them. "It's important to fully understand how customers want their homes to feel, as well as look," Sacks asserts. What has set Ann Sacks apart from the crowd is the very personal approach taken with each client, combined with the firm's tremendous variety of colors, patterns and textures.

*A*nn Sacks, above, started her business out of her home and has been called the "Queen of Tile" because of her industry leadership and impeccable taste. Today, the firm sells tile and stone through showrooms and dealers nationwide. Pictured left is Roman Stone with Roman Border.

ince the mid-1980s,
Kohler Co. has greatly
expanded its product
offerings for the kitchen
and the bath. The kitchen
pictured here features
Canac cabinets and Kohler
brand plumbing products.

Even as it has diversified into new businesses, Kohler Co. has devoted significant financial resources and management attention to the continued development of its traditional core business, plumbing products.

Since Herb Kohler became chairman and chief executive officer in 1972, he has taken the plumbing products business that was started by his grandfather, John Michael Kohler — and that was built into the industry's design and quality leader during the tenures of his uncle, Walter Kohler, and his father, Herbert V. Kohler Sr. — and has lifted that business to an entirely new level of performance.

Moreover, continuing in the tradition of active family oversight of the Kohler brand, the Kitchen & Bath Group is headed today by Herb's son, David Kohler, group president. David grew up in the business, working in various manufacturing jobs during his summer vacations while in high school and college. After earning a bachelor's degree in political science from Duke University in 1988, he joined Kohler Co. full-time in manufacturing, soon becoming a foreman in the cast-iron division.

He left in 1990 to attend the Kellogg Graduate School of Management at Northwestern University, receiving a master's degree in marketing in 1992 and joining retailer Dayton Hudson Corporation as a buyer of fine china. One year later, Herb asked David to return to Kohler Co. as director of fixtures marketing. "I had no intention of coming back so quickly," David says, "but I realized marketing was the heart and soul of Kohler Co., and I couldn't turn down the opportunity."

Following his initial assignment in marketing, David was promoted to vice president-sales and then sector vice president and general manager-plumbing North America, becoming sector president in 1997. He was elected group president in 1999, joining Kohler Co.'s board of directors that same year.

David believes his career has been shaped by his background in marketing and sales, as well as by his having worked in manufacturing. "Understanding our business at all levels has been essential for my effectiveness and is also something that my father did," he states.

David describes his business philosophy as "very growth oriented, very optimistic."

Dynamic Growth Opportunities

Plumbing products is an exciting, fast-moving business for Kohler. *Newsweek* magazine reported recently that the typical new American home today has three bathrooms, twice as many as in 1960, and that bathrooms keep getting more spacious and fancier. Products for the bath have reached "a level of opulence in design and materials that would have turned heads in Pompeii," the magazine opined.

The Kathryn Fireclay Console Top, above, is inspired by the artistry of Kohler products at The Metropolitan Museum of Art in 1929 (see page 73). The Kohler Iron Works Historic bath, opposite, is evocative of the materials and icons of the Industrial Revolution. The color of the bath is Cashmere, an organic brown-gray, one of more than 50 colors in the Kohler palette.

*D*avid Kohler is group president-kitchen & bath, heading the company's worldwide plumbing products business. He holds a bachelor's degree in political science from Duke University and a master's degree in marketing from the Kellogg Graduate School of Management at Northwestern University. He worked in various manufacturing, marketing and sales positions at Kohler Co. before assuming his current position in 1999. He describes his management style as "very growth oriented, very optimistic."

Equally powerful is the trend toward larger, more stylish kitchens. Many Americans talk about their "dream kitchen," beautifully laid out with expansive counter space, elegant tile, handsome cabinetry, state-of-the-art plumbing fixtures and the latest appliances.

In addition, outside the United States demand for plumbing products is booming in many developing nations as living standards improve.

To capitalize on these trends, Kohler Co. — the number-one plumbing products manufacturer in the United States, with a growing presence overseas — has been adding new products, new brands, new production technologies, new distribution channels and new geographic markets.

Two decades ago, the company's plumbing products business consisted solely of the Kohler brand. Today, the business encompasses the Kohler brand — healthier than ever — and much more. The Kitchen & Bath Group includes:

Plumbing Americas — The Kohler brand, the mid-priced Sterling brand and the high-end Kallista line in North America, Central America, the Caribbean and South America.

Kohler Europe — The Mira brand in the United Kingdom and Ireland; the Jacob Delafon, Neomediam and Sanijura brands, sold primarily in France, Spain, Morocco and the Middle East; and the Kohler brand in Germany and the Middle East.

Kohler Asia-Pacific — Kohler China, which manufactures and markets Kohler brand products in the People's Republic of China; Kohler Australasia, which manufactures the Kohler and Englefield brands for distribution in Australia, New Zealand and other Pacific nations; Kohler Thailand, which produces Karat brand sanitaryware; and Kohler Japan KK, which provides Kohler products for the Japanese market.

Cabinetry — Canac kitchen cabinets and Robern mirrored bath cabinetry.

Global Faucets — The company's faucet business worldwide.

How the company got from point A (the Kohler brand) to point B (an even more successful Kohler brand, plus other powerful brands in the United States and around the globe) is a pivotal chapter in Kohler Co.'s history.

Kohler Brand: On the Leading Edge of Innovation

Speaking of the diversity, quality and style of the company's products, David Kohler states, "Our goal is to keep advancing the state of the art of the kitchen and the bath, because that's what customers expect from Kohler and that's the way we win in the market."

Indeed, Kohler Co. has a long and

celebrated history of innovation in the plumbing products business. Since 1972, when Herb Kohler became chairman and chief executive officer, one of his priorities has been to continue and even accelerate the pace of innovation, and this has resulted in an outpouring of new Kohler brand products and technologies.

In 1974, Kohler introduced a line of low-consumption toilets, faucets and showerheads to conserve water and reduce the strain on municipal and private sewage systems.

Three years later, in 1977, Kohler launched a line of enameled cast-iron whirlpool baths, the first to be offered by a major full-line plumbing products manufacturer.

Also in 1977, Kohler introduced Environment, the world's first environmental enclosure. With the touch of a button, the user could program the unit to create the effects of sun, gentle rain or warm breezes.

This was followed in 1980 by Super Spa, a fiberglass unit that comfortably seated four to six people, marking Kohler's entry into the spa market.

In 1986, Kohler introduced Autofill, a high-tech bathing system that allows the user to program a whirlpool to fill automatically to a desired level and temperature at a specified time — perfect for the consumer who wants to have a hot bath already drawn on getting up in the morning or on arriving home from work in the evening.

Nineteen ninety-two saw the intro-

Karat Sanitaryware, renamed Kohler Thailand, makes vitreous china products at modern facilities. Its acquisition allows Kohler Co. to further develop its business in Thailand and China, expand in the Asia-Pacific region and serve the U.S. with an additional source of world-class products.

duction of barrier-free plumbing products in response to the issue of universal design for persons with physical limitations and disabilities, as well as the launch of the Peacekeeper seat-actuated flushing system, which keeps peace in the family by flushing the toilet only when the lid is closed.

In 1995, Kohler introduced the high-volume, water-conserving BodySpa bathing system, described by the *Los Angeles Times* as "the Rolls-Royce of home-massage bathing." The unit is a fully enclosed shower stall with a waterfall and a series of six to 10 massage jets mounted on the walls. It recirculates water up to two times per minute. The result is about 80 gallons per minute of hydro-powered jets of water, more than the combined delivery of 25 average showerheads, directed at all the right places to work away tension and stress.

For those who prefer to be hydro-massaged while relaxing in a whirlpool, the Vigora Whirlpool, also new in 1995, is just the ticket. Vigora

features 10 Bodyssage water backjets and two neckjets, as well as two Flexjet whirlpool jets at the bather's feet. For added comfort and support, the ergonomically designed unit cradles the bather in a reclining position. With the touch of a button, the bather can easily adjust both the water massage intensity and pulsation speed, making Vigora ideal for various bathers in a single household or the varying moods of a single bather.

New in the late 1990s were Vessels lavatories — elegant, above-the-counter basins for the bathroom — and the Avatar kitchen faucet, which features sleek, sophisticated styling and a pull-out sprayhead designed around natural hand movements.

Continuing its product leadership, in 1999 Kohler introduced the RiverBath Whirlpool, which massages the body and relaxes the mind by creating the sounds and sensations of an exhilarating waterfall, invigorating rapids or gentle river flow.

One of Kohler Co.'s more unusual

*T*he WaterHaven Shower System integrates a collection of custom showering components with one plumbing connection. Centered around a shower tower with seven easily adjustable water ports, WaterHaven features two dual-direction telescopic shower arms, four ultra-low flow body sprays and a personal hand shower. Each is individually adjustable, up or down and left or right.

new products is the PRO CookCenter, launched in 2000. It combines a kitchen sink and a separate stainless steel "cooking sink," with a heating element, in which to boil, steam and poach food. The cooking sink can be filled directly from the faucet and can be drained with the turn of a dial, eliminating the need to tote water between sink and stove. The *Wall Street Journal* commented with a touch of playful humor, "People have been using kitchen sinks to wash their dishes, rinse fresh vegetables, clean dirty clothes and even bathe babies. Now, they'll be using them to cook pasta." And indeed they are.

Who says there is nothing new in plumbing products? These and numerous other Kohler advances demonstrate the rapid pace of change. A technology seemingly as simple as the flushing mechanism of a toilet has, in fact, undergone a revolution, led by Kohler. By 1974, Kohler had reduced the water consumption of its Wellworth toilet to 3.5 gallons per flush. Today's Wellworth does even better, using 1.6 gallons of water per flush while delivering a superior flushing performance. In comparison to toilets that use more than twice as much water per flush, the Wellworth conserves up to 11,000 gallons per year for a family of four. This water saving not only makes the Wellworth environmentally friendly, it also lowers water and sewer bills and extends the life of a well and septic system. Although many people think all toilets flush alike, that is not the case. The superior performance of the Wellworth and many other Kohler toilets is provided by a siphon jet flushing system. By rapidly filling the trapway with water, the system creates a strong siphonic action that quickly and effectively pulls waste from the bowl. A jet of water finishes the job by cleaning the drain line and removing any waste that may affect the next flush.

Taking flushing technology even further, Kohler offers an exclusive Power Lite system, which employs a 0.2-horsepower electric pump to propel water through the toilet. In combination with the Twin-Touch side-mounted push button, the system allows users to save water by choosing either a 1.1- or 1.6-gallon flush.

The Kohler Mobile Plumbing Systems division, formed in 2002, offers yet another new twist. It makes emergency decontamination units and upscale washrooms housed in trailers. Kohler employees designed and built the company's first mobile washroom in six days as a contribution to rescue workers at the World Trade Center site. As demand poured in from potential customers, Kohler created the new division. Kohler Co.'s decontamination trailers are designed for use by first responders, medical personnel and victims in major fires and biological, chemical or nuclear incidents. Individuals who have been contaminated enter the trailer at one end and go through a six-step showering and decontamination process designed in cooperation with the U.S. Army Biological Task Force. They emerge from the other end "clean." Kohler's mobile washrooms provide

luxurious facilities for concerts, festivals and other events. "Talk about a royal flush," the *Los Angeles Times* said. "Step inside the cushy portable

restroom built by Kohler, and you'll encounter blasts of air-conditioning, a stereo playing New Age music, gold-plated faucets, designer cabinets and a bank of private stalls with solid cherry doors…. If that's too low-rent for your tastes, Kohler can add a whirlpool bath, steam room, waterfall shower and crystal chandeliers."

The list of Kohler technical innovations and creative designs goes on and on, helping propel the company's success in plumbing products. "We take innovation and new products very seriously," David Kohler says, "because we think they are critical to our premium brand positions. We ask

The RiverBath Whirlool, above, envelops the senses by bringing the natural elements, sounds and sensations of a river to the bather's fingertips. The Waterscape Whirlpool, right, includes an integral pillow with neckjet massages for the most stress-sensitive area of the neck.

The Kohler Fairfax single-control faucet, left, blends traditional styling with the ease of single-handle operation at an affordable price. Right, this Kohler PRO CookCenter features the high-arch ProAvatar faucet with a flexible pull-out spray.

each of our businesses to drive a vitality index of at least 20 percent, meaning that we want at least 20 percent of current sales to come from products introduced in the last three years."

Leadership in Consumer Advertising

Kohler has been equally innovative in its advertising — from its pioneering consumer ads of the 1920s to its acclaimed print and television ads of more recent vintage. Herb Kohler says, "There are two primary drivers of the success of the Kohler brand. One is the imaginative concept and design of the products. The other is the very imaginative advertising that allows us to communicate directly with the consumer."

Unlike most competitors, which seek to push sales through their distribution channels by advertising primarily to distributors, plumbing contractors and builders, Kohler seeks to pull sales through its channels by advertising to consumers. Kohler's

goal is to build brand image and create consumer excitement, thereby getting consumers to specify Kohler products for the kitchen and bath.

Two of the company's better-known ad campaigns are the "Edge of Imagination" series of the 1970s, featuring unusual images of plumbing products in surreal settings (see page 151), and the more recent "As I See It" series, illustrated with photographs and paintings by contemporary artists.

David Kohler observes, "Kohler is never going to be about mainstream brand advertising. We're always going to be about unique, provocative, impactful, intriguing advertising that has stopping power and makes people interested in our brand."

Investments in Production Capacity and Technology

As sales of the Kohler brand have increased, Kohler Co. has supported those increases by investing in new manufacturing capacity and advanced

production technologies.

In 1969, the company opened a plant in Toledo, Ohio, complementing existing manufacturing facilities in Kohler, Wisconsin, and Spartanburg, South Carolina. The Toledo plant took Kohler into a new product line — fiberglass-reinforced plastic (FRP) fixtures, including one-piece shower modules and tub-showers. Fiberglass fixtures continue today as a core product area. The Toledo facility operated for 14 years before being closed in 1983 as FRP manufacturing capacity was brought on stream at other Kohler factories.

In 1975, the company opened a plant in Brownwood, Texas, to produce vitreous china, fiberglass and acrylic fixtures. "We needed additional capacity and wanted a site that was well located to serve customers in the Southwest and West," Frank Williams, retired vice president-vitreous and plastics manufacturing, states. "Brownwood has been very successful. We have expanded the facility three times, in 1982, 1995 and 1998, and it is now our largest plumbing products manufacturing operation."

In 1991, Kohler built Sanimex, then the world's most modern vitreous china plant, in Monterrey, Mexico. This facility is not only highly efficient, but is also considered a model of environmental responsibility by the Mexican government. It makes products for the North American market as well as for export beyond.

To ensure that all its plants

Sterling products for the bathroom include the stylish sinks and other products seen here. A lower-to-middle priced brand, Sterling complements the higher-priced Kohler brand. Price differentials between the two are distinguished through materials and levels of detail, not through quality.

continue to be among the most efficient in the industry, Kohler Co. has invested extensively in robotics and other advanced manufacturing technologies. Anthony F. Bocchini, retired vice president-metals and general manager-Kohler Shanghai, says, "In the cast-iron business, we probably have invested more in new technologies in the past 10 to 15 years than any other company. For instance, nobody else in the world has anything near what we have in our use of robotics for cast-iron manufacturing. It took us two years to develop and install our robotics, but Herb had the patience to let us do that."

Also vital is the Kohler Operating System (KOS), a company-wide initiative to infuse lean manufacturing principles in every aspect of the business. Lean manufacturing refers to various techniques aimed at

simplifying processes in order to eliminate waste and improve quality, productivity, safety and responsiveness to the customer. These principles have even been adapted by Kohler to non-manufacturing areas, such as supply chain management and customer service.

KOS brings together techniques such as Kaizen (pioneered by Toyota in Japan) and Six Sigma (developed by General Electric in the United States). Dale Snyder, senior vice president-technical services, says, "We used to build products in large batches and move them in bins down the production line." This sometimes resulted in unneeded effort and wasted material, and it took up large amounts of manufacturing space and tied up large amounts of money in work-in-process and inventory. "The new paradigm," Snyder says, "is a very lean process

where we build pieces one at a time in response to demand." Whereas it used to require as long as two months to produce a finished part, some production processes are now leaned down to as few as four hours.

David Kohler says, "Our core manufacturing strategy is continuous improvement in quality, delivery, cost and safety. Through KOS, we have created tens of millions of dollars of benefits for the organization, and we expect those benefits to continue to grow."

Adding Resources Via Acquisitions

In addition to expanding its plumbing products business through internal development, Kohler has utilized acquisitions as a strategic tool. In its entire 111-year history prior to 1984, Kohler had acquired just one other company. Since 1984, in a dramatic shift, it has purchased more than 20 companies and product lines, not only in products for the kitchen and bath but also in fine furniture and accessories.

"Acquisitions per se are not key to our strategy," Herb Kohler asserts. "They are important only in terms of the capabilities and resources they bring to us." The company has used acquisitions to fill specific needs, including:

- extending its plumbing product line to lower price points, notably with the Sterling brand, and new materials, such as Vikrell;
- entering product areas, such as bathroom and kitchen cabinets and tile, where it did not previously compete;
- expanding into Europe; and
- broadening into new distribution channels, including direct distribution to retail store chains.

In 2001, in its largest acquisition ever, Kohler Co. acquired Mira (subsequently renamed Kohler Mira Ltd.), the leading shower manufacturer in the United Kingdom, for approximately $430 million. Its brands include Mira Showers, Alstone shower enclosures, Meynell valves and Rada shower controls. One trade publication called Mira "the premium name in showers" in the U.K. David Kohler says, "Mira is a terrific fit for us culturally. It's a very well run company with a strong executive team and a significant market share pres-

*S*enior executives posed at the 1984 purchase of Sterling, Kohler's first acquisition in its history. Front row, left to right, are Sam Davis and William Boyd; back row, Herb Kohler, Natalie Black, David Wright and Richard Wells.

ence in the United Kingdom." He adds, "We intend to capitalize on their market presence, bring in other products and build a significant U.K. plumbing products business over time."

Because Kohler Co. is privately owned, it does not have a publicly traded stock that can be used to buy other businesses. Acquisitions have been financed entirely with internal funds and bank loans. Jeffrey P. Cheney, senior vice president-finance and chief financial officer, observes, "We generate a lot of cash internally,

*J*effrey Cheney, senior vice president-finance and chief financial officer, is responsible for financial, accounting, tax and acquisition functions worldwide. He joined Kohler in 1979 and was elected to his current position in 1999.

and the company has a policy to reinvest 90 percent of earnings in the business, including acquisitions. Only 10 percent is paid out to shareholders." Because the company retains such a large portion of its income, Cheney says, "We have never found ourselves in a position where we could not make a planned acquisition for lack of resources."

Kohler Co.'s goal is to achieve an after-tax annual return of at least 12 percent on each investment, whether internal or external.

Acquisitions present a special challenge in this regard. Herb Kohler explains, "Let's say we want to buy a business that is performing well. Perhaps we will have to pay 20 times earnings to acquire that business. If we do, the existing earnings of that business will generate only a five percent

annual return on our investment. We have to get an earnings leap to reach 12 percent. Our objective, therefore, is to buy resources which we can meld with existing resources to make that leap happen." He adds, "If you buy a company and don't find a way to improve its earnings, you have squandered capital."

Developing the Sterling Brand
The acquisition of Sterling Faucet Co. in 1984, and the subsequent development of the full-line Sterling brand, is a prime example of leveraging acquisitions to increase their value.

Sterling was founded in 1907 and

prospered for many years as a leading independent manufacturer of faucets and other brassware. It fell on hard times, however, after being acquired by Rockwell International in 1969. Rockwell de-emphasized wholesale distribution to concentrate on sales of faucets through hardware stores to the do-it-yourself market. That plan did not work as expected, and Sterling lost market share and became unprofitable during its nine years of ownership by Rockwell.

In 1978, Kohler Co. tried to acquire Sterling from Rockwell, but was outbid by an investment group headed by William W. Boyd and David Wright, senior executives of United States Gypsum Company (today called USG Corporation). "Boyd and Wright were able to bid a slightly higher price," Herb Kohler says, "because they had some inexpensive financing from the State of West Virginia that we didn't know about." On acquiring Sterling, Boyd and Wright left USG to manage the company. Over the next six years, they nearly doubled Sterling's sales and restored its profitability by expanding its customer base and reducing its costs. "Then they turned around and sold the company to us at a pretty good profit," Herb remarks, shaking his head as if he still can't believe what happened. Sterling's annual sales were approximately $70 million, primarily from faucets and other brassware, when the company was sold to Kohler. Boyd continued as Sterling's CEO following the transaction.

Kohler was attracted to Sterling for two reasons: it provided a foundation on which to build a mid-priced, full-line plumbing brand, and it gave Kohler entrée to sales through retail stores, a distribution channel that was beginning to grow rapidly. Over the next several years, Kohler acquired other companies to meld with Sterling and fill out the brand. In 1986, Kohler purchased Polar Stainless Products, Inc., the second largest U.S. manufacturer of stainless steel sinks; in 1987, the compressed fiberglass bathtubs and enclosures business of Owens-Corning; and in 1988, USG Corporation's Kinkead Division, the leading manufacturer of tub enclosures and shower doors. The brand name of each was changed to Sterling, contributing to the building of the full-line Sterling brand. In addition, in 1987 Kohler acquired Hytec Manufacturing Ltd., a Canadian manufacturer of fiberglass and acrylic fixtures. Hytec continues to manufacture gelcoat and acrylic bathtubs and showers for wholesale distribution in western Canada and also distributes Sterling products made of solid Vikrell material. To complete the Sterling brand, Kohler Co. began supplying vitreous china products, including toilets and lavatories, from Kohler factories.

To further leverage Sterling, Kohler Co. now manages the Kohler and Sterling brands to achieve

*L*os Angeles interior designer Michael S Smith's classically inspired bathroom fixtures for Kallista include these console table legs. Kallista's designs take their cues from the classics of the past but are refined for today.

manufacturing efficiencies. Just as Kohler factories supply certain products for Sterling, but at different price points and at a different level of design and functionality than Kohler brand products, Sterling's factories manufacture stainless steel sinks and shower doors for the Kohler brand to Kohler specifications. This arrangement is less expensive than having separate manufacturing facilities for the two brands.

In 1991, Boyd stepped aside from day-to-day management to become Sterling's chairman. He continues today as a member of the Kohler board of directors.

It has now been more than a decade and a half since Kohler Co.

acquired Sterling. In that period, Kohler has turned a modest-sized faucet company into a significant full-line brand. Kohler continues to be the number-one selling plumbing products brand in the United States. Sterling has climbed to number three — and continues to grow.

"These two brands, Kohler and Sterling, working in combination with each other in different price segments, become a formidable force going forward," David Kohler remarks.

Kallista: High-End Elegance
Some of Kohler Co.'s acquisitions, such as Kallista, Inc., in 1989, have filled specialty product niches. Whereas Sterling makes products in

Frank Williams, above, retired vice president-vitreous and plastics manufacturing, and Anthony Bocchini, left, retired vice president-metals and general manager-Kohler Shanghai, were key players in opening Kohler Co. manufacturing sites in China.

the mid-to-lower price range, Kallista is at the market's uppermost end. Its products have been described as "the best of the best."

The Kallista line includes luxurious sinks and faucets, vitreous china lavatories, basins and toilets, whirlpools, and two special collections, Retro Kallista and Decorative Kallista. Some of its products are hand crafted, such as an exquisite copper bathtub imported from France.

Much in the way that Kohler Co. has expanded its furniture business by working with leading-edge designers, it has brought influential artists and designers to the table at Kallista as well. These include Barbara Barry, Michael S Smith, Baccarat Inc., Tracy Porter and Mottahedeh & Company. Barry's and Smith's products for Kallista include "glamorous bath fixtures with retro-themed looks from the 1930s and 1940s," in the words of *USA Today*. Baccarat has created a series of high-end faucets featuring crystal knobs. Tracy Porter, the noted Wisconsin artist, has created fanciful painted lavatories and vanities and a magnificent, hand-painted claw-foot bath, while Mottahedeh, the china and dinnerware manufacturer, designs elegant lavatories for Kallista.

Vikrell: Perfecting a New Material

Other acquisitions have brought unique technical capabilities to Kohler Co. Owens-Corning's FRP Components Division, acquired in

1987, had developed a process for making bath and shower enclosures of compressed fiberglass, but the process had limitations. "Owens-Corning got to a point where it could make a bath and wall system with an etched surface," Herb Kohler says. However, an etched surface hides flaws and is therefore considered to be of low to moderate quality. The product was sold primarily to builders of multi-family homes, a relatively small and volatile market. The real challenge was to take the material to its full potential by developing a glossy, flaw-free finish so it could be sold to more profitable end markets, including single-family homes and home remodeling.

"We bought the division from Owens-Corning and through research, through trial and error, and through a hell of a lot of persistence, we were able to develop a high-gloss surface without defects," Herb says. "Today we have an exclusive position as the only manufacturer of this product."

The material carries the brand name Vikrell and competes successfully with enameled steel and fiberglass. "The material not only has a beautiful look, but also is extremely durable and doesn't crack or chip," David Kohler points out. Vikrell material is used for tubs, shower enclosures and other fixtures in both the Kohler and Sterling product lines. Ease of installation is a key benefit. Components made of Vikrell material are modular in design and are

*S*anijura is the largest bathroom cabinet and vanity manufacturer in France. Based in Champagnole, it produces 20 complete lines of bath vanities and other furniture in melamine, laminated and lacquered finishes and is recognized for its product quality and innovation.

shipped in flat packs, and their patented tongue-in-groove interlocking wall system provides a watertight seal and seamless appearance without caulking. "We have focused during the past five years on driving the growth of Vikrell in the U.S. market," David says. "Now we are looking for opportunities to develop markets around the world."

Developing a Global Market Presence

In the late 1980s, with its development of the Sterling brand in full swing, Kohler Co. turned to a second major element of its growth plan in plumbing products — building a strong international presence. Kohler had expanded overseas later than did many of its competitors. Once Kohler got started, however, it proceeded full-bore. As a result, international sales today account for more than 25 percent of Kohler Co.'s revenues, versus approximately five percent when Herb Kohler became CEO in 1972.

Kohler initially stepped up its global sales through exports, particularly to Asia. By 1983, Kohler Co. was the leading exporter of plumbing products to the People's Republic of

China. Three years later, it established Kohler Japan KK, a marketing organization in Tokyo. It has since expanded its export presence worldwide.

But that was only the beginning. With exports climbing, the company began to develop an overseas manufacturing capability, initially through acquisitions in Europe and more recently by building plants in China.

In 1986, Kohler expanded to France by acquiring Jacob Delafon (formerly Compagnie Internationale Des Produits Sanitaires), subsequently renaming the company Kohler France, SAS. The Jacob Delafon brand, more than a century old, is that nation's best-known plumbing

*K*ohler France, SAS, is headquartered on the rue de Turenne in Paris. It manufactures and markets the Jacob Delafon brand, one of Europe's oldest and most esteemed names in bathroom fixtures.

products line. It includes cast-iron, steel and vitreous china fixtures, faucets and small vanity cabinets made at factories in France, Spain, Morocco and Egypt. Products are distributed not only in France, but also in much of the rest of Europe and in the Middle East.

Seven years after acquiring Jacob Delafon, Kohler Co. purchased Sanijura S.A., the largest bathroom cabinet and vanity manufacturer in France. In 1995, it acquired Holdiam S.A., a leading French manufacturer of acrylic baths and whirlpools, synthetic kitchen sinks and artistic faucets.

Kohler now has a major position

*P*ictured is an elegant bath by Holdiam, a leading French manufacturer of acrylic baths, whirlpools, synthetic kitchen sinks and artistic faucets. Kohler acquired Holdiam in 1995.

In 1995, Kohler Co. formed its Foshan Kohler Ltd. joint venture pottery in Guangdong Province in the People's Republic of China to manufacture select models from Kohler, Jacob Delafon and Sterling for the Chinese market. The facility is one of three Kohler plants in China opened since the mid-1990s.

in the French plumbing products market through the continued development of the businesses it acquired there.

In Germany, Kohler is breaking the mold of how it does business elsewhere in the world. Herb says, "Here was Kohler, manufacturing in Europe, yet not selling anything in Germany, Europe's largest market. We debated for years how to enter that market." In 1998, Kohler Co. resolved the matter by signing on with OBI, Germany's leading home-improvement chain. Selling at retail in Germany through OBI stores contrasts with Kohler Co.'s primary use of wholesale distributors elsewhere and represents an interesting twist.

In the United States, the growth of home-improvement retail stores is putting pressure on wholesalers. In Germany, Kohler Co. is the one exerting the pressure. Plumbing product wholesalers in Germany typically cherry pick each manufacturer's goods — that is, they distribute ceramics from one company, cast-iron enamelware from another, faucets from another and so on. "We chose retail," Herb explains, "because it is the only distribution channel in Germany that could offer a full presentation of our products." He adds, "In going retail, we've done an end run around the German plumbing products industry. German manufacturers cannot do what we have done

because they are dependent on the wholesalers."

In a further innovation, Kohler Co. is taking several of its brands — including Canac, Robern and Jacob Delafon, as well as Kohler — and marketing all of them in Germany under the Kohler name to build a single brand identity. Products are being supplied from Kohler Co. plants in Europe and the United States.

"With so much communications clutter, it has become more important than ever to establish and protect our brands," says Laura Kohler, senior vice president-human resources and former vice president-communications. "The companies that have been most successful globally, such as Coca-Cola, have built a consistent and recognizable brand image worldwide. We are doing the same with the Kohler brand."

Following up on its approach in Germany, in 2000 Kohler Co. formed an alliance with Internacional de Cerámica (Interceramic) to sell Kohler brand plumbing products at retail in Mexico. Interceramic is Mexico's leading retailer of tile, with approximately 200 stores across the nation. "The Interceramic relationship gives us excellent representation in their showrooms, which are very beautiful," David Kohler says. Kohler Co. also acquired a minority equity position in Interceramic.

In Asia, Kohler Co.'s major focus is on the People's Republic of China, where the company is manufacturing

Kohler brand plumbing products for domestic consumption. Three production facilities, all commissioned between 1995 and 1998, are a pottery in Foshan, a faucet plant in Beijing, and a cast iron and acrylics plant near Shanghai. Tony Bocchini says the three facilities provide a starting point as Kohler develops a market presence in China, including establishing distribution channels and building a brand identity through consumer advertis-

*A*bove, Kohler Co. had already established a leading export position in China when Herb Kohler visited the nation in 1983. Left, the Shanghai Kohler, Ltd., plant, opened in 1998, manufactures cast-iron and acrylic bathtubs and whirlpools.

*I*n 1998, Kohler Co. established a separate global faucet business to support the sector's growth. The business is headed by James Westdorp, sector president. He directs all aspects of global faucets, encompassing eight manufacturing sites and covering the Kohler, Sterling, Jacob Delafon, Meynell, Mira and Rada faucet brands.

ing and other marketing techniques. The Chinese plumbing products market is growing robustly and one day may surpass the United States as the world's largest. In 2001, Kohler became the number-one selling brand at the highest end of the Chinese market. "We have a great foothold in China," David Kohler points out, adding, "Our opportunity throughout Asia is unlimited. More than 60 percent of the world's population lives in Asia, and over half that population is under 25. We intend to build a large business in the Asia-Pacific region over the next 10 to 15 years."

Kohler Co. further extended its market presence in 2000 by acquiring Englefield Bathroomware of Auckland, New Zealand. The company is the number-one manufacturer of acrylic bathroom fixtures, including shower enclosures, baths, spa baths, vanities and accessories, in New Zealand and

number two in Australia. Products are distributed not only in those countries, but also in Europe, the Middle East, South America and Asia. A chief benefit for Kohler is aligning with a leading regional bathroom fixture manufacturer that has plants, people and distribution throughout the Pacific Rim. Most of Englefield's products have been rebranded as Kohler.

In the 1970s, Kohler Co. captured the lead in the U.S. plumbing products market. It has now set its sights on gaining world leadership.

Bolstering Worldwide Sales of Faucets

As part of its globalization, in 1998 Kohler Co. established a separate global faucet business within the Kitchen & Bath Group. Kohler manufactures faucets at plants in Wisconsin, Arkansas, England, Egypt and

China. The new unit directs all aspects of the company's faucet business across brands, worldwide. It is led by James Westdorp, sector president, who has been with Kohler since 1981.

As is true of other products for the kitchen and bath, faucets are an exciting, highly competitive category. New designs continue to capture the imagination of consumers. *Architectural Record* magazine said, for instance, that the Kohler wall-mounted Falling Water faucet, with its spare elegance, is "sure to appeal to any architect." And the Sterling Progression faucet, targeted to the do-it-yourself market, simplifies installation by allowing the job to be completed almost entirely from above the sink. Even *Popular Mechanics* magazine has taken up the subject, stating, "If you haven't shopped for a faucet lately, you may be surprised at the swell of options. Not only is there more variety today, but warranties are longer, water-control mechanisms are improved, more features are available, safety and conservation are frequently built in, and many design flourishes are genuinely impressive."

Global coordination of Kohler Co.'s faucet business provides manufacturing efficiencies and facilitates the worldwide introduction of new faucet designs. "The components for most of our faucets are made on more than one continent," David Kohler states. "As a result, we can be

*L*aura Kohler is senior vice president-human resources with worldwide responsibility for human resources development. After earning a bachelor's degree from Duke and a master's degree from Catholic University, she worked in theater and as a teamwork instructor at Outward Bound. She became executive director of Kohler Foundation, Inc., in 1992, joining Kohler Co. in 1995 as director-public affairs. She became vice president-communications in 1998 and assumed her current position in 1999.

cost effective with standard manufacturing platforms worldwide, while adapting products to local markets."

Recruiting, Training, Compensating and Keeping the Best People

Globalization has also led to changes in Kohler Co.'s human resource programs, not just in plumbing products, but throughout the company.

This effort is led by Laura Kohler, senior vice president-human resources. Laura, who is Herb's oldest child, graduated from Duke University in 1984 with majors in political science and theater and earned a master's degree from Catholic University. She enjoyed a career in theater — performing with the National Players, a classical company in Washington, D.C., and founding Address Unknown, a Chicago-based performing ensemble of homeless people — before joining Outward Bound as an instructor in corporate teamwork development. She was appointed executive director of Kohler Foundation, Inc., in 1992 and

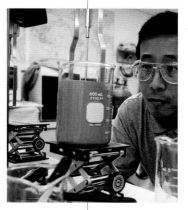

*K*ou Yang is a slip and glaze technician in the pottery in Kohler Village.

The sôk overflowing bath is a tub within a tub. Its gently bubbling water continuously overflows into the outer tub, where it is maintained at a constant temperature and recirculated. The sôk bath at right is pictured with a ceiling-mount laminar flow bath filler. Laminar flow technology allows the flowing water to impact the bath surface with barely a ripple. Left, a bather relaxes in a sôk bath with chromatherapy.

joined Kohler Co. as director-public affairs in 1995, becoming vice president-communications in 1998. In 1999, she was appointed vice president-human resources and was elected to the Kohler Co. board of directors, becoming senior vice president in 2002.

Laura notes that Kohler Co. used to compete for employees primarily in Wisconsin and against other plumbing products manufacturers. "We have to operate differently as a global company," she adds. "We are now competing with every other business in the world for talented people." Consequently, the company has strengthened and refocused its human resource programs in all areas, including performance man-agement, recruitment, compensation, benefits, associate learning and suc-cession planning, to ensure they are world class.

A primary thrust has been to decentralize the human resource function, integrating it more effec-tively into each of the business units. "We are giving each business the flexi-bility to respond to local needs and local cultural distinctions," she says. "At the same time, all our businesses must adhere to a common set of cor-porate policies."

"This is a time of huge change for the company," she says. "As we become more global, how we hire, train, compensate and keep people will be very important to our success."

Growth in Cabinetry: New Designs for the Home

In addition to the creation of the Sterling brand and international expansion, cabinetry and tile is a third major element of Kohler Co.'s growth strategy for the kitchen and bath. Kohler has entered these businesses through the acquisition of premier brands, including Ann Sacks in 1989, Robern in 1995 and Canac in 1996. The Ann Sacks business is part of the Interiors Group, while Robern and Canac reside within the Kitchen & Bath Group.

"Our plumbing products business has become much stronger because of cabinetry and tile," Herb Kohler submits. "We are driving for the entire bathroom and the entire kitchen. And as we go after the kitchen, with the evolving definition of the home — the kitchen and the great room merging, and the great room melding into the living room — furniture and furnishings start creeping in. So they all begin to work together."

The Robern cabinetry firm got its start in 1968 when Bernard Meyers, then a regional sales manager for a bathroom accessories manufacturer, decided to go into business for himself. The name of the company derives from the first two letters of his wife's name, Rosa, and the first four

Bernard Meyers is founder and past president of Robern, a Kohler company since 1995. Robern makes top-of-the-line mirrored bathroom cabinets, lighting, accessories and glass consoles. Many of its products are modular and can be mixed and matched to create a system unique to the customer's bathroom. At left are a Robern glass console and mirrored cabinet with dimmable fluorescent lights, in combination with a Kohler Vessels lavatory and Falling Water faucet. The cabinet at right features a door defogger, interior electrical outlets and safety lock box for drugs and valuables.

of his, Bernard. With money he and Rosa were saving for a new house, Meyers started distributing bathroom and building supply products from the garage of their Philadelphia home. In the early 1970s, recognizing that the market lacked an easy-to-install mirrored sliding-door bathroom cabinet, Robern designed and began manufacturing its first product, the MirroWall. Ten years later, Robern upgraded its products to include top-of-the-line cabinets, and that has been the focus ever since. "At first we struggled. It was really a new direction for us," Meyers says. "But our staff was loyal and persevered, and Robern developed the best in product and services."

"Fifty years ago," Meyers adds, "all the things you used in a bathroom could fit into a 14-inch-by-18-inch metal cabinet. Now we have drug stores as large as supermarkets and lots of electrical appliances that need recharging. Robern takes care of all of that, and more, by building in user-friendly features like a defogging door, interior electrical outlets, a safety lock box for drugs and valuables, and a magnifying mirror for up-close tasks."

Canac Kitchens, Kohler Co.'s other major unit in cabinetry, was founded in 1966 in Thornhill, Ontario. It is a premier manufacturer of wood cabinetry for the kitchen and bath, selling its products through 120 company-exclusive showrooms across North America. Kohler bought the

company not only because of the quality and distinctiveness of its products, but also because Canac possesses three major competitive advantages: 1) the highest unit production per square foot of manufacturing space in the industry; 2) a distribution system that is devoted entirely to Canac; and 3) Canac's policy, unusual in its industry, of guaranteeing the final installation of its products.

Canac's cabinetry products consist of the Signature Series, Cellini Series and Ultra Series, each of which embraces Canac's pride of craftsman-

*P*ictured here and opposite are examples of Canac products for the kitchen. The company makes custom kitchen and bathroom cabinetry, as well as peninsulas and islands, for discriminating homeowners. Canac became part of Kohler in 1996.

ship and its "eye towards style in every product we create," in the words of Michael Golden, president of Kohler Cabinetry. *FDM Magazine*, which covers the furniture industry, remarked that "just as spices add flavor to a meal," new designs in wood cabinets "are adding flavor to the kitchen." The magazine praised the style and originality of Canac products, singling out designs such as a Mission-style oak door featuring "an intricate stained glass pattern…and distinctive wrought-iron enhancements" and an Oxford maple cabinet door lacquered in a honey stain.

Seeking Synergies Across Product Lines

Having diversified its plumbing products business, Kohler Co. is addressing some significant opportunities

and concerns. One issue is whether Kohler can capitalize on potential synergies by selling various products in conjunction with one another. As Herb puts it, "Will the sale of a medicine cabinet enhance the opportunity for selling a bathroom lavatory? Or a kitchen cabinet a kitchen sink? Or will all these products continue to sell independently of each other through their own distribution channels?"

The company is cross-selling various brands by offering incentives to buyers of multiple products. "We can leverage a bundle of products with some effectiveness to builders, big retailers and wholesalers," Herb says. The cost of the discount is less than the cost to Kohler of selling each product independently. And in Germany, as we have seen, the company is selling Kohler and Jacob

David Kohler meets with Kohler Thailand executives. Left to right are Mr. Visit Ruttanastian, manager, plant no. 2; Capt. Roongroj Komolmal, technology manager; Mr. Jaru Narksen, product development manager; and Mr. Chanchai Homsethie, assistant managing director. Kohler Thailand is one of the largest manufacturers of vitreous china sanitaryware in Asia.

ment retailer. David Kohler says, "We finally decided that to maintain and enhance our position with the consumer, we had to add this retail chain to our portfolio." Subsequently, Kohler extended its retail distribution to Lowe's Home Improvement Warehouse, another major do-it-yourself home products retailer.

David Kohler continues, "When we initiated this policy of selling through Home Depot, there was a lot of consternation in our wholesale community. But I think for the most part that community has adjusted very well. They've found ways to compete against do-it-yourself chains and thrive."

Abe Kogan, president of Builders Plumbing & Heating Supply Co., a major Kohler distributor near Chicago, says, "Kohler was really the last major company in the industry to resist selling to the retail market. Therefore, when Kohler changed its mind, I did not call Herb Kohler to complain. He was the last one and I could understand his viewpoint. I feel he will protect his distributors, who have helped make Kohler Co. what it is today."

Like many wholesalers, Kogan is himself adjusting, finding new ways to meet the evolving needs and preferences of consumers. His company has opened a public showroom to compete directly with retail chains, something he never would have considered in the past. "I don't worry about Home Depot," he says. "I can compete because I carry a much larger

Delafon fixtures and faucets, together with Canac cabinetry and Robern mirrored cabinets, under the single brand name of Kohler. The company continues to experiment with ways in which to cross-sell products.

Changes in distribution patterns are another crucial question. In the United States, Kohler Co. has traditionally distributed Kohler brand products exclusively through a network of 700 independent wholesalers. That network has been vital to the company's success. However, as in many other industries, established distribution methods are being challenged by new channels, including retail store chains and the Internet.

For many years, Kohler Co. resisted direct sales of the Kohler

brand to retailers. "Then along comes this phenomenon called the home center store," Herb points out. "And the home center starts to sell 50 percent of the faucets sold in the United States. And it starts to sell high percentages of fixtures. And it's growing at double-digit rates per year. So you have to make a decision. Do you play on this side of the road [wholesalers] and only on this side? Can you have any hope of maintaining your position if you only play on this side of the road, when the other side is attracting more and more consumers?"

In 1995, Kohler Co. began selling Kohler brand products directly to The Home Depot, the nation's largest and fastest-growing home improve-

stock and I service better."

Herb Kohler mentions another wholesaler that is opening retail stores next to Home Depot outlets, knowing there will be a concentration of consumer traffic.

Kohler Co. has gone about selling products through The Home Depot in an unusual way. "We have taken over the responsibility of the presentation of our product in Home Depot stores even though it adds to our costs," according to Ronald Pace, sector president-plumbing Americas. "This was done at Herb Kohler's insistence, to make sure the presentation is correct and the experience of the consumer is positive. He is very concerned about maintaining the Kohler image. He gets very upset if that image is tarnished in any way."

Even as it explores new distribution methods, Kohler Co. remains committed to wholesale distributors as its primary customers. They continue to represent the lion's share of Kohler brand sales and are central to the company's past, present and future. To support its wholesalers' continued growth, Kohler Co. has developed a premier showroom concept that it shares with them. In addition, the company is opening the first Kohler-owned retail store, which it is refining as a prototype for its wholesale distributors.

Herb makes clear, "We will be very careful not to do anything to damage the value of the Kohler brand to our distributors."

*M*ary Reid is director-advanced concept development, Kitchen & Bath Group. Formerly vice president-industrial design, she has helped build a strong Kohler design competence that supports the company's leadership in the kitchen and bath market.

Kohler Co.'s plumbing products business has come a long way in the past two decades in terms of new products, new brands, new production technologies, new distribution channels and new geographic markets. By keeping on the leading edge of design, innovation and marketing, it continues to deliver strong revenue and earnings growth.

*R*onald Pace is sector president-plumbing Americas. He recently said, "There's a concept called 'brand experience,' which goes beyond style and delivery. It goes to quality, to service, to packaging, to instructions. The value that brand experience has to consumers is what we consider important. The supreme compliment would be for anyone to say, 'You're a pleasure to do business with and I'd like to do business with you again.' That's what the brand experience means to us."

The Kohler Co.
mission is to enhance the
gracious living of all those
touched by its products and
services. The American
Club, shown here in a
beautiful winter setting, is
an example of that mission
in action.

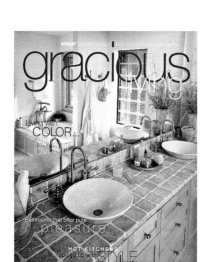

*G*racious Living

magazine highlights Kohler

products for the home.

Right, the sôk overflowing

bath with chromatherapy

relaxes the bather not

only with gently bubbling

water, but also with colors

transmitted via four internal

LED light ports. Research

has shown that color can

enhance feelings of

well-being and comfort.

*A*s Kohler Co. looks to the future, it is guided by one of the most unusual mission statements in corporate America.

Many companies have mission statements that emphasize the need to maximize earnings or achieve a specified rate of return on capital. Kohler Co.'s mission, by contrast, is to "contribute to a higher level of gracious living for those who are touched by our products and services." "Gracious living," the Kohler mission statement explains, "is marked by qualities of charm, good taste and generosity of spirit. It is further characterized by self-fulfillment and the enhancement of nature."

Is this mission statement merely pie in the sky? Or does it have real meaning in today's harsh and highly competitive business world?

Herb Kohler insists that Kohler Co.'s mission statement provides clear direction to the company and its business groups — and, in doing so, helps link the four groups by ensuring that each is focused on the same values and objectives.

What "Gracious Living" Means to Kohler Co.

Part of "gracious living" is to create distinctive, beautiful products and provide first-class services. "To realize our mission," Herb Kohler says, "our quality must be superb across all price points and our products must be unique and innovative across all categories. They cannot be copies or

*R*espect for the environment is a core Kohler value, as exemplified by the Sheboygan River, which weaves its way through Kohler Village. Kohler Co. has preserved rather than developed the river valley, safeguarding it for future generations.

we won't contribute to gracious living for anybody."

Indeed, as we have seen throughout this book, Kohler Co. has a long and remarkable history of developing cutting-edge products and services that add value for the customer — from the first one-piece enameled bathtub in 1911 to the many innovative plumbing products introduced in the '70s, '80s and '90s and now into the twenty-first century; from superb furniture that is in the vanguard of quality and design to four of the world's most renowned golf courses at Blackwolf Run and Whistling Straits. Even Kohler engines and generators, although hardly thought of as elegant, contribute to gracious living through their technical innovation, reliability and trouble-free maintenance.

However, gracious living goes well beyond products and services to encompass every aspect of the relationship between Kohler Co. and its customers. "To fulfill our mission," Laura Kohler says, "we must make the customer's overall experience of dealing with Kohler Co. as pleasant and trouble-free as possible." This means, for instance, that Kohler products and services should be easy to understand, easy to buy and easy to use. In addition, customer complaints must be answered promptly and courteously, and any product or service flaws must be acknowledged and rectified.

Because it encompasses every

detail of the company's relationship with its customers, the Kohler Co. mission statement sets an exacting standard for the company and its people. Consequently, the mission statement is anything but "pie in the sky." To the contrary, it is grounded in the tried-and-true principle that the customer comes first — that by doing a superior job for the customer and managing operations efficiently, profitability will follow. Such a philosophy is a smart way to run any business.

Summing up, Herb says, "Gracious living to me is being delighted by a product or service every time you experience it or remember it. You're delighted. It continues to stand out in your mind as something you have enjoyed amidst all the material things we encounter in life. This means that the product or experience hasn't given you a hassle. It has truly delighted. How many things in life delight you day in and day out? Not that many. That's what gracious living is about. We are trying to give people a higher sense of well-being. And we have to work hard to do so and stay on top in each of our businesses."

Sensitivity to the Natural Environment

The mission statement also makes clear that gracious living includes "the enhancement of nature," meaning that operations are conducted in harmony with the natural

environment. In this book, we have seen several examples of this commitment, including the development of Blackwolf Run with sensitivity to the surrounding landscape and the preservation of a valley where eagles roost on company-owned land on the Mississippi River. Moreover, long before "environmental protection" was a phrase in the American lexicon, Walter Kohler developed Kohler Village with a goal of preserving the Sheboygan River valley, local woodlands and other natural resources. No one forced him to do that. There were few if any environmental laws on the books at the time. He did so simply because he thought it was the right thing to do and was the best way to safeguard the natural environment for future generations.

Kohler Co.'s environmental programs and sensitivity to nature have been recognized with numerous awards ranging from the Wisconsin Wildlife Habitat Award to the 1995 and 1996 Wisconsin Governor's Award for Hazardous Waste Reduction, the first time any company ever received the Governor's Award two years in a row. The National Association for Environmental Management, in honoring Kohler Co., noted that its growth in Kohler Village and the growth of the village itself have been successfully guided by a long-range plan that emphasizes the delicate balance between man and nature, and between a company, a community and the river valley they share.

*B*eginning with a 560-acre pancake-flat parcel of land on the Lake Michigan shore, Kohler Co. and designer Pete Dye brought in 13,126 truckloads of sand to create Whistling Straits, one of the most acclaimed golf venues in the United States. Pictured is the par four 13th hole, Cliff Hanger, of the Straits Course. The Straits Course is characterized by open, rugged and windswept terrain, while the grass-land-and-dunes Irish Course — just inland and interspersed by four streams — offers a more tranquil landscape.

Four Keys to Kohler Co.'s Long-Term Success

Although Kohler Co.'s mission statement is of relatively recent vintage, it reflects the fundamental principles that have guided the company since its founding in 1873. In fact, four major attributes help explain the company's staying power through two world wars, the Great Depression and other momentous events and underpin its success as one of the premier privately owned businesses in the world today:

The creativity of its leaders and their willingness to take risk. The company has been blessed with extraordinary leadership. Each family member who has headed the company — John Michael Kohler, his sons Robert, Walter, and Herbert Sr., and Herbert's son, Herbert Jr. — has been an individualist who has thought and acted boldly. "This is a company where the leaders don't always think in conventional ways or solve problems in conventional ways," Natalie Black comments. Many of Kohler Co.'s most unconventional decisions — such as moving the foundry to farmland in 1900, entering the electrical generator business in the 1920s, resisting a union shop in the late 1950s and creating "Destination Kohler" beginning in the 1980s — were so controversial or misunderstood at the time that they were frowned upon or even mocked. Yet, in each

case, they reflected the judgment of a leader who managed the company with confidence and was willing to take decisive action regardless of what others thought.

Long-term perspective. Throughout its history, Kohler Co. has maintained a "generational" approach to investing — that is, it has invested to create lasting value rather than for a quick payoff. This approach sets Kohler apart from the thousands of companies engaged in a frenzied race for ever-higher quarterly profits. Of course, increasing earnings quarter

*N*ew York interior architect Bill Sofield's collection for Baker includes the formal dining room, left, and the Kiosk Butler's Cabinet, Tusk Table (which looks like a footstool) and Library Case, above. Featured in the dining room are the Cheval Dining Room Table, Cheval Arm and Side Chairs, Steamer Sideboard (left) and Pavilion Storer (right). Sofield's work is known for its modernist simplicity and functionality. *House Beautiful* has described his designs as "super-stylish and resoundingly trendsetting."

by quarter is a noteworthy accomplishment for any company, and Kohler cannot ignore its near-term financial results. However, as a privately owned enterprise, Kohler Co. has great leeway to think and act long-term to build value for the next generation of consumers, not for the mutual fund that bought the stock yesterday and hopes to sell at a profit tomorrow.

Not many corporations would have created a 50-year master plan for the coordinated development of a village, and then created a second 50-year plan when the first one expired. Generational investing also enables

A removable personal hand shower is one of seven easily adjustable water ports in the WaterHaven Showering System. "The latest technology, innovative options and creative thinking," a company publication states, "result in showering experiences that move beyond the ordinary to customized environments."

Japanese plumbing products supplier, followed suit in 1994. Kohler finally commissioned its first plant in 1995. "We were a bit late to invest in manufacturing facilities," Herb acknowledges. However, when Kohler Co. made its move, it did so aggressively, opening three plants in China between 1995 and 1998. Having established a manufacturing base, the company began to build its market presence by applying the same principles it has applied to capture the number-one position in plumbing products in the United States: leading-edge design and a continuous flow of new products; creative advertising targeted directly to the consumer; and efficient operations. By investing for the long term and following these principles, Kohler is now the top-selling brand in the mid-to-high end of the Chinese plumbing products market, with significant opportunities for ongoing growth.

Kohler Co. to undertake projects that do not pay off immediately but can add tremendous value over time. The building of a successful hospitality business over a period of two decades is one example. The company's investments in the People's Republic of China are another. Kohler Co. first exported plumbing fixtures to China in the 1920s. Then in 1978, as that nation was being reopened to foreign trade and investment, Herb Kohler personally visited China. This led to renewed Kohler exports beginning

with a landmark order from five major hotels in 1980 — the first sales in China by an international plumbing products company in four decades. Herb returned to China in 1983 with a team of Kohler Co. executives to explore potential investments in manufacturing. Rather than investing at that time, however, Kohler Co. elected to wait until the right opportunities came along. Meanwhile, American Standard opened its first joint venture factory in China in 1984 and TOTO Ltd., the

Single level of quality and history of innovation. Quality and innovation are deeply ingrained in the Kohler Co. culture. Few other corporations in the world have been innovation leaders in their industries so consistently for so long, and few brands can match Kohler as an imprimatur of excellence. Other Kohler Co. brands, including Robern, Kallista, Mira, Neomediam, Canac, Sterling, Sanijura, Jacob Delafon, Ann Sacks, Baker and McGuire, are equally prestigious in their markets.

Kohler has not only invented specific products and services, but has also created entire new product categories, such as two-person bathtubs; environmental enclosures that envelop the user in sun, gentle rain or wind; pump toilets that use less water by employing an electric pump to help flush the bowl; and "flat" sinks based on the application of laminar flow technology. It has also pioneered innovative business concepts, such as enlisting top interior designers to create distinctive furniture and bath products.

Herb Kohler states that innova-

*H*ome computers and other electronic equipment, above, are spurring demand for reliable electrical power. The Kohler standby generator, right, switches on automatically when utility power is interrupted. It can be fueled by natural gas or propane, and its housing is weatherproof and sound-deadened.

Private ownership. Because their family name is imprinted on the corporate letterhead and on the company's products, Kohler Co. is, to the Kohlers, more than just a business being run to make a profit. They are guided by a commitment to good stewardship. Each generation has sought to preserve the company and hand it on, in better shape, to the next generation. "That is both the blessing and the burden," Natalie Black says. The intense personal involvement of the Kohlers in the company has been true since Kohler Co.'s beginnings and is true today. Indeed, if you know Herb Kohler, you realize he is motivated by an incredible passion for the family heritage and a desire to lead the company to ever greater success, building on what his father, uncles and grandfather accomplished before him. The Kohler family heritage provides a competitive advantage by ensuring that the owners of the business will do everything within their power to maintain the highest standards of product quality and customer service.

A Heritage of Quality, and the Ability to Lead Change
Established in Sheboygan, Wisconsin, in 1873 in the midst of a depression by an immigrant salesman turned foundryman, Kohler Co. is today the world design leader in products for the kitchen and bath and holds strong positions as well in the generator and engine, furniture, and hospitality busi-

*T*he major theme of Kohler Co.'s 125th birthday celebration in 1998 was the craftsmanship of its employees. Kohler continues as one of the oldest and most successful privately owned companies in America.

tion and quality remain keys to Kohler Co.'s future, adding that one of his priorities as CEO is to ensure that Kohler Co. never succumbs to the ordinary or imitative. "It is human nature for people to copy or take a me-too approach," he observes. "The proven idea is a lot safer than the adventurous. However, reliance on proven ideas can destroy a company in the long run. I've always fashioned my job as president of this company as trying to keep people on the forefront."

*T*he Purist lavatory is a unique flat sink. It is pictured with a laminar flow faucet that aligns water molecules so they do not splash. The water rolls gently off the hands, onto the surface and into the surrounding channel. Laminar flow conserves water by getting hands wet faster and allowing lower flows to feel like higher flows.

nesses. The company has grown from a small cast-iron and steel foundry with 21 employees serving local markets to a world-class enterprise with 25,000 associates and 46 manufacturing plants encircling the globe.

John Michael Kohler, the company's founder, would doubtless be astonished by the scope of the company's operations today. He would not be surprised in the least, however

— and would certainly be pleased — by the high quality of Kohler Co.'s products and services and the company's dedication to innovation through a mix of technology and art, attributes that have characterized Kohler Co. from its beginning.

Kohler Co. has been on a remarkable journey of growth and change for well over a century. The journey continues. Each and every day,

Kohler and its people are forging ahead, creating new products and services and capitalizing on opportunities around the world — succeeding through excellence and by staying at the forefront of change. As Herb Kohler makes clear, "We are a strong, independent company with a rich heritage and youthful eyes, focused on that considerable potential we have yet to accomplish."

Acknowledgments

In writing about Kohler Co., I have had a great deal of help from many people. I am deeply grateful to them all and wish, in particular, to thank the following.

Few executives are as passionate about corporate history as Herb Kohler. He believes the history of Kohler Co. is not only an interesting story in its own right, but also provides guidance for managing the company today and tomorrow. His management philosophy is based on leveraging the company's traditions and values, rather than ignoring or rejecting them. In Herb's view, the time had come to put Kohler Co.'s story in print so it would not be lost. Thus, this book was born. Herb spent dozens of hours with me, sharing his ideas and discussing his business plans and strategies. I love immersing myself in writing corporate histories, and I found my match in Herb. Over a period of six years, this book became as much of an obsession for him as it did for me.

Preparing the book was a collaborative process. Natalie Black, Kohler Co.'s senior vice president, general counsel and corporate secretary, and Laura Kohler, senior vice president-human resources, were actively involved every step of the way, helping shape the book's contents.

Pete Fetterer, who retired recently as Kohler Co.'s manager of civic services, and Cheryl Prepster, the company's archivist, made vital contributions. Time and again, when I needed help in researching questions about the company or the family, they not only found the information I needed but also delved further to come up with colorful anecdotes and interesting facts — just the type of material any author would die for.

Others who contributed significantly include Ruth Kohler, director of the John Michael Kohler Arts Center, who shared many wonderful stories about the family and the company; Mike Kohler, a member of the Kohler Co. board of directors and retired vice president, whose knowledge of the company's history is extraordinary; and Cindy Howley, Kohler Co.'s manager-Design Center and civic services, who provided valuable editorial guidance.

Sadly, Mowry Mann, the founder and president of Greenwich Publishing Group, Inc., the publisher of this book, died in early 2002 before its publication. He was personally active in the development of the book and would be proud, I think, of the finished product. John Hostnik, Mowry's colleague at Greenwich Publishing, was enthusiastic in his support and skilled in his editing. He carries on Mowry's tradition of quality corporate history publishing.

When I began this book, I knew nothing about Kohler Co. except that the toilet and lavatory in my apartment bear the Kohler brand, an imprimatur of the highest quality. My journey in learning about the company, and in putting what I have learned into writing, was not only fascinating but also great fun.

Richard Blodgett
New York
September 2003

Timeline

1844
John Michael Kohler, Kohler Co.'s founder, is born in Austria.

1854
Kohler family immigrates to the United States.

1871
John Michael Kohler marries Lillie Vollrath of Sheboygan, Wisconsin.

1873
Kohler Co. is founded when John Michael Kohler and a partner, Charles Silberzahn, purchase a Sheboygan foundry from John Michael's father-in-law, Jacob Vollrath, for $5,000. John Michael is 29 years old. The company, initially named Kohler & Silberzahn, makes plows and other farm implements.

1878
Charles Silberzahn sells his minority interest to two employees, Herman Hayssen and John Stehn. Company is renamed Kohler, Hayssen & Stehn.

1880
The Kohler factory burns to the ground. Company moves to a new facility, also in Sheboygan, adding an enameling shop.

1883
Company makes its first plumbing product when John Michael enamels a cast-iron hog trough and adds ornamental feet, selling it as a bathtub. Within four years, plumbing fixtures account for 70 percent of revenues.

1887
The company, which has operated as a partnership, incorporates.

1897
Twenty-one employees go on strike in a dispute over changes made in molding pay rates. Some of the 21 later return to work, and a few of the openings are filled by job applicants. Although meetings are held with the union's representatives, no record of a formal settlement exists today.

1899
John Michael purchases 21 acres of farmland in Riverside, four miles west of Sheboygan, to build a new foundry and move the company there.

1900
John Michael dies at age 56, just days after the new foundry is completed. Three of his sons assume management — Robert as president, Walter as treasurer and Carl as secretary.

1901
The new foundry is destroyed by fire. Operations are returned temporarily to Sheboygan while the Riverside foundry is rebuilt.

The Kohler family assumes full ownership when it purchases the shares of Herman Hayssen and Magdalena Stehn (John Stehn's widow). The company is renamed J. M. Kohler Sons Co.

1902
The rebuilding of the foundry is completed. The company returns to Riverside.

1904
Carl Kohler dies at age 24.

1905
Robert Kohler dies at 31. Walter Kohler, 30, becomes president, heading the company for the next 35 years.

1911
Kohler Co. introduces the industry's first one-piece built-in bathtub with an integral apron.

Company becomes one of the first in America to provide workers' compensation coverage for its employees.

1912
The company adopts its current name, Kohler Co.

Riverside is incorporated as Kohler Village.

1913
Walter Kohler travels to Europe with architect Richard Philipp to study "planned communities" which provide clean, affordable housing for workers. They conclude their journey by meeting with Sir Ebenezer Howard, father of the European garden city movement. This trip generates ideas for the development of Kohler Village.

1916

Company designates an annual Naturalization Day. Foreign-born employees are given the day off with pay to file their "first papers" for U.S. citizenship.

1917

Under Walter Kohler's auspices, Olmsted Brothers of Boston completes a 50-year master plan for the development of Kohler Village, including provisions for parks and the controlled growth of housing.

Kohler Co. starts building houses in the village, selling the houses and land to employees at cost.

Company becomes one of the first in America to provide free life and health insurance for employees.

1917-1918

Company produces mine anchors, projectiles and shells for U.S. forces in World War I.

1918

Kohler Co. opens The American Club to house single male employees in comfortable surroundings at affordable cost.

1920

Kohler Co. enters the power systems business with the introduction of the Kohler Automatic, the world's first engine-powered electrical generator.

1924

Company forms a Quarter Century Club, one of the first in American industry, to honor employees with 25 years or more of service.

At Walter Kohler's initiative, company starts the Kohler Stables, which later becomes famous for the breeding of Morgan and Warmblood horses.

1925

Until now a manufacturer of cast-iron enamelware, Kohler diversifies into the manufacture of vitreous china products by purchasing the Cochran, Drugan & Co. pottery of Trenton, New Jersey.

1926

Company begins construction of a pottery in Kohler Village based on Cochran, Drugan technology.

Company opens a plant in Kohler Village to manufacture faucets and other brass accessories.

Company begins offering tours of its factory. Free two-and-one-half-hour tours continue today, attracting some 8,000 visitors a year.

Company introduces the Kohler Electric Sink. Product is discontinued during the Great Depression.

1927

Kohler begins production at its new pottery, becoming a full-line plumbing products manufacturer.

Company introduces enameled bathtubs and vitreous china toilets and sinks in matching pastel colors, an industry first.

1928

Walter Kohler purchases a Ryan monoplane, a replica of Lindbergh's *Spirit of St. Louis*, becoming one of the first business executives in the nation to travel routinely by air.

1929

Kohler jet-black products are exhibited at The Metropolitan Museum of Art in New York.

Walter Kohler is sworn in as governor of Wisconsin, serving one two-year term. He continues as Kohler Co. chairman, president and CEO while governor, traveling back and forth between the state capital, Madison, and Kohler Village.

1931

Kohler Co. initially maintains full employment and full production despite the Depression.

1933

As the Depression continues, Kohler lays off employees for the first time.

1934

Federal Union No. 18545 of the AFL strikes for three months, claiming the right to represent Kohler Co. production and maintenance employees. In a government-supervised election, the Kohler Workers' Association outpolls the AFL and is certified as the employees' bargaining agent.

1937

Herbert V. Kohler Sr. becomes president, succeeding his brother, Walter, who continues as chairman and chief executive officer.

1940

Walter Kohler dies at age 65. Herbert V. Kohler Sr., 48, becomes chairman and chief executive officer, continuing also as president.

Walter's three sisters, Marie, Evangeline and Lillie, together with Herbert Sr. and Executive Vice President O. A. Kroos, organize Kohler Foundation, Inc., which to this day supports cultural, educational, environmental and other civic causes.

Company is awarded the world's largest plumbing contract for more than 50,000 products for the Parkchester Development in New York City, then the largest residential development in American history.

1941

Kohler converts production to torpedo tubes, shell fuses and other military components in support of the war effort.

1942

Kohler begins manufacturing valves and fittings for military aircraft, continuing in the precision controls business for the next 34 years.

1948

Company begins producing and marketing small engines.

1952

Production and maintenance employees vote to affiliate with the United Auto Workers, becoming UAW-CIO Local 833.

1954

UAW-CIO Local 833 strikes. The factory reopens within two months, but the strike continues for six years primarily over issues of a union shop and strict seniority in promotion.

1958

Company begins manufacturing plumbing products at a new plant in Spartanburg, South Carolina, its first outside Kohler Village.

1962

James L. "Les" Kuplic, 50, becomes president (the first from outside the Kohler family), succeeding Herbert V. Kohler Sr., who continues as chairman and chief executive officer.

1964

Kohler opens a plant in Mexico City to produce small engines. Kohler de Mexico is today the leading producer of engines for the Mexican market, and also produces for export.

1965

Kohler Co. introduces bathroom fixtures in "accent" colors, richer and more vibrant than the pastels of the 1920s.

1967

The advertising theme, The Bold Look of Kohler, is introduced.

1968

Les Kuplic, president, dies at age 56. Six days later, Herbert V. Kohler Sr., chairman, dies at age 76.

Lyman Conger, 66, is elected chairman. Walter Cleveland, 52, is elected president. Herbert V. Kohler Jr. becomes vice president-operations.

1972

Lyman Conger, chairman, retires. Herbert V. Kohler Jr., 33, grandson of founder John Michael Kohler, becomes chairman and chief executive officer.

1973

Kohler Co. celebrates its 100th birthday with gala parties, new products and a "demonstration house" in Kohler Village that is featured in *Better Homes & Gardens* magazine.

1974

Walter Cleveland, president, retires. He is succeeded by Herbert V. Kohler Jr., who continues also as chairman and chief executive officer.

A unique Arts/Industry residency program is established with the John Michael Kohler Arts Center. This program, which continues today, allows artists to work in studios within the Kohler Co. factory, utilizing the factory's materials and equipment to create whatever art they want.

1975

Kohler begins producing vitreous plumbing products at a plant in Brownwood, Texas, helping strengthen distribution in the Southwest and western states.

1976

Company divests its precision controls business.

1977

The Frank Lloyd Wright Foundation completes a new 50-year master plan for the development of Kohler Village.

1978

Shareholders approve a 1-for-20 reverse stock split.

The American Club is closed to allow its renovation as a luxury hotel. The building is placed on the National Register of Historic Places, ensuring it can never be torn down.

Company opens River Wildlife.

1979

Company opens Sports Core.

1980

Kohler receives orders from five major hotels in the People's Republic of China, the first sales in China by an international plumbing products company since the 1930s.

1981

Following extensive renovations, The American Club is reopened as a resort hotel.

1983

The UAW strikes briefly.

1984

Kohler purchases Sterling Faucet Co., beginning an active acquisition program.

Sales surpass $500 million for the first time.

1985

Company establishes the Kohler Design Center in the village, open to the public, serving as a design resource and product showcase for the Kohler family of companies.

1986

The American Club is awarded Five Diamonds, the highest rating of the American Automobile Association.

Acquisitions include Jacob Delafon, a leading French plumbing products company, and Polar Stainless Products, Inc., a U.S. manufacturer of stainless steel sinks.

Kohler Co. enters the furniture business through the acquisition of Baker Knapp & Tubbs, Inc.

Company expands its exports to Asia by forming Kohler Japan KK, a marketing and sales organization in Tokyo.

1987

Acquisitions include Hytec Manufacturing Ltd. (fiberglass and acrylic fixtures) and the FRP Components Division (sheet molded compound bathtubs and enclosures) of Owens-Corning Fiberglas Corp.

Sales reach $1 billion.

1988

Acquisitions include Bathroom Jewelry (faucets) and the Kinkead Division of USG Corp. (tub and shower enclosures and other plumbing products).

Kohler opens its first golf course, Blackwolf Run, named the year's best new public course by *Golf Digest* magazine.

1989

Acquisitions include Ann Sacks Tile & Stone, Kallista, Inc. (bathroom fixtures and fittings) and Dupont Sanitaire-Chauffage (French plumbing and heating products wholesaler).

1990

Kohler Co. expands its Interiors Group by acquiring McGuire Furniture Company.

The American Club is named the seventh best resort hotel on the U.S. mainland by *Condé Nast Traveler* magazine.

Kohler Stables' world champion stallion, Noble Flaire, is named Morgan Horse of the Decade by *Horse World* magazine.

1991

Company begins making vitreous china products at a plant in Monterrey, Mexico.

1993

Company acquires Sanijura, S.A., a French manufacturer of bathroom cabinets.

1994

Company opens The Inn on Woodlake in Kohler Village.

1995

Acquisitions include Robern, Inc. (mirrored bathroom cabinets, lighting fixtures, accessories and aluminum railings), Holdiam, Inc. (French manufacturer of acrylic bathtubs, whirlpools and kitchen sinks) and Aqualux (Pty.) Limited (South African producer of luxury shower enclosures).

Kohler forms a joint venture, Foshan Kohler Limited, to manufacture toilets and other vitreous china products in the People's Republic of China.

1996

Acquisitions include Canac Kitchens, Ltd. (Canadian manufacturer of kitchen and bathroom cabinets) and Lumatech International Inc. (manufacturer of acrylic plumbing fixtures in the Dominican Republic).

Kohler forms a second joint venture in China, this one to make faucets.

Company enters generator rental market by forming Kohler Rental Power.

McGuire Furniture subsidiary opens a factory in Indonesia.

Sales reach $2 billion.

1997

Company builds engine-manufacturing plant in Hattiesburg, Mississippi, and opens a plant in Singapore to manufacture generators for the Asian market.

1998

Kohler Co. recapitalizes to establish separate voting and non-voting classes of stock, solidifying the company's privately held status and providing an effective means to transfer control to future generations.

Company enters German plumbing products market by selling Kohler brand products through OBI, that nation's largest home-improvement products retail chain.

Company begins producing cast-iron and acrylic plumbing products at a wholly owned plant in China, near Shanghai.

Baker Furniture subsidiary opens PT Port Rush plant in Indonesia.

Kohler expands in golf by opening the Straits Course at Whistling Straits on the shore of Lake Michigan, northeast of Kohler Village.

Blackwolf Run hosts the U.S. Women's Open Championship.

1999

Baker Furniture subsidiary opens a plant in Hildebran, North Carolina.

PGA of America selects Whistling Straits for its 2004 PGA Championship, one of the four tournaments in golf's "grand slam."

2000

Company expands in the Pacific Rim by acquiring Englefield Bathroomware of New Zealand.

Company acquires a minority equity position in Internacional de Cerámica (Interceramic), which begins distributing Kohler plumbing products through its retail stores in Mexico.

Kohler Waters Spa opens.

2001

Company acquires Mira, the leading shower manufacturer in the U.K.

Construction begins on stainless steel sink plant in Reynosa, Mexico.

Following refurbishing, the Riverbend estate opens as a private membership club. Herb Kohler calls it "the cherry on the Kohler cake."

Annual capacity of the Kohler Sanimex plant in Mexico is increased to five million units, making it one of the largest vitreous china plants in the world.

Kohler Co. donates a unique mobile showering trailer for use by workers at the World Trade Center site. The unit, containing nine showering stalls and four sinks, is designed and built in six days by a team of 150 Kohler associates.

2002

Jacob Delafon expands pottery in Tangier, Morocco.

Kohler breaks ground for injection molding plastics plant expansion in Sheridan, Arkansas.

The American Club earns an AAA Five Diamond rating for the 16th consecutive year.

Condé Nast Traveler recognizes Kohler Waters Spa as one of the "top 40 spas in North America and the Caribbean."

Kohler acquires Karat Sanitaryware plc, which makes vitreous china products in Thailand for customers worldwide.

Herbert V. Kohler Jr. named national Entrepreneur of the Year in manufacturing by Ernst & Young.

Sales reach $3 billion.

Index

Bold listings indicate illustrated material.